The Evidence Liberal Arts Needs

The Evidence Liberal Arts Needs

Lives of Consequence, Inquiry, and Accomplishment

Richard A. Detweiler

The MIT Press

Cambridge, Massachusetts | London, England

The MIT Press would like to thank the anonymous peer reviewers who provided comments on drafts of this book. The generous work of academic experts is essential for establishing the authority and quality of our publications. We acknowledge with gratitude the contributions of these otherwise uncredited readers.

This book was set in Stone Serif and Stone Sans by Westchester Publishing Services. Printed and bound in the United States of America.

Library of Congress Cataloging-in-Publication Data

Names: Detweiler, Richard A., author.
Title: The evidence liberal arts needs : lives of consequence, inquiry, and
    accomplishment / Richard A. Detweiler.
Description: Cambridge, Massachusetts : The MIT Press, [2021] | Includes
    bibliographical references and index.
Identifiers: LCCN 2021000492 | ISBN 9780262543101 (paperback)
Subjects: LCSH: Education, Humanistic. | Education, Higher—Aims and objectives
Classification: LCC LC1011 .D38 2021 | DDC 370.11/2—dc23
LC record available at https://lccn.loc.gov/2021000492

10 9 8 7 6 5 4

For Carol,
My partner in life,
In a life well lived, and
In a life of learning

Contents

Preface

In my judgment, one of the most vexing issues facing higher education in the United States today is the role of the liberal arts. It is blamed by some for making college expensive, impractical, and worthless, but by others, it is credited with making our society innovative, creative, and civically involved. As a long-ago college-bound student, I inadvertently chose to attend a liberal arts college—inadvertently because I decided I wanted to attend a smaller college without understanding that I was, at the same time, choosing an education of liberal arts character—and I had no idea what that meant. But of course, at that time, there was little controversy about what should be studied in college; everyone at almost every college and university in the United States, regardless of major, was expected to take courses in the humanities, social sciences, and sciences because breadth of study (which is inherent to the liberal arts approach) was standard everywhere, as it had been for centuries on this continent.

But for many reasons—economic, political, social, and religious—for the past several decades, many long-standing assumptions about American higher education have been challenged. Two of the issues that have dominated discussion have been the cost and the value of a college degree (and with those, the associated issue of who has access to higher education). The cost (or more accurately, the price that colleges charge as their tuition) has risen inexorably, driven by a number of factors, including decreases in government support (especially the shift from federal grants to students to attend college to student loans, as well as decreases in state aid), the expenses of high-tech equipment (especially in the science and technology areas), improved compensation for faculty and staff, dramatically increased financial aid funded by the institutions themselves, and the increase in amenities that are now expected (such as fancy facilities ranging from classrooms to gyms). As the price inexorably increased, attention began to focus on the question of value: is a college education worth the money?

Colleges and universities ultimately responded to this question by arguing that college graduates earn more, so obviously higher education is a good investment. And research supported this assertion not only in the case of salary, but also in work advancement and health, among other benefits. By embracing graduates' employment upon graduation as proof that their price was worth it, and with this simple-to-measure outcome, colleges inadvertently helped unleash a change in view about the nature and purpose of higher education. With jobs and income as the rationale for going to college, what should students study? "Practical and useful and resulting in a good-paying job at graduation" became the new watchwords for students, parents, regulators, and legislators.

Whereas higher education had long been viewed as a mechanism for social mobility, this fresh emphasis on economic value to the person made a college degree a private good (e.g., like buying a car, it benefits the individual) rather than a public good (e.g., necessary for a successful democracy, as had been the primary assertion). From this shift in perspective, it was a short step to lots of new issues, including questions as to whether governments should really be funding a private good, ever-higher expectations about what colleges must offer if they are going to attract students to enroll, and who was being excluded from access to this life benefit. Like other aspects of consumer behavior, college became increasingly competitive for both the prospective students (who often feel they need to get admitted to the most prestigious college possible when quality educations are available at hundreds of institutions) and the colleges (needing to attract students in a competitive environment through scholarships, services, and wonderful campus amenities).

That brings me back to the first sentence of this preface: in my judgment, one of the most vexing issues now facing higher education in the United States is the role of the liberal arts.

Two simple questions indicate why this issue is vexing. First, should all college students be required to take courses in history and philosophy as well as more obviously practical courses that are directly related to a good job? Second, do graduates who have studied in a liberal arts context live a more successful or better life? The first question assumes that study in the tradition of the liberal arts is defined by the courses that one takes. But it turns out, as you will learn from this book, not only is there is no agreed-upon definition or description of the liberal arts, but importantly, the research findings make it clear there is much more to a liberal arts education than merely the courses that one takes. The second question assumes that we know which life outcomes are most important or valuable—is it personal success, or making contributions to society, or being fulfilled, or something else? Again, as you will find in this book, while there are countless books, articles, and speeches on this subject, there is no agreement on what life outcomes actually matter most.

In developing the work reported in this book, my goal was to take a fresh look at higher education in general, and liberal arts education in particular. Rather than adopting a particular theoretical or philosophical position, or simply accepting the assertions of some of the many impressive thinkers who have written on this subject, I endeavored to objectively catalog both the practices of liberal arts education over the centuries and the goals that institutions have identified for their graduates' life outcomes. Then it was a simple process (well, actually, it was quite challenging and complicated) to see whether, based on the actual experiences of college graduates, there is any relationship between particular aspects of liberal arts study and specific life outcomes.

As you will learn, I concluded that liberal arts study always involves serving a common purpose (of value to both society and the individual) and involves not only the content of study (the courses taken), but also the context of study (the nature of the educational environment). And the desired outcomes include those of individual value (success and fulfillment), societal value (leadership and altruism), and intellectual value (continuing study and cultural involvement). Importantly, there are some aspects of the content and context of the liberal arts that are related to some of the life outcomes, and other aspects that are related to other life outcomes. So the results reported in this book can be useful to many people: students, as they choose the type of college to attend based on their own life goals; institutions, as they allocate resources for particular outcomes; regulators, as they decide how to hold colleges accountable; and others.

This endeavor was, not surprisingly, not a solo journey. In partial acknowledgment, I must start with the leadership of many liberal arts–based institutions outside the United States which, by showing me their different approaches to the liberal arts, stimulated me to ask new questions about the essence of this educational approach. Next, my abiding gratitude goes to presidents associated with the Great Lakes Colleges Association (GLCA), who encouraged me to invest time and attention to this issue: Brian Casey, Grant Cornwell, David Dawson, Sean Decatur, Mauri Ditzler, Gregory Hess, Rock Jones, John Knapp, James Mullen, Georgia Nugent, Adam Weinberg, and Eileen Wilson-Oyelaran. The following members of the GLCA staff were supportive in countless ways: Derek Vaughan, Gregory Wegner, Simon Gray, Colleen Monahan Smith, Charla White, and Maryann

Hafner. And then, without the generous financial support of the Teagle Foundation, the Spencer Foundation, and the GLCA, the research reported here could not have been undertaken in the first place.

As this project developed, many people and organizations contributed substantially to shaping it: Julie Kidd, president of the Endeavor Foundation, who relentlessly supports education in the tradition of the liberal arts; the Andrew W. Mellon Foundation through their long support of education at liberal arts institutions; the presidents, deans, and faculty of colleges and universities in the United States and abroad through their involvement in workshops and discussions; numerous higher education thinkers and leaders who patiently spent time responding to my questions about the nature of higher education; and David Strauss and Shanaysha Sauls of the Art & Science Group, who thoughtfully and skillfully turned messy concepts into useful interview questions. I am also indebted to the 1,000 graduates of decades past who invested substantial time in being interviewed and reflecting on the nature of their higher education experience, and the additional 85 graduates who contributed lengthy narratives about their college experiences; without them, there would have been no research findings to report. Finally, my exploration of Islam and its role in the history and development of the liberal arts through the Islamic Golden Age was greatly advanced by the wisdom shared by Dr. Haifa Reda Jamal Al-Lail, president of Effat University; and Dr. Driss Ouaouicha, then the president of Al Akhawayn University and now the minister delegate to Morocco's Minister of National Education.

As the preliminary results became public, I am particularly grateful to Scott Jascik for his interest in reporting on the results, and to Elizabeth Branch Dyson, who encouraged me to write a book on this work. At that point, Richard Ekman, president of the Council of Independent Colleges, and the enthusiastic comments of Howard Gardner of the Harvard Graduate School of Education were fortifying as I slogged through the detailed analyses. In addition, I wish to acknowledge the superb final manuscript editing by Susan McClung. And very importantly, I express my deep appreciation to Susan Buckley, my editor at MIT Press, whose strong interest and continuing support have brought this work to you as the book you now hold.

Finally, there were the numerous people who provided reviews and suggestions for improving the work, ranging from professional colleagues and anonymous readers to members of my academically involved family, who shared expertise on the educational concepts (Jerusha Detweiler-Bedell), analytic strategy (Brian Detweiler-Bedell), publication process (Courtney Hillebrecht and Carrick Detweiler), social justice (Natasha Detweiler-Daby), and the public case (Doug Detweiler). Through all of this, my wife, Carol—my partner in higher education as well as in life—not only unceasingly gave me the time for this work, but also kept pressing me onward both through encouragement and candid critiques of countless drafts; without her, this book would not exist.

1

Our Puzzle

Who in the world am I? Ah, that's the great puzzle!
—Alice, in Lewis Carroll, *Alice's Adventures in Wonderland*

America's higher education system is considered by many to be the best in the world. Nearly 1 million international students come to the US for college or university studies every year[1]—twice the number as any other country, and in many cases, they need to pay for an education that would have been very inexpensive or free at home. At the same time, numerous educational leaders in other countries assert that their higher education systems should be improved by adopting essential aspects of the American approach. Many of us in the US scratch our heads at this acclaim, which is in stark contrast to critics who persistently lament what they describe as our broken and ineffective colleges.

So, what about the American approach has made people in other countries believe it to be exceptional and impactful in ways not typically reported elsewhere? It is probably not the football teams, though they are distinctively American. It is probably not the disproportionate number of Nobel Prize winners that have come from

US universities because, while this is an impressive accomplishment, Nobel laureates rarely teach classes or spend much time with undergraduate students. It also doesn't seem likely that it is how hard students must work to gain admission—some US colleges accept almost everyone who applies. Indeed, in many other countries, more extreme demands are placed on students to qualify for university admissions than in the US.

The fact is that what has made undergraduate education in the US unique, and makes it the darling of the world, is that it is based on the liberal arts. And while US colleges are currently feeling intense pressure to eliminate this approach, and students are being encouraged to focus exclusively on mastering immediately practical, job-specific information, this is a grave error, as the research reported in this volume demonstrates. *Higher education based on six essential aspects of education in the tradition of the liberal arts is an educational ecology that has a uniquely powerful and positive impact on the life and achievements of college graduates and the society in which they live.* This impact is not simply the result of the subjects studied (its content); much more important, it is the result of the use of a deliberately crafted educational environment (its context). In this era of educational reform, the challenge facing higher education today should not be to eliminate liberal arts in favor of the wrongly perceived value of an exclusive focus on specialized education, but rather to strengthen those liberal arts practices that have been demonstrated to increase the lifelong value of the education provided.

*   *   *

From its early days, American-style higher education was intentionally designed to be different from the higher education being offered in other countries. Two centuries ago, when European universities were considered the best in the world, a decision by the faculty of Yale University led to the US taking a different path to higher education. This was an approach that American educators of that time believed would not only better serve the needs of the individuals being educated, but also more constructively shape the development of the nation. So, instead of trying to copy the European approach, which focused on the development of job-oriented, specialized, and professional training, educators in the US concluded that it was more important to equip American youth with the broader talents and values they would need to thrive in, and contribute to, individual and societal progress during a time of challenge and change. Their belief was that the payoff from this approach would be far greater in the longer term than the shorter-term benefits that come from a narrow focus on specialized higher education.

Choosing not to follow the world's educational leaders of the time, but instead to take a distinctive path, was a courageous experiment—seeing whether higher education designed to prepare people for a lifetime of contributions and achievement, not just for a particular job, would be successful at projecting a nation and its people forward. And successful it has been, as judged by the attainments of graduates, its contribution to the progress of society, and its well-deserved global reputation for impact and effectiveness.*

This distinctive American approach to higher education carries the label "liberal arts"—which, unlike what many believe, does not merely describe the types of courses students take, but rather the totality of an educational approach, both inside and outside the classroom. In recent years, interest in this liberal arts approach

---

*While the focus of this book is on undergraduate degree education rather than technical or trade programs, the same argument can be made for those in noncollegiate educational programs, which prepare so many of our society's essential workers. As described in chapter 11, in this time of constant change, people will hold ten to fifteen different jobs over their careers. The analysis by the World Economic Forum reported in that chapter also indicates that liberal arts skills—leadership, communication effectiveness, problem-solving ability, a collaborative mindset, and so on—are equally important for those without a traditional college degree, in order to prepare them to successfully navigate the constantly changing and evolving world of work.

to education in other countries has been encouraged by newspaper articles emphasizing the need for the development of creativity, adaptability, insight, and personal responsibility, outcomes that international observers believe are among the hallmarks of a liberal arts education. The handful of American-style colleges founded in other countries at a time of American idealism more than a century ago have earned new attention and respect; new liberal arts colleges have been created and are now operating within traditional European universities,* and Africa, Asia, and the Middle East are the homes of a growing number of liberal arts colleges.† In Asia, there are serious efforts to replace narrow specialization, career focus, and rote memorization with education in the tradition of the liberal arts: "It's past time for colleges to introduce a broader range of subjects, to promote greater intellectual curiosity, and to foster creative thinking. And they're convinced that these changes will, in turn, build a workforce of rigorous, creative thinkers—just what they think is needed to meet the fast-changing needs of a transforming global economy."[2]

In India, well known for its engineering and technology universities, there is a growing realization that longer-term success comes from rejecting the narrow specialization of these institutions and developing "in students a spirit of inquiry, critical thinking and analysis as well as verbal and written communication skills" through "a broad-ranging education aimed at holistic development."[3] A major new initiative of the Indian government is to require liberal arts

---

*See the work of the European Consortium of Liberal Arts Colleges at www.ecolas.eu /eng/.
† A few examples of these institutions are Al Akhawayn University in Ifrane, Morocco; Ashesi University in Berekuso, Ghana; Bratislava International School of the Liberal Arts in Slovakia; Effat University in Jeddah, Saudi Arabia; FLAME University in Pune, India; the International University of Grand-Bassam in Côte d'Ivoire, the American University in Cairo; American College of Greece in Athens; the American University of Nigeria in Yola; the American University of Paris; Lingnan University in Hong Kong; Universidad San Francisco de Quito in Ecuador; and Yale-NUS College in Singapore.

study for all college students not only by creating many new public liberal arts institutions, but also by overhauling the university curriculum, including at its well-known technological institutes.[4] One need only read the books *American Universities Abroad*[5] or *Doing Liberal Arts Education—Global Case Studies*,[6] or consider the work of organizations such as the Global Liberal Arts Alliance,[7] which links thirty institutions internationally, in order to be convinced of the importance of this growing international liberal arts wave.

I first became aware of the significance of this difference in 1993, not long after the fall of the Berlin Wall and in the early days of the reunification of West and East Germany. As president of an American liberal arts college, I committed to supporting interested German students from the East's best high-tech university to come to my college for a year of study—the kind of opportunity that did not exist when they were under communist rule. Our interest was in helping to bridge the East/West divide through a linkage between Hartwick College and Mittweida University, which indeed happened.* But it turned out that I was in store for an important learning experience myself. These students regularly came to talk with me about the profound impact of taking courses in literature and philosophy and psychology and history and more; taking a range of courses unrelated to their area of specialization was not allowed at their German university. They found that by studying a broader span of knowledge and developing some understanding of how areas of knowledge interrelate, their ways of thinking about their future life and profession (many in engineering) fundamentally changed.

And they also spoke enthusiastically about their professors at this American college—how they invested time and effort getting to know each student and were committed to helping them succeed.

---

*I express my gratitude to Hartwick College faculty members John Clemens, Tom Sears, Steve Kolenda, and Doug Mayer for recommending, developing, and implementing this project.

The professors spent out-of-class time with students exploring both academic and nonacademic issues; rather than giving passive lectures, they used teaching methods that involved the students. At their eastern German university, a prime example of the traditional European university, the focus was on the development of specialized knowledge within an area of study in preparation for a specific vocation; memorization was essential and there were no opportunities for broader study. There, my students said that the professors focused on the degree to which students could accurately regurgitate facts they were given, and professors did not express much interest in the intellectual or personal development of individual students.

The time that professors at my college spent with students outside of class and the range of courses that students took, as well as their active involvement with students of different values and life experiences, generated fresh insights, broader interests, heightened creativity, a desire for continued opportunities to learn, and a new awareness of and commitment to ways they could contribute to the development of their nation in the future. In short, they found the experience to be one that they believed would help them be more successful over the longer term, for both themselves and their society. Their enthusiasm about their learning experience upon returning home resulted in the chancellor of their university coming to my college to learn about this very different liberal arts approach to higher education.

This label, "liberal arts," is frequently used pejoratively in the US. In part, this is because it is often interpreted as political, although its actual meaning comes from the Latin word "liberalis," which means "free"—an education for a free person. In addition, some people believe that it describes a type of college study that is impractical, useless, designed for those lost souls who don't know what to do with their lives; it is an education that leads directly to unemployment, with the horrifying outcome of graduates having to move back home with their parents. There is an often-told joke about liberal arts education:

How can you tell the difference between graduates with different college degrees?

The graduate with a science degree asks, "Why does it work?"
The graduate with an engineering degree asks, "How does it work?"
The graduate with an accounting degree asks, "How much will it cost?"
The graduate with a liberal arts degree asks, "Do you want fries with that?"

As a result, many parents encourage their children to specialize and take courses that prepare them for their first job. Governors and legislators have taken actions to ban liberal arts majors or eliminate humanities subjects at state colleges. Some opinion writers ridicule this approach to education. As described in the *New York Times*, students attending a liberal arts college, or perhaps even worse, majoring in a humanities subject, can face astonishment bordering on ridicule, or at the very least, can expect this uncomfortable conversation:[8]

Parent: What's your major?
Student: History and the classics.
Parent: What are you going to do with that?

This negative assessment of education in the tradition of the liberal arts is not shared by knowledgeable people who appreciate and respect the demonstrated success of graduates of American-style, liberal arts–based colleges. Indeed, there are significant voices in the US who advocate for education in the liberal arts tradition: 80% of US employers believe that, regardless of major, every college student should acquire broad knowledge in the liberal arts and sciences, and 93% agree that "a candidate's demonstrated capacity to think critically, communicate clearly, and solve complex problems is more important than their undergraduate major."[9] According to a recent study by the National Association of Colleges and Employers, the top ten attributes of job candidates sought by employers are communication skills (82%), problem-solving skills (81%), ability to work on a team (79%), initiative (74%), analytical/quantitative skills (72%), strong work ethic (71%), communication skills (67%), leadership (67%), detail-oriented (60%), and technical skills (60%). It is noteworthy that seven of the top ten are associated with liberal arts education, and that specialization, while still included, is at the bottom of this list. Technology entrepreneur Mark Cuban states that the longer-term value of nontechnical expertise is clear: "Creativity, collaboration, communication skills. Those things are super important and are going to be the difference between make or break . . . In an [artificial intelligence] world, you have to be knowledgeable about something, right?"[10]

Further, the noted journalist Fareed Zakaria writes eloquently about the power of a liberal arts education: "A liberal education gives us a greater capacity to be good workers. But it will also give us the capacity to be good partners, friends, parents, and citizens."[11] The conservative social and political commentator David Brooks describes the importance of studying the humanities in developing people with a strong "inner character"[12] and of cultivating an inner life.[13] And for many years, Apple cofounder Steve Jobs spoke of the centrality of the liberal arts to innovation. While he never graduated, he took many college courses in the humanities, which he later reported shaped his approach not only to life, but to his groundbreaking work humanizing computers. One of these courses was calligraphy, about which he stated, "It was beautiful, historical, artistically subtle in a way that science can't capture, and I found it fascinating. None of this had even a hope of any practical application in my life. But 10 years later, when we were designing the first Macintosh computer, it all came back to me. And we designed it all into the Mac."[14]

And more recently, Microsoft president Brad Smith and artificial intelligence (AI) vice president Harry Shum, in a book about the future distributed at Davos, said that their most important conclusion may relate to the value of the liberal arts: "One of us grew up learning computer science and the other started in the liberal arts. Having worked together for many years at Microsoft, it's clear to both of us that it will be even more important to connect these fields in the future."[15]

There is an irony here: in the US today, there are substantial public and governmental pressures to change higher education to be more as it is in most other countries—a vocational, specialized, professional education—and our colleges are complying. Yet these changes threaten the very features that have made the American approach to higher learning different and powerful. Those advocates of changing higher education so that it is specialized and prepares a graduate to perform a specific job do not realize that they are emulating an approach first championed in nineteenth-century Prussia and subsequently adopted throughout Europe and their colonial world. Their calls to action are the result of a fundamental misunderstanding (and rejection) of education based on liberal arts principles.

What you will learn in this book is that the liberal arts approach to higher education has developed, evolved, and improved over a period of 3,500 years in ways designed to maximize learning impact and positive life outcomes—in the past through trial and error, and today through the insights provided by rigorous research. It is important to note that while the most complete education in the liberal arts tradition is usually found at smaller liberal arts colleges, virtually every American college and university, regardless of major, involves at least some liberal arts requirements or experiences. The analyses reported in this book demonstrate that people who live more consequential, wise, and accomplished lives have experienced most of the six essential aspects of liberal arts education.

Education in the tradition of the liberal arts, as I develop it in this book and use it in the research to be reported, includes both the content of study and the educational context within which learning occurs—the whole educational ecology. As with any ecological analysis, these attributes are interlinked; we must consider them together to fully understand the liberal arts educational experience. This increased understanding creates opportunities to enhance the impact of this

American approach to higher education; contrarily, a lack of understanding is now leading to changes that diminish its impact and erode
its value. The purpose of this book is to bring the liberal arts back to the
center of higher education, based both on a newly clear understanding of its purpose and methods and on evidence about its long-term
impact on the lives of individuals and the societies in which they live.

*   *   *

I have now used the term "liberal arts" many times in this chapter.
While I have worked in and taught at liberal arts colleges for many
decades, I began to develop fundamentally new insights into the
meaning of the liberal arts when I became involved in partnerships
with more than a dozen colleges and universities in other countries. These institutions had adapted the liberal arts to fit their own
national, cultural, and educational needs. Just like Alexis de Toc-
queville, writing from the perspective of an outsider to the US 150
years ago, my experience as an outsider looking at liberal arts education abroad stimulated fresh insights about a subject that I previously thought I knew very well.

In my discussions with liberal arts educators in other countries,
I learned they believed that American undergraduate education—and
they used the terms "American-style" and "liberal arts" interchange-
ably—is distinctly different from higher education in their own
countries. They said it is unusually valuable for a number of reasons,
including:[16]

- It prepares people to be successful over their lifetimes by educating them to lead their societies forward, not just to become prepared for a specific job upon graduation.
- It respects and values students, and student learning is the first
  priority.
- It places faculty themselves as participants in the learning process, while also being engaged with developments in their own
  areas of expertise.

Previously, like most liberal arts advocates in the US, I had focused primarily on the content of a liberal arts education—the courses required. In contrast, a majority of the ideas expressed by these non-US liberal arts educators focused instead on the nature of the educational experience and on the life outcomes expected.

This simple insight launched me on a renewed liberal arts journey that involves learning the answers to three questions:

- What is the impact of a liberal arts education?
- What are the implications of an education in the tradition of the liberal arts, and what is the value of it?

The answers to these questions are overwhelmingly positive and surprisingly conclusive. For those of you looking for "ammunition for the liberal arts," as I once heard a college president put it, look no further.

The First Question: What Is Education in the Liberal Arts Tradition?

The next several chapters of this volume explore the nature and development of liberal arts education. This is not a philosophical analysis (Kimball's *Orators and Philosophers* nicely fulfills this purpose[17]), but rather an examination of the practice of the liberal arts. These chapters begin by noting that the liberal arts is described in many ways: some say that it is the study of humanities subjects (such as philosophy and history); some say that it involves the study of a broad range of subjects, as well as one subject in depth; some say that it includes the sciences, as well as the social sciences and humanities; some say that it involves the development of citizenship or responsibility; some say that it occurs at residential liberal arts colleges; and so on. Indeed, a systematic review of descriptions of liberal arts education yields hundreds of words and terms used by various writers, educators, and colleges. While these descriptions often include inspiring rhetoric, the lack of consistency among them is striking.

With such a variety of contemporary descriptions, it is little wonder that people have different ideas about the nature and value of liberal arts education. To unscramble this jumble of ideas, I concluded that it would be enlightening to take a fresh look at the character of education in the tradition of the liberal arts as it has developed over its many years of existence. Have there been consistent ideas about what is involved in the liberal arts that are (or should be) considered today as essential aspects of this educational approach?

Indeed, the most important insight that I developed as a result of my investigations of liberal arts education over the past 3,500 years, and as practiced today, is that three aspects of this educational approach must be considered: the outcomes intended for the education (its *purpose*), what is studied (its *content*), and the educational environment (its *context*).

The earliest roots of liberal arts in ancient Greece stemmed from the purpose of training warriors for compulsory military service—an urgent societal need at that time. This seems like an odd beginning for what many today see as a wishy-washy approach to education. Over the next 1,000 years, studies involving the intellect—arts, music, and philosophy—were added and gymnastics and athletic competitions were substituted for military training. An understanding of this broader range of subjects was seen as necessary in order for leading citizens to contribute effectively to the progress of society through informed civil discourse and decision-making. In this earliest era of the liberal arts, the way that education occurred—the educational context—remained constant: it involved a close relationship among students and teachers learning together. The purpose evolved, although it was always based on fulfilling the highest needs of both society and the individual: it consistently served the "common good."* However, the content of the study changed substantially over time in ways that served the societal and individual outcomes described in its purpose.

This approach to higher learning was transplanted from Greece to ancient Rome and, indicative of continuing changes in the content of study, was ultimately described as involving music, logic, rhetoric, grammar, geometry, arithmetic, and astronomy. This content was believed to be important for educating individuals who could best contribute to the "common good"—at that time, an education for a free person to be an effective and successful contributor to society. Throughout the Greek and Roman millennia, the educational context continued to involve teachers and students learning together in a very personal way: tutors worked with individuals or small groups, and intellectual interaction among all of them was central to teaching and learning.

When Europe entered the early medieval period (sometimes referred to as the "Dark Ages"), most of the writings from the Greek and Roman periods were deliberately destroyed because they were thought to be pagan. Scholars who knew about them were driven from Europe to the largely Muslim Near East. This resulted, as it turns out, in a critical phase in the development of a liberal arts approach to higher education. It was described as the Islamic Golden Age, an era when the nonsectarian and open pursuit of knowledge and understanding was a sacred calling for Muslims. Major efforts were undertaken to collect the knowledge of the known world; all sources were pursued, including (but not limited to) ancient Greek and Roman writings. The "House of Wisdom" (located in what is

---

*Philosophers, economists, political scientists, and social activists have developed many definitions and interpretations of this term. It is also important in Buddhist, Confucian, Christian, Hindu, and Islamic thinking and teaching. My use of the term is similar to current common usage and is largely consistent with Aristotle's conception that it involves benefits shared by individuals and society more broadly.

now Iraq) was founded, and scholarly collectors ventured through South Asia and went as far as China to bring together many of humanity's contributions to knowledge.

Documents were translated into Arabic by interdisciplinary teams of scholars, thereby preserving them for the future. Over several centuries, not only was knowledge gathered, but major new advances were made in mathematics, sciences, astronomy, medicine, philosophy, and other subjects. Schools, universities, and libraries were pervasive from Spain through North Africa and the Middle East. In this era, the content of study changed dramatically as areas of knowledge expanded exponentially. But the higher purpose remained constant—the common good—and the educational approach (its context) continued to emphasize effective teaching and learning through close relationships among teachers and students with numerous circle schools (where students would literally gather around a scholar), as well as residential centers of learning.

Much later, as Europe moved from the early medieval period, followed several hundred years during which the much deeper and broader human knowledge that had been developed and accumulated during the Islamic Golden Age was translated from Arabic into European languages. To prepare those who would be ecclesiastical and secular leaders, European universities were founded and grew. The course of study began with a narrow definition of the content of the liberal arts, but as stimulated by the new translations from Arabic, as well as significant new European contributions, a vastly expanded range of knowledge became a part of liberal arts education. Like their Islamic-world forebears, the educational context involved bringing students and teachers into residential communities, with them living and learning together. And the higher, common good purpose of this education remained a constant—both the individual and society benefited. Ultimately, English graduates of Oxford and Cambridge brought education in the liberal arts tradition to colonial America and founded institutions such as Harvard and Yale.

Then, in the early 1800s, a different approach to higher education was established; an approach that rejected liberal arts education. The king of Prussia, Frederick William III, concluded that education at all levels must serve a different purpose. Rather than serving the common good, its purpose was to strengthen the kingdom and protect the monarchy through the creation of bureaucrats to run the growing number of state agencies and researchers who would contribute to the economic success of the state. Ideas of breadth of education were replaced by early specializations in primary and secondary school because students needed to begin their higher education with their choice of profession already made. This Prussian approach was adopted by monarchies throughout Europe as they also wanted to strengthen their rule. And because this was the age of European colonial empires, the monarchy-serving Prussian approach spread throughout the world. With this change in the purpose and content of study, the educational context also changed, focusing on the mastery of specialized information rather than fostering a learning environment that engaged students in broader intellectual and societal learning.

In response to this development, the faculty of Yale paused in 1828 to ask whether they should copy the Prussian specialization model. After careful consideration, they rejected that approach and reaffirmed a liberal arts–based education. This conclusion was based on a number of insights about what they believed should be the character of a truly valuable higher education. First, its *purpose* needed to be for the common good: to educate people who could effectively contribute to the development of a growing democratic society in a time of change—a benefit not only to the individual, but also to the progress of society. Second, to accomplish this purpose, the *content* of a higher education needed to include fluency in the full span of human knowledge. Third, the educational *context* should involve learning in a residential educational community in which faculty and students lived and learned together; this was seen as necessary not only because the population was relatively dispersed, but also because this familial approach was the best way to educate the whole person in ways that served the common good.

To these three aspects of the liberal arts approach—its purpose, content, and context—was added a uniquely American contribution: this education was to be available to *all* people. Whereas a higher education had formerly been offered only to the elite, they believed that it was a necessary education for all people because everyone in American society was expected to have the knowledge and ability to be contributing and responsible citizens.*

And from the East Coast of the US, this renewed liberal arts approach to higher education spread voraciously west across the rapidly growing nation through the creation of hundreds of residential liberal arts colleges. Ultimately, virtually all American colleges and universities, even those that developed noteworthy specialized programs and research universities, took a liberal arts approach to undergraduate education.

Although this summary description of the development and evolution of the liberal arts is very brief—I present more information in the next three chapters of this book—it points to the following six attributes of education in the tradition of the liberal arts:

- Regarding the *content* of study:
  a. It is nonvocational (not designed for a specific job or profession),
  b. involves the full span of knowledge (studying broadly while understanding ways in which areas of knowledge are interrelated), and
  c. develops intellectual skills (analytic and reasoning ability, creativity)

---

*Of course, in the early 1800s, the phrase "all people" included only white males. Most Blacks were enslaved through 1868 and did not have the right to vote before 1870, and women did not have the right to vote until 1920. With the exception of a few liberal arts colleges, higher education for women and for nonwhites was rarely available before the 1860s. The lasting impact of this inequity persists today, and as discussed in chapter 11, higher education can be a tool to support equity, inclusion, and social justice efforts.

- Regarding the educational *context* of the education:
  a. It uses engaging pedagogy (methods of teaching that actively involves students),
  b. it develops larger perspectives (broadens understanding and challenges narrow thinking), and
  c. occurs in an authentic learning community (students, faculty, and staff interact with each other in meaningful ways, both formally and informally outside of class time).

And what is the purpose of a liberal arts education—the desired common good? Identifying common good outcomes that are relevant today involved analyzing the mission statements of 241 undergraduate liberal arts colleges.* Consistent with the historical types of higher good outcomes, today's mission statements indicate that liberal arts graduates could exhibit some or all of these socially and/or personally valued behaviors:

- Living lives of consequence:
  a. as leaders in communities, organizations, and with others;
  b. as altruists (civically involved and contributing to society).

- Living lives of inquiry:
  a. be continuing learners (being involved in learning activities throughout life);
  b. be culturally involved (with arts, museums, music, and other artistic pursuits).

- Living lives of accomplishment:
  a. attain a fulfilling life (satisfaction with life and career, reflective on the meaning of life);
  b. be personally successful (through professional contributions and success).

---

*I express my gratitude to Colleen Smith of the Great Lakes Colleges Association for her help on this analysis.

Of course, colleges vary in which of these six outcomes they seek to create or focus on, but the overwhelming majority of colleges state that their mission purpose is to fulfill one or more of them.

The answer to the first question, then, is clearly defined. A liberal arts education involves *fulfilling a common good purpose by creating an educational ecology involving both the content of study and the educational context.*

The Second Question: What Is the Impact of a Liberal Arts Education?

In the words of the noted entrepreneur John Doerr, who provides counsel on organizational impact to philanthropists and companies alike, every effective organization must keep their focus on what matters most: being clear about their mission and purpose and then identifying and assessing a limited number of truly key outcomes.[18] In the case of liberal arts education, the "what" is the content of study and the educational context, and the key outcome is the common good purpose of preparing people to be effective in their adult lives. Or, to state it more specifically, *the key question is whether there is a relationship between any of the six aspects of a liberal arts education (its content and context) and any of the six longer-term life outcomes.*

The answer to this question is presented in the middle four chapters of this book. First, we developed a series of interview questions related to each of the *content attributes* (e.g., amount of humanities study, kinds of course assignments, major), the *context attributes* (e.g., out-of-class interaction with faculty and other students, campus involvement, teaching methods experienced), and each of the *purpose attributes* described as adult life outcomes (e.g., leadership, altruism, continued learning, cultural involvement, fulfillment, and success). Using these questions, we then interviewed 1,000 graduates of a wide range of types of colleges and universities across the US:

small and large, private and public, teaching-focused and research-focused. Some of these graduates had experienced many of the aspects of a liberal arts education, whereas others received a college education involving few of these aspects. These differences made it possible to draw comparisons between people who had experienced each of the liberal arts attributes with those who did not—for example, those with vocational majors compared to those with non-vocational majors, those who experienced teaching that is highly involving of students compared to those who experienced less personalized education, or those who spent time with faculty outside of class compared to those who did not. And because the goal was to understand the impact over one's lifespan—not merely new college graduates—the interviews involved people who ranged in age from twenty-five to sixty-five.

Participants were not asked their opinions about the relationship between their college experiences and later life activities; rather, the interview questions asked them to describe various aspects of their college experiences and their adult lives. Statistical analyses were then used to assess whether there was any relationship between each of the six aspects of a liberal arts college education and each of the six adult outcomes.

What did we learn from this research? Based on statistical analyses of the interview responses, we can objectively document significant and substantial relationships between many aspects of a liberal arts educational experience and various life outcomes. *Overall, while both the content of study and the educational context are associated with significant life outcomes, the content of study* (i.e., subjects studied) *has less relationship to positive adult life outcomes than the educational context* (i.e., frequently talking with faculty outside of class about both nonacademic and academic matters, professors knowing students' first names, being mentored, frequent out-of-class discussions with other students of their different values and life experiences, and campus involvement).

Among many other statistically significant specific findings, college graduates who, in their adult life, are:

- *Leaders of organizations*—more likely to report having developed larger perspectives that broaden understanding and challenge narrow thinking and to have been more involved with faculty and other students outside of class
- *Altruistic*—more likely to have been more involved with faculty and other students in their college community
- *Continuing learners*—more likely to have studied a broader range of subjects, have a nonvocational major, develop larger perspectives and intellectual skills, and engage with their college community
- *Culturally involved*—more likely to have had a nonvocational major, study a broad span of knowledge, have closer out-of-class relations with faculty and with students of different backgrounds, develop intellectual skills, and experience engaging pedagogy
- *Fulfilled*—more likely to have taken more courses in the humanities, to have taken many courses where humanities issues were considered, have had a nonvocational major, have experienced engaging pedagogy, and have had their professors challenge their thinking and writing
- *Successful* (in more senior positions and with higher income) over the long term (as their lives and careers mature)—more likely to have taken more than half their courses outside their major, to have had greater involvement in the college educational community, and to have discussed issues of significance to humanity with other students outside of class more frequently

Study in the tradition of the liberal arts indeed has a great impact.* But it is important to point out that through this research, we have

---

*The question of causation is addressed in chapter 10 and in appendix 1. In brief, the strongest case for demonstrating long-term causation requires making experimental changes in educational practices and then waiting twenty-five or fifty years

also learned that liberal arts education is not a singular concept. Rather, "liberal arts study" is an educational ecology involving a number of educational approaches (the attributes of a liberal arts education as described earlier); each bears a distinct and often different relationship to adult life. For example, the "development of intellectual skills" educational experience is related to three life outcomes: continued learning, cultural involvement, and fulfillment. In contrast, a higher degree of involvement in an "authentic educational community" (interaction with faculty outside of class, out-of-class serious discussions with other students, and so on) is related to all six adult life outcomes. Therefore, it begins to be possible for a college, a student, or a policymaker to think about the life outcomes desired and to design an education tailored to that purpose.

It is also noteworthy that whereas vocational or professional study does have value (e.g., the salary of a graduate's first job), over the longer term, it was either unrelated or negatively related to positive life outcomes, including leadership, altruism, fulfillment, and personal success. Indeed, people who were more successful over the longer term took more than half their courses outside their major and were more engaged with faculty and other students. In contrast to specialization, the span of college study—an education beyond the major that includes the humanities, social sciences, and sciences—is frequently associated with many positive life outcomes

---

to assess the impact. The problem, of course, is that the delay would likely make any results valueless. Instead, the approach used here is to analyze the statistical relationship between reported college experiences and long-term life outcomes, and then to assess whether those relationships are consistent with experimental and nonexperimental research on short-term impact and are also supported by experimental findings in the fields of human learning and affective social neuroscience. The fact that the findings reported here align with research in these other fields increases confidence that the reported liberal arts effects are meaningful and consequential; that it is not merely the fact that, for example, people who report that at age eighteen they like to live in an environment with faculty were destined (by dint of their character or personality) to become leaders, altruists, and culturally involved.

over the longer term, including professional success, continued learning, cultural involvement, and personal fulfillment.

This research, then, objectively documents the relationship between specific aspects of the college educational environment and specific types of life outcomes. *So not only can we confidently describe the relationship between liberal arts education and positive adult life outcomes, but we can describe what specific types of liberal arts experiences are associated with those life outcomes.*

The Third Question: What Are the Implications of an Education in the Tradition of the Liberal Arts, and What Is the Value of It?

In the final four chapters of this book, I explore the implications of the research findings for higher education. Among the many specific implications discussed, several broad insights emerge. The first is the important positive impact of the educational context (e.g., personal involvement with faculty, mentoring, frequent out-of-class discussions with other students of different values and life experiences, campus involvement). This finding is no surprise to those who have followed Howard Gardner's extensive work on how college affects students: "the community surrounding a cognizing individual is critical,"[19] a view that has guided his pioneering work on learning since that time.

Indeed, educational context has a more consistently positive, long-term relationship to life outcomes than does the content of study. How can this be? Contemporary research on human cognition—in the area of affective social neuroscience especially—provides strong evidence that the learning context is essential: educational impact occurs in the context of more socially and emotionally based approaches to learning. Human connection is essential. It isn't that content doesn't matter; after all, an educational experience by definition involves the study of something. But because most discussions of what should happen in college focus strictly on the content of study, not on the significance of the educational context, the lesser impact of content is surprising. Indeed, the disproportionate focus on content that is typical of discussions of what college study should involve is a significant mistake if we wish to have a higher education with a life impact.

The second general insight relates to the content of college study. What becomes clear is that it is primarily the broadening aspects of the content of study that is more important than the specific courses taken (e.g., taking more than half of one's courses outside one's major, discussing issues of significance to humanity in most classes, and taking a nonvocational major).

The third is fresh insight into current conflicts about the purpose of a higher education: should college education be redesigned so that it focuses only on practical outcomes such as getting a particular job or maximizing income? Or should it fulfill a larger purpose, as our history of the liberal arts suggests? As Johann Neem insightfully describes a liberal arts education, "the goal is not just to give all people what they want (as utilitarianism would have it) or to accommodate every worldly need (as some pragmatists suggest) but instead to help students and professors orient their lives around new purpose."[20] While Neem believes that these goals indeed are not exclusive—that a liberal arts education can provide all these outcomes even though it is aimed at the last goal—the good news is that the research findings reported here objectively support this view. While different specific aspects of a liberal arts education have different kinds of relationship to life outcomes, the individual who experiences all aspects of the liberal arts is the person who as an adult is more likely to be a leader, an altruist, a continued learner, culturally involved, fulfilled, and successful.

Indeed, contemporary pressures from students, parents, legislators, and regulators to Prussianize our American education by emphasizing specialization and eliminating other aspects of learning are destroying higher education's long-term, constructive impact on graduates' lives and society. Over the longer term, people who not only are more successful professionally, but are more fulfilled, are leaders, and become more involved in the advancement of our society are those who experience the full educational ecology of the liberal arts.

In the final chapters, I also explore many other implications of the research findings. Where can college educations with the most impact be found? How should a prospective college student decide what college to attend? How should faculty think about the higher education they provide and the desired priorities for their academic programs and professional lives? How do college and university policies support or interfere with creating an impactful educational experience? How should colleges think about marketing themselves in this liberal arts–skeptical era? What is the role of diversity, equity, inclusion, and social justice in educational practice? What is the implication of technology for a liberal arts approach to education? What government policies encourage or discourage an education that has a positive impact on the progress of a region or a nation? Are there lessons to be learned regarding education in a pandemic and postpandemic era? Can liberal arts education contribute to the complex challenges facing our society regarding inequity? And what about the cost of college? Overall, the findings provide numerous insights into how both students and society benefit from an education in the tradition of the liberal arts, and how, by applying liberal arts educational principles, higher education can be made more impactful for all.

The Value of the Liberal Arts for Higher Education

Questions about the value of the liberal arts specifically, and higher education in general, typically include three issues: is the outcome useful; is the cost reasonable; and is it accessible to all who could benefit from it? For outcomes, as the research summarized thus far amply demonstrates, experiencing a liberal arts education is highly related to very positive life outcomes for both the individual and society. While, as described in chapters 10 and 11, the impactful practices of the liberal arts are fully present in only some colleges and universities, they can be adopted more broadly and thereby enhance the outcome of higher education for all institutions.

Would adopting liberal arts practices increase the cost of higher education? As chapter 11 will also demonstrate, adopting or enhancing many liberal arts practices need not be expensive; it has to do with priorities and use of time, not with adding expensive personnel or programs. In fact, it may be less expensive: undergraduate-only institutions, which are more intensely student-focused, spend less per student on education and student support than do well-known research universities* whose focus is more on graduate and specialized programs.[21]

What about access to a college degree? There is no reason why a liberal arts–based education should not be accessible to all who seek an education that has the greatest impact on longer-term life outcomes. While the advertised tuition for attending the most famous liberal arts colleges is high, those schools represent a tiny proportion of undergraduate colleges in the US. Indeed, contrary to the perception that private, undergraduate-focused colleges are the bastion of the wealthy, the percentage of low-income students (as measured by Pell grants) is higher at these institutions than at other types of colleges, including at the typically well-known research universities.[22] Private four-year colleges invariably offer substantial financial support to students with financial needs, and graduation rates are substantially higher[23] and default on debt lower.[24] So the issue of access to a liberal arts education well may be more limited by perception—lack of understanding of its value and affordability.

---

*The National Center for Education Statistics does not separate expenditures by degree program, so it is impossible to know how much of this very substantial difference can be accounted for by educational and student services for graduate students as opposed to undergraduate students.

Those who seek value—students, higher education institutions, policymakers, and funders—should start with the question of purpose. If one's singular purpose is for a graduate to have a higher-paying job on the day of graduation, then specialization can be the answer and most of the liberal arts can be stripped away. If the purpose is longer-term success, however, then critical aspects of the liberal arts must be added to the college experience. If the educational goal is to maximize value by developing people who will contribute to the leadership and advancement of our society, will live fulfilled lives, and will be more personally successful over the longer term, then all aspects of the liberal arts educational ecology become important. By starting with this question of purpose and considering the findings of the research on educational content and context as reported in this book, both individuals and organizations can make more informed choices about the best way to enhance the value of a college degree.

In Closing

This chapter has provided a brief sketch of the story told in greater detail in the rest of this book. It describes essential ways in which this book is different from the myriad other books and articles on liberal arts and higher education. *Most fundamentally, it moves beyond broad assertions about the association between college and life or between the liberal arts and life after college; this work identifies which specific types of liberal arts experiences are directly associated with specific types of longer-term life outcomes.* Further, it does the following:

- Begins by identifying six key aspects of an education in the tradition of the liberal arts through a fresh historical assessment of the essence of this approach to higher learning
- Examines purposes of liberal arts education, identifying six categories of desired life outcome through an exhaustive analysis of college mission statements

- Involves an examination of longer-term, rather than short-term, impacts through interviews of 1,000 college graduates varying in age from twenty-five to sixty-five from a diverse array of institutions, ranging from small liberal arts colleges to large research universities

- Statistically analyzes the relationship between specific types of liberal arts experiences and specific adult behaviors that are indicative of the life outcomes of leadership, altruism, continued learning, cultural involvement, fulfillment, and personal success

As a result of this process, we can now answer the question posed at the beginning of this chapter: what in the world is liberal arts? The answer provided here is not only historically based, but also is empirically documented across a wide range of types of colleges and universities. The research findings impart the following lesson:

> *A bona fide liberal arts education is impactful—fulfilling the common good and serving the future of both the individual and society—by educating people for lives of consequence, inquiry, and accomplishment. This impact is brought about through a learning environment that is socially and affectively engaging and involves the study of the full span of human knowledge, intellectual challenge, and the exploration of different perspectives on issues of significance to humanity.*

This statement is not just another nice, generalized description of liberal arts education; the specific findings supporting this statement as reported in this book are filled with significant insights regarding the choices that students, faculty, institutions, and policymakers should make if their goal is for higher education to have a real and lasting impact on the lives of college graduates and our society.

While I base the work in this book on a systematic investigation of the history of the liberal arts, and frequently refer to "education in the tradition of the liberal arts," the research findings and their implications are not a call for higher education to resist change, nor to return to the practices of an idealized past. Quite the contrary, this presentation urges colleges and universities to shed many of today's engrained assumptions and practices and to focus on those liberal arts educational approaches that have demonstrable life impact. By doing so, we will be able to confidently attest to the value of the liberal arts—benefitting the individual and our society—and enhance our ability to provide an education of life impact.

*   *   *

In developing a fresh understanding of education in the tradition of the liberal arts, you may choose to read the rest of this book selectively. If you are interested in understanding what the term "liberal arts" means, read chapters 2, 3, and 4. What you will find there is not the usual philosophical exposition, nor a defense of particular beliefs about what must be studied in college. Rather, you will find a description of an approach to education comprising specific practices and goals that have been developed and perfected over millennia—an educational method consistent in its higher purpose, using methods designed to maximize its impact and with a curriculum embracing the span of knowledge and insight.

If you are most interested in the research findings regarding the lifetime impact of a college education and the specific educational experiences related to those outcomes, read chapters 5 through 8, as well as the appendices. There, you will find a description of how our research on college experience and life outcomes was carried out, and the essential findings regarding those aspects of higher education most related to long-term life outcomes: living lives of impact, inquiry, and accomplishment. Or, if you are interested in more information on the research and findings but wading through the details and graphs of those chapters is more than you wish to do, just read the first and last few pages of each of those research chapters, as they will give you both an introduction and a summary of the findings.

And if you are most interested in why and how the essential aspects of an education in the tradition of the liberal arts have impact, as well as the implications of this understanding for higher education, read chapters 9 through 12. In these chapters, I explore the educational ecology comprising the liberal arts and the reasons for the powerful importance of learning in a deliberately constructed social environment, as well as the implications of our research insights for colleges, students, and policymakers.

And, of course, if your interest is in developing a full range of fresh insights into what it means to truly be higher educated—to best serve the future of the individual and the society in which we live—then each of the chapters will contribute to your understanding.

2

An Educational Ecology: Higher Learning through Purpose, Content, and Context

What a piece of work is a man, how noble in reason,
how infinite in faculties, in form and moving,
how express and admirable in action,
how like an angel in apprehension,
how like a god!
— *Hamlet, Prince of Denmark*, Act II, Scene 2

The longest-standing approach to higher education in the United States carries the label "liberal arts." What is liberal arts education? It is often assumed to be an education with particular characteristics: some say that it is a study emphasizing humanities subjects such as philosophy, history, and art; others say that it is the study of one subject in depth and many subjects broadly. But there are literally hundreds of other definitions. While there is no single definition of the desired results of a liberal arts education, the outcome of this approach to education is supposed to involve the development of people who know how to think, learn, be creative, and adapt to change.

Of course, to skeptics the liberal arts encompasses the study of subjects with no practical application, such as philosophy, history, and art, as well as most of the social sciences. From the skeptic's point of view, the outcome is unemployment or low-paying and futureless jobs. Their belief is that specialization is key, getting jobs is the outcome, and the key indicator, first and foremost, is job income.

Both proponents and detractors are skilled users of anecdote, with alumni stories of success or failure cited as proof of their position, as well as some objective outcomes research (summarized in appendix 1), which most often focuses on intellectual impact while in college or on jobs shortly after graduation.

Contrary to these viewpoints, it is my position that study in the tradition of the liberal arts consists of a three-part educational ecology, and as is the case with an ecological approach to any endeavor, it is the network of relationships among multiple factors that results in the various outcomes. In the case of the liberal arts, its coequal components are the higher learning purpose, the content of study, and the educational context. The purpose describes the life outcomes intended, and the importance of the educational content and context can be tested by examining the relationship they have to life outcomes. This view arises from a careful rereading of the history and development of the liberal arts as it journeyed from ancient Greece and Rome, through the Middle East and back to Europe, from there to a newly independent United States, and now globally.

This chapter gives a summary of the development of the *purpose, content,* and *context* of the liberal arts approach to higher learning, which is a necessary step toward understanding why the analyses presented in later chapters focus on these three attributes of higher education. You will learn that a view currently espoused by some liberal arts proponents and detractors—that the content of liberal arts study has remained consistent over time (e.g., it is simply the study of the humanities)—is, in fact, inaccurate. While the humanities have been included for millennia, so have the sciences; the content of liberal arts study has consistently broadened as the span of knowledge has increased. Contrarily, the educational context (how the education is delivered) and the purpose of higher learning (life outcomes expected) have been very consistent over time.

The story of the evolution of education in the tradition of the liberal arts, which continues today, is neither boring nor staid; while always driven by the goal of maximizing a higher good, its progress has not infrequently been ironic, strange, and humorous. But the result of its innovations has been the creation of an educational experience that more effectively contributes to the progress and success of the individual and of humanity—much more than competing approaches to higher learning. People who today demand that higher education change to be jobs-based do not understand how essential aspects of higher learning interrelate to create an impact; they are putting at risk the very aspects of collegiate education that have a significant life impact for both the individual and our society.

*   *   *

You might think that, with roots going back millennia to ancient Greece as well as two centuries of experience in the United States, educators would have a clear, succinct, and agreed-upon description of liberal arts education. While I have studied in and worked at liberal arts colleges for over fifty years, have read countless articles and books on the subject, and given many talks about it, I decided it was important to explore this question systematically rather than simply relying on my personal experience. To that end, I have reviewed dozens of books and articles; examined statements on the liberal arts by educational and scholarly organizations; interviewed college presidents, academic officers, foundation executives, and writers; carried out a research project on this topic;[1] ran faculty workshops to learn their perspectives; and read the mission statements of hundreds of colleges and universities. The list of descriptive statements developed from these sources turned out to be a long one, with 141 words and phrases used to describe liberal arts education.

Indeed, the hundreds of well-thought-out, but different, statements about the essential nature of the liberal arts led me to four interesting, but also disturbing, insights:

- Educators believe that they know what a liberal arts education is—they always say, "I know it when I see it."
- When groups of educators (faculty, administrators, or a combination of the two) are convened and asked to agree on a description of liberal arts education, they enthusiastically engage in discussion and invariably come up with a list of essential features. While each group writes eloquent and well-reasoned definitions, each group's definition includes a somewhat or very different list of so-called essential attributes.
- While the various lists describing the essential nature of liberal arts education will usually overlap, nearly everyone has their own favored, often unique, set of inspiring words or phrases or principles to describe what liberal arts education means.
- The descriptions nearly invariably include terms or phrases that educators love but that are unclear, confusing, or opaque to noneducators.

I was disturbed by these insights because if educators don't agree and can't communicate clearly, is it any wonder that nearly everyone else is at best confused, or at worst confident that the liberal arts is focused on useless purposes? Is it any wonder that the liberal arts approach is under siege?

Because it wasn't clear to me whether the challenge of cutting through the complexity of the meaning of "liberal arts" was a Gordian knot requiring creative insight to solve or merely a tangled knot requiring patience to unscramble, I decided on a different way of trying to bring clarity to the liberal arts. Rather than reading others' conclusions about the liberal arts or endless philosophical statements on the subject, I decided to go back to basics by reading about how education in the tradition of the liberal arts developed—its purpose, content of study, and methods. It turned out that this story was far more interesting than how it is usually presented, as simply a list of required areas of study or generalized statements about good citizenship. Study in the tradition of the liberal arts is an educational ecology involving not merely the content of study, but also the ways in which education is delivered and the purposes that it is to fulfill. While the roots of liberal arts study are several thousand years old, it has evolved in ways that make its life impact even more consequential today than it was in ancient Greece.

In the following summary of the development of the liberal arts, I focus exclusively on the actual character of liberal arts study: its purpose, content, and educational context. The reader is encouraged to read other books on the liberal arts to fill in philosophical and historical facts that I judged less relevant to the focus of this presentation.

Ancient Roots

The origins of liberal arts study began in Greece about 3,500 years ago. Its *purpose* was to educate people who would contribute to the most urgent needs of society at that time: the need for effective warriors trained for compulsory military service. While an ironic purpose from the viewpoint of contemporary educators, this was a common need at that time—a higher, common purpose—that was being served because it improved the ability of both the individual and the society to survive and progress.

While at its earliest inception the content of this Greek education was limited and directly practical, it occurred in the context of direct and personally very involving interaction with both instructors and peers. As Greek civilization developed over the next 1,000 years, innovative changes included changes in *content* (e.g., substituting symbolic warfare through gymnastics and athletic competitions for military training) and the addition of the study of culture through arts and music.[2] Ultimately, the content of ancient Greek schooling[3] changed to involve a number of areas of intellectual study—classical poets and writers, composition, mathematics, and music—which "prepared the mind for the more advanced stages of education and culture."[4] While the specifics varied, the two areas of study "most typical of advanced education [were] philosophy and rhetoric."[5] This change in content was tied to the larger societal purpose: what the leaders of the time felt was needed to make increasingly democratic states successful. This education was to prepare "free citizens for their new role in democracy."[6]

These free citizens, who were rich and powerful men (never women, slaves, laborers, or foreigners) were thought to need special personal and interpersonal competencies, although there was no general agreement about just what this required proficiency was. In many ways reminiscent of the social and political controversies of today, there were differences of opinion about the most critical components of higher education. Some prioritized teaching the skills of oratory so that their students could develop and deliver persuasive arguments in civic discourse (e.g., Gorgias, Protagoras); others focused on the development of ideals of intellect and the pursuit of truth (based on Socratic ideals, including Plato and his followers); and still others felt that people should learn to live their lives and adopt civic values based on traditional, noble virtues (e.g., Isocrates and his persuasive oratory).

Thus, while the content of this higher education was inconsistent over time and place in ancient Greece (it changed and expanded as societal needs and the extent of knowledge grew), there was consistency in the underlying purpose of this education. This purpose was to serve the higher, common good—the needs of both the individual and society—through the formation of a responsible adult. Education involved the whole person ("the whole man, body and soul, sense and reason, character and mind"); the development of morality ("an ideal standard"); and the development of the person as opposed to the creation of a specialist. In sum: "the classical ideal . . . preceded any specialized technical considerations. It preceded them for once the mind had been trained it was pure power, completely free, ready for any demands that might be made on it."[7]

In ancient Greece, education consistently occurred in the context of the personal relations among teachers and students. Most often, it involved a tutor who traveled to homes or other community locations where they worked with individuals or small groups of students. Additionally, collecting teachers and students into learning communities was another approach to creating a social learning context, such as Plato's Academy and its descendent organizations. It is important to note that a close relationship between student and teacher was consistently seen as essential: "advanced education involved a deep and absolutely personal bond between teacher and pupil, a bond in which . . . emotion, if not passion, played a considerable part."[8] Indeed, Plato, in the Dialogues, supported the active engagement of students in learning.[9] Much of what was learned occurred through these interpersonal oral relationships rather than through written materials.[10]

In the second century BC, the Roman Republic conquered ancient Greece, eliminating its political independence but extending its cultural and educational impact. Before being influenced by Grecian norms, Roman education was "nothing really intellectual"[11]—it was an education designed for a peasant people, for farmers, and for the maintenance of traditional values. But Rome quickly assimilated early Greek culture in general, as well as the purpose, content, and context of higher learning. Becoming an educated aristocrat in Rome was now based directly on a Greek educational context: "the Roman aristocracy adopted Greek education for its sons. Teachers were readily at hand amongst the great numbers of slaves that conquest had provided . . ."[12] The content of study changed somewhat: Romans rejected disciplines such as music and athletics (especially the nudity associated with the latter), continued Greek philosophy and science, and added Cicero's Latin approach to oration and Roman medicine, among others. Very interestingly, persuasive public speaking was given the highest value, as indicated by the fact that teachers of rhetoric were paid four or five times as much as other teachers.[13]

And what higher purpose was this Roman education supposed to fulfill? Its purpose was to provide a "liberal" education—reflecting the Latin word "liberalis." "In Roman antiquity liberalis denoted 'of or relating to free men.' Quite significantly, this denotation implied both the status of social and political freedom, as opposed to slavery, and the possession of wealth, affording free time for leisure."[14] These were virtuous, knowledgeable, and articulate people who could contribute to the public good by participating in public debate, defending themselves in court, serving on juries, and providing military leadership.

Ironically, it was not until the end of the Roman Empire—indeed merely a few decades before its final demise in the fifth century— when a North African in the Roman province of what we now call Algeria wrote a book that for the first time defined the necessary content of a liberal arts education. Martianus Capella's book, *On the Marriage of Philology and Mercury*,[15] described the content of a liberal arts education as requiring the study of seven essential disciplines which, when combined, describe the knowledge of a learned person. The first three of these seven, later labeled the "trivium," were well established in ancient Greece and related to thinking and communicating: logic, grammar, and rhetoric. An understanding of these disciplines was believed to be necessary before going on to the study of the other four. These latter four, described by Plato in *The Republic*, were later called the "quadrivium," and they involved an understanding of physical reality: arithmetic, music, geometry, and astronomy.

Martianus's book was written from a perspective that today would be seen as a somewhat bizarre allegory: a man describes to his son the marriage of a young woman called Philology (whose name means "love of learning and literature") to Mercury (the god of commerce and communication). As wedding gifts, Philology receives from Mercury seven handmaidens, each individually representing one of the essential disciplines of the liberal arts. The description of each discipline is given in an extensive allegorical style. For example, the maiden named Grammar is described as carrying a beautiful polished box, out of which "she took a pruning knife with a shining point, with which she could prune the faults of pronunciation in children; then they could be restored to health with a certain black powder."[16] The specific aspects of each discipline are described: in the case of Grammar, the discipline is both mechanical and intellectual, with the handmaiden stating: "My duty in the early stages was to read and write correctly; but now there is the added duty of understanding and criticizing knowledgeably."[17] Each handmaiden's story includes an extensive elaboration of the aspects of the discipline to be learned.

It is important to reiterate that while education continued to serve a higher, common purpose—advancing society as well as the individual—and to use a personally engaging educational context, the content of study changed. It was no longer confined to the ideas of the ancient Greek philosophers: as the span of human knowledge grew over millennia, it was necessary to innovate by broadening the number of areas to be studied. Early on, the highly educated person's learning included only music and rhetoric, but as new areas of knowledge developed, math and astronomy were also essential.

The Span of Knowledge Globalizes

Unfortunately, the descent of Europe into the early medieval period (sometimes called the "Dark Ages") created a hostile environment for higher learning. Greek knowledge largely disappeared; indeed, in 529 AD the East Roman (Byzantine) emperor Justinian banned and ordered the destruction of the works of the ancient Greeks because he believed them to be pagan, and therefore contrary to his view of the purposes of Christianity. The Academy—founded by Plato nearly a thousand years earlier—was closed.

Yet these developments ultimately resulted in a tremendous increase in the *content* of higher learning, which would later reenter European liberal arts education. The scholars of the Greek classics found refuge outside Europe, at the Academy of Jundhi-Shapur (a city in what is now western Iran) in Persia. There, "they preserved these traditions, improved upon and added to them."[18] A hundred years later, in 636, Islamic forces conquered this Near East region, but the Academy of Jundhi-Shapur was left undisturbed; indeed, it "flourished as an extensive intellectual reservoir having much influence on Islamic learning."[19]

Dramatically furthering this commitment to enhancing knowledge, another hundred years later in the middle of the eighth century, Caliph al-Mansur established a new Muslim capital by creating the city of Baghdad. This city was to be the center of an empire stretching from Spain, through the Middle East, and into South Asia and the edges of China. A central feature of Baghdad was the House of Wisdom. Based on the Islamic ideal that "to pursue knowledge is a way to come closer to God,"[20] al-Mansur's purpose was to ensure that this new center of learning would become an intellectual superpower, and he invested substantial funds to accomplish this. He acquired Greek, Sumerian, Persian, Byzantine, Indian, and Chinese knowledge by purchasing or negotiating the receipt of thousands of manuscripts from many nations and eras.* His emissaries traveled

---

*As Cheng and Wei report, it is noteworthy that ancient Chinese education involved a broad curriculum and whole-person development based on Confucian Boya or Wenhua Shuzi principles. It is also the case that ancient Buddhist-based education involved close relationships between teacher and student and fulfilled the higher purpose of bettering society. Universities such as Nalanda and the University of Ancient Taxila in what is now India, providing instruction 2,500 to 3,500 years ago,

extensively, not infrequently at the cost of their own lives, to acquire knowledge from throughout the known world. He brought together a diverse range of scholars—Muslims, Christians, Jews, Hindus, Buddhists, and others with different areas of expertise, exchanging ideas with and teaching each other. The pursuit was interdisciplinary, intercultural, international, and interreligious. He supported the translation of works[21] of scholars ranging from classical Greek philosophers to Hindu scientists. These were all preserved by translating them into Arabic. By bringing the Chinese technology of paper making to Baghdad, these translations could be made into books, a far more useful and compact form of information storage than animal hides and scrolls. He established a royal library, complete with not only a staff of scholars but administrative and financial support.[22]

The result was an era described as the "Golden Age of Islam" (750–1150)—a time characterized by the open pursuit of knowledge as a divine calling.[23] Scholars took seriously the first word of the Holy Koran—*Iqra*—meaning "read," and, unlike Europe at that time, theology and dogma were not allowed to limit scholarship. It was a society "based on reason and invention, for a world empire of faith filtered through the lens of reason,"[24] and it yielded "centuries of uninterrupted, organized research and steady advances in mathematics, philosophy, astronomy, medicine, optics, and other pursuits."[25] Arabic was the language of science and all other areas of advanced knowledge. Indeed, much of the knowledge we now possess about the great Greek and Roman philosophers and writers—having been systematically destroyed as anti-Christian in Europe—was preserved through these translations into Arabic.

The northwesternmost end of the Islamic world, Cordoba (located in today's Spain) became a center of learning when its caliph

offered a range of subjects suggestive of a liberal arts approach. It is reasonable to assume that these approaches may have been included among the ideas brought back to the House of Wisdom.

established one of the most renowned of the many hundreds of libraries established during the Islamic Golden Age, as well as twenty-seven free schools. This "gave Cordoba a reputation for learning that spread throughout Europe, attracting Christian scholars as well as Muslims, not to mention the Jews who lived under Islamic rule."[26] As will be described later in this chapter, this region subsequently played an essential role in the reintroduction of classical and more contemporary knowledge to Europe. As noted earlier, Arabic was the language of the educated and of scholarly discourse.

This was a dynamic environment, with innovations shaping education in what subsequently became liberal arts education in its more contemporary form. Learning continued to serve a higher, common purpose of advancing humanity through personal and public enlightenment. The ancient Greek and Roman content was combined with a dramatically increased span of human knowledge from all the nations and cultures known at that time with the new ideas of Islamic scholars in the arts, philosophy, medicine, and sciences.

As was the case in ancient Greece and Rome, the educational context involved a carefully constructed personal and interpersonal community. Students would travel long distances to sit with a great teacher and hear and discuss his lectures in convenings known as "circle schools." In this authentic learning community, "students showed great devotion to teachers and often preferred direct intellectual association with them than with their writings."[27] Great universities were founded in the Muslim world, including the still-operating al-Karaouine in Morocco (founded by a woman, Fatima al-Fihri, in 859) and al-Azhar in Egypt (founded in 970). These universities provided a rich educational context involving complete residential learning communities, including housing, kitchens, bathhouses, and medical care.[28] The teacher/student relationship was central, with "the educational model relying not simply on close study of the text, but on intensive, personal interaction with a shaykh (scholar)."[29] The importance of engaging pedagogy was emphasized: "It is the duty of the teacher, then, to study the qualities of a student and direct him to the most suitable branch of learning."[30] Further, "students were encouraged to debate their views with their teachers" and "to question the teacher on any point and feel free to disagree with his point of view or even to challenge and correct his statements."[31] Until the eleventh century, these schools and universities were privately supported and secular; with the subsequent rise of the religious madrasa, education became a function of the state, and sectarian and political education was added.[32]

The Islamic Golden Age saved classical Greek and Roman knowledge and added very significantly to the span of knowledge, with far more extensive content in mathematics, natural sciences, engineering, social sciences, health and medicine, arts, poetry, architecture, and many other areas of inquiry. But it then started a period of rapid decline due to invasions from the East and the West. With the spirit of open intellectual inquiry already being progressively constrained by increasing sectarianism, the Crusaders in the eleventh to the thirteenth centuries destroyed the places of Islamic learning and knowledge in the Middle East, and the Spaniards did the same following their elimination of Islamic rule on the Iberian Peninsula. Genghis Khan and his followers destroyed Baghdad and the House of Wisdom in 1258; the "greatest calamity which came to Muslim learning was the Mongol invasion of the thirteenth century. The Mongols destroyed most of the great institutions of learning . . . the mosques, the universities, the libraries. After the Mongols, these Islamic universities never regained their old spirit and beauty."[33]

The Shepherd Boy and the Reintroduction of Purpose, Content, and Context to Europe

Fortunately, several hundred years before the end of the Islamic Golden Age, a peasant shepherd boy in France was offered a place in a monastery school by an abbot who was impressed with his apparent intelligence after having a chance conversation with him.[34] This boy, Gerbert of Aurillac, gave up his sheep and moved to the monastery school. A bright student, he exhausted the learning resources of that school before too many years elapsed. In contrast to Arabic libraries, in the mid- and late-900s, monasteries (being the only schools and libraries of Europe) had collections of only a few dozen books. Indeed, the great European libraries at that time had a collection of only hundreds of books.[35]

Gerbert, having consumed the learning resources of France and mastered grammar, logic, and rhetoric, found no place in that nation where he could progress to more advanced subjects. Therefore, "in 967, his superiors sent him for three years of advanced studies at the monastery of Vich in Catalonia, then a distant Christian frontier outpost abutting the scientific and cultural powerhouse of Muslim Spain."[36] There, he had access not only to teachers with greater knowledge, but also to the estimated 40,000 Arabic-language books in the library in the nearby Muslim city of Cordoba.[37] The fact that Gerbert was Christian was not a problem—Muslims, Jews, and Christians in Spain lived and worked together—and he undoubtedly mastered Arabic because it was the lingua franca of that time. (Christians in Spain even sang Mass in Arabic.)[38] According to an imam of the mosque in ancient al-Karaouine, Gerbert traveled all the way to Morocco to study at that ancient university.[39]

Thus, not only did Gerbert learn Arabic and the great diversity of subjects advanced during the Islamic Golden Age—sciences, mathematics, social sciences, arts, poetry, and others—but he also learned about religious tolerance and intellectual openness, which were not attributes characteristic of Christian Europe. He brought this new knowledge and open perspective back to France, where he took up a series of teaching posts. He introduced Europe to a number of innovative concepts that he learned in Cordoba, including not only new understanding of subjects such as arithmetic and geometry, but also Arabic numerals, the abacus, and the astrolabe. Gerbert's growing fame resulted in his being named by the emperor of the Holy Roman Empire, Otto II, to be the abbot of a monastery in Italy with a library of 690 books—an immense number for Europe.[40] When Europe entered a period of great tumult in 983 Gerbert fled Italy, but a number of years later he returned, and was named an archbishop in 998 and became the trusted advisor to emperor Otto III.

Finally, in 999, Gerbert was named pope by that emperor. Calling himself Pope Sylvester II, he encouraged the flow of knowledge and intellectual openness from the Islamic world to Europe. As a result, even though he was the pope, he was accused by some of being a sorcerer because of his unusual knowledge. While he served as pope for only four years before his death, his introduction of knowledge and educational perspectives from the Islamic Golden Age unleashed a tidal wave of new knowledge into Europe as the earlier translation of Greek texts into Arabic—which occurred hundreds of years earlier—now reversed direction, with translations from Arabic to Latin and other European languages.

Whereas in the ninth century, an Islamic scholar traveling in Europe "found the Europeans 'humorless, gross and dull,'"[41] intellectual life was now returning. European students ventured to Muslim universities and libraries, as did Gerbert, to study a wide range of subjects, from philosophy to cosmography. Martianus's book *On the Marriage of Philology and Mercury,* and his seven-component definition of the liberal arts, were "quickly taken up as a textbook for the septem (seven) artes liberales" and became one of the most popular books in Western Europe.[42]

However, the speed with which knowledge returned to Europe from the immense Muslim collections was slow. Around 1100, a century after Pope Sylvester II, an Englishman called Adelard of Bath returned after spending seven years in the Middle East with a massive collection of *Studia Arabum* (meaning "scholarly materials" in Arabic) and spent a lifetime translating the materials. Through the work of Adelard and many others who translated Arabic writings into Latin or other European languages, it took nearly 300 years for the knowledge from the Golden Age of Islam to fully penetrate Europe.*

In the eastern Mediterranean, the Byzantine Empire, centered in what today is Turkey, remained a home for the scholars of ancient Greece. In the early 1400s, following the Italian merchants who traded with the Byzantines, Italian scholars traveled east to study with these scholars of classical Greece, creating another flow of knowledge back into Europe. This stimulated a migration of experts from East to West, where "Byzantine scholars who taught in Italy represented the richness of the Greek heritage to their Western admirers."[43] In 1454, after many years of conflict with various invaders, the empire fell to the Ottomans, and then many more scholars fled to the West, stimulating the development of the Renaissance as they brought with them additional ancient Greek wisdom and writings. The Renaissance now swept across Europe, further broadening knowledge and insight. European nations became deeply involved in the Age of Discovery through exploration, trade, and colonization around the world.

The impact of this slow flood of knowledge was enormous, and the stage was set for the rebirth of higher education in Europe. Translations "were destined for Italy, France, and England—home to groupings of scholars and students who came together around the early thirteenth century to create the West's earliest universities in Bologna, Paris, and Oxford."[44] The beginnings of these universities were "obscure" and "intricate";[45] indeed, students of that time would not have thought of themselves as attending a university,

---

*The volume of these scholarly materials in Arabic is so great that even today, not all have been examined or translated—see, for example, the work of Staatsbibliothek zu Berlin, which has a large collection of original documents (described in blog.sbb .berlin/uncovering-the-history-of-islamicate-astronomy/).

nor would we recognize these early institutions as universities today. The word *universitas* ("university" in Latin) was not used anywhere until 1215.[46]

Although similar in many ways, these institutions had important differences. Governance varied widely; for example, Paris was ruled by teachers who organized themselves into a guild "resembling those that had long dominated any other craft or profession"; and Bologna was ruled by students, where "teaching doctors in consequence were reduced to an almost incredible state of subservience. It was the students through their representatives who hired and fired the faculty, fixed their salaries, required each professor to swear allegiance and obedience to whatever statutes were enacted, granted and limited leaves of absence, and in other ways controlled even the smallest details of daily academic life."[47]

There were important common characteristics of these newly emerging European institutions: they often grew out of a cathedral- or monastery-associated school; they attracted students of many nationalities, from near and far; they were located in towns so that the relatively large number of students could live together and be fed and housed; and all instruction was in Latin as it was the common language of education and the educated in a time when there were many scores of languages in Europe. The result of this combination of characteristics—the need to travel, live away from home, and to study and converse in Latin—meant that this education was generally limited to the privileged who had the family resources to have received tutoring in Latin, to afford the expense of living away from home, and to pay the costs of instruction. While all students were required to complete an extensive liberal arts education before receiving any professional instruction, institutions tended to specialize—for example, Bologna (established in 1088) specialized in law, and Paris (1150) specialized in philosophy and religion.[48]

The essential purpose of higher education in this era was to inform and support the constructive development of society. Given the roots of universities in cathedral schools, as well as the dominance of the Catholic Church in that era, it is not surprising that the higher education of the clergy took high priority.

For the content of study, Martianus's "septum artes liberales" (seven liberal arts areas of study) "came to be adopted as the education necessary for the study of higher truth in Scripture."[49] The receipt of the bachelor of arts (liberal arts) degree was the prerequisite for master's degrees in more specialized fields such as law, medicine, and theology. At both Paris and Oxford, four to five years of liberal arts study was required before specialization could be considered, including a thorough study of Latin translations (from Arabic initially, and much later from Greek) related to grammar, rhetoric, logic, arithmetic, music, geometry, and astronomy.[50] The development of law—moving from Roman law to canon law—was essential; "law was viewed as a part of rhetoric, and could be formally incorporated into artes liberales."[51]

The educational context revolved around a residential educational community involving people of a wide range of backgrounds, cultures, and life experiences. Students lived and studied together as people from many nations traveled long distances to join these educational communities. In 1265, for example, one university listed fourteen nationalities of students from north of the Alps alone.[52] In this era, these people of different nationalities who spoke different languages brought true differences in life experience, culture, and beliefs; as a result, disputes were frequent and negative stereotypes common.[53] It is very important to note that liberal arts learning was enriched through intellectual and personal interaction with these very different others.

At Oxford and Cambridge, residential colleges were the norm, with groupings of colleges making up a larger, somewhat loosely organized university. Each college had its own faculty and instructional spaces; classrooms and eating facilities were often on the ground floor and student and faculty residences were on the upper floors.

A porter stood guard at the entrance to each college—in this context, a "porter" was not a person who carries bags in the contemporary meaning of the word; rather, it was a man who, as a respected college official, knew nearly everything about the community and decided who could enter and who could not. The notion of the authentic learning community had reached a new level of refinement.

With the large number of students and lack of written materials in this era, the lecture became central to European higher education. But lecturing was not meant to be either impersonal or unengaging. Mirroring the emphasis on the importance of effective student engagement found during the Islamic Golden Age, teaching guides were developed. With hauntingly contemporary advice, requirements for effective lecturing included that a lecture should be "clear, short, relevant, and easy to listen to"; it should "start with generally well-known things, so as gradually to penetrate deeper into the material and [help students] learn to distinguish between essentials and inessentials"; and it should lead "to independent reflection outside hours, and to a personal engagement with problems . . . that would supply the scholar lastingly with a 'life full of inward joy and all possible comfort in this vale of sorrows.'"[54] An effective teacher was described as a "'classroom entertainer,' bold, original, lucid, sharply polemical, always fresh and stimulating, and withal 'able to move to laughter the minds of serious men.'"[55] Students were encouraged to request debates among scholars on particular topics or issues, and out-of-class teaching and learning opportunities were created.[56]

As was the case in ancient Greece and Rome, higher education was available only to the select few—the so-called betters of society. People of that era spoke many regional native languages, so higher education was offered in Latin, the language of the educated. As a result, relatively few people could attend a university; in general, only the children of men holding significant roles in their nations had the requisite knowledge and the financial resources. To be highly educated was the province of men of influence and significance, and such knowledge was a necessary precondition for studying for a profession.

At this point, we will jump forward five hundred years since the founding of the earliest European universities, to the time when England was colonizing North America. American higher education began during the colonial period of the 1600s and 1700s, when educational institutions based on the model of Oxford and Cambridge were founded, most often by Protestants intent on advancing humanity by bringing civilization to a newly developing land. The founding of Harvard—America's oldest university—is described as follows:

> Approximately a hundred Cambridge men and a third as many Oxford men emigrated to New England before 1646; among them were the founders of Harvard, the fathers of the first generation of Harvard students. Their purposes were complex, but among other things, they intended to re-create a little bit of old England in America. . . . Of course, a religious commonwealth required an educated clergy, but it also needed leaders disciplined by knowledge and learning, it needed followers disciplined by leaders, it needed order.[57]

With the higher purpose of "preparing men of refinement and culture, those destined to positions of responsibility and leadership,"[58] the content of the curricula was heavily classical, including rhetoric, philosophy, ethics, and math. But for these English speakers, there were new and different requirements as well, including the need to learn Latin and ancient Greek (the language of the classical texts), as well as Hebrew. Newer fields of knowledge resulting from discoveries by Islamic scholars and Europe's subsequent scientific revolution were included, ranging from physics to aspects of economics and sociology,[59] which significantly added to the span of subject areas included in liberal arts study. Specialized study came after an education grounded in this elaborated version of the liberal arts. Indeed, specialized education in this era was often accomplished through apprenticeships in professions like law and medicine rather than through academic study.

A total of nine colleges were founded in English North America between 1636 and 1769, with Harvard, William and Mary, and the Collegiate School of New Haven (later renamed Yale) being the oldest.[60] These institutions often began with a single building (as both the educational facility and residence) and included as much of the surrounding land as was available.[61]

The educational context was described by some as the "collegiate way." The belief was that "a curriculum, a library, a faculty, and students are not enough to make a college. It is an adherence to the residential scheme of things"[62]—an intentional learning community involving students and faculty inside and outside the classroom. In these residential colleges, it was typical to have strict codes of conduct—at Union College, "card playing, swearing, drunkenness, striking instructors or locking them in their rooms" were among the prohibited activities; Princeton students were "instructed to raise their hats to the president at a distance of ten rods and to tutors at five"; and frontier colleges required "pledges from students that they were not carrying guns or bowie knives."[63] As was the case in medieval Europe and even before, students were frequently rowdy or ribald, and they occasionally rioted—there are many humorous (from today's perspective) reports of these extreme events—although learning expectations were high.

This education was designed for the elite, as also had been the case in ancient Greece and Rome and medieval and Renaissance Europe. One need only read an excerpt from a Harvard commencement address in the 1670s to believe this. The speaker asserted that were it not for a Harvard education, the "everyday person" might be in charge: "The ruling class would have been subjected to mechanics, cobblers, and tailors . . . the laws would not have been made by senatus consulta (decree) . . . but plebiscites, appeals to base passions, and revolutionary ramblings."[64] A statement typical of the times referring to the founding of William and Mary described it as "ensuring 'that the youth . . . (be) piously educated in good letters and manners.'"[65]

This liberal arts approach to being highly educated took root in the newly colonized North America during the seventeenth and eighteenth centuries. As in Europe, the liberal arts was the first course of study—the first level—of a higher education, possibly followed by professional education, often through apprenticeships; it was designed with the purpose of strengthening the abilities of the select few, who, as the leaders of their time, would further the goals of their society—emphasizing "civic virtue over private advantage."[66]

In Summary: An Educational Ecology of Purpose, Content, and Context

Looking across the millennia at the development of approaches to higher learning, several things become clear. First, this approach to higher learning has always served the *purpose* of preparing people to play significant roles in their society in ways of value to both the individual and the society—a higher, common good. As described by the economics scholar Robert Reich, this common good represents "what we owe one another as citizens who are bound together in the same society," and further, that it "recognizes that we're all in it together."[67]

Second, what was studied—its *content*—has changed over time. While the oldest origin of the liberal arts involved the specialized training of warriors, as the needs and complexities of society increased, it broadened to include subjects described today as the humanities (poetry, music, philosophy, public discourse) and subjects that today are called science (including mathematics and physics). During the Islamic Golden Age, when the knowledge of diverse nations from Europe through Asia was brought together and the advances of Islamic scholars in many disciplines were added, the span of knowledge to be considered in the arts and sciences expanded. When the liberal arts reentered the knowledge-starved Europe, and then the North American colonies, the areas of study broadened to include many newly developed understandings in the sciences, mathematics, natural sciences, engineering, social sciences, health and medicine, arts, poetry, architecture, philosophy, and other subjects.

Finally, the approach to teaching and learning, the educational *context*, invariably involved learning in a social or community setting, with close relationships among teachers and students and the use of what was understood to be effective pedagogy. In ancient Greece and Rome, the most common approach to higher learning involved a tutor who, often working within homes, taught individuals or small groups of students. In the Islamic Golden Age, there were advances in the approaches to teaching, apparently stimulated by the numbers of people seeking higher education. That is, students traveled to places where education was offered—gathering around a scholar in Circle Schools or attending a residential university. Although this approach now involved groups of students rather than a student alone with a tutor, close and personal interactions between and among students and teachers were viewed as essential.

As higher learning returned to Europe after the early medieval period, those who sought higher learning came to towns where collections of books and scholars were available and substantial universities developed. These were residential communities—sometimes within the walls of a school, but often encompassing an entire town—but including places for everyone to live and eat and converse and learn together. Now involving a broad diversity of nations, people, ideas, cultures, and knowledge, personal relationships among faculty and students were essential, and engaging methods of learning both in and out of class was emphasized.

Of course, for such a relationship-based experience to be educational, it must also involve content-based learning; and for it to be liberal arts in character, it must, as described in the last section of this chapter, involve the full span of human knowledge and how areas of knowledge interrelate.

Overall, then, this combination of purpose, content, and context is an educational ecology designed to transform lives: these attributes are interlinked, and we must consider them all to understand the liberal arts educational experience. And this liberal arts approach characterized higher learning in the Western Hemisphere for centuries until it was displaced by an approach designed for an entirely different purpose. This is the subject of the next chapter.

3

The Liberal Arts versus the World

A college should not be a haven from worldly contention, but a place where young people fight out among and within themselves contending ideas of the meaning of life, and where they discover that self-interest need not be at odds with concern for one another.

—Andrew Delbanco, *College: What It Was, Is, and Should Be*, 177

Education in the tradition of the liberal arts was well established in North America by 1769. Imported from England, it served the higher, common good—namely, preparing leading citizens in a deliberately designed educational context and with an evolving content of study. This approach to education was challenged in the early 1800s by the new needs of European monarchs, who demanded a different kind of higher education—one that fulfilled a different purpose and therefore involved a change in both content and context.

Because this was the era of European colonial powers, this monarchical approach was exported around the world, with the exception of the young United States, where its purposes and methods were rejected in favor of those associated with the liberal arts tradition.

What follows is neither a history nor an analysis of higher education as it developed in the United States—that is worthy of a volume
of its own, and I particularly recommend Andrew Delbanco's *College*[1] as an insightful presentation on this complex topic. As was the
case in the last chapter, this is simply an exploration of the purpose,
content, and context of education in the tradition of the liberal arts
as it developed in the United States. This analysis begins in Prussia,
for that old European nation represents the backdrop against which
American liberal arts was renewed.

A European Invention: Specialized Education Serving the State

While liberal arts education was growing deep roots in North America in the eighteenth century, Europe was simultaneously becoming a
land of empires. The countries of Europe were neither stable nor fixed;
multiethnic, multilingual regions were ruled by emperors or kings, and
borders changed due to intermarriages and conflicts. The beginning
of the nineteenth century was characterized by particular upheaval as
national borders changed as alliances for and against Napoleon developed, and battles were won and lost. European higher education was
demolished in the process: 50% of the universities in Prussia and 40%
of the universities in Europe as a whole disappeared.[2] But the era of
the nation-state was emerging, in which national borders were increasingly seen to be inviolate; this created the need for a state-imposed
national identity to unite often-diverse ethnic and language groups.

A different educational purpose emerged as states had to "gov-
ern effectively and [have] dynamic industrial economies."[3] Napoleon "transformed French universities into specialized academies
designed to produce efficient bureaucrats for the state."[4] With most
Prussian universities destroyed and the entire educational system

in shambles, the king of Prussia, Frederick William III, appointed Wilhelm von Humboldt, a diplomat then serving in Rome, as head of the educational department in the Prussian ministry of the interior. The king asked him to "lay the foundations of a new education system in Prussia,"[5] whose purpose was to serve the needs of the state. As the beneficiary of a liberal education himself,[6] Humboldt believed that education should be about the "'complete training of the human personality," even in the poorest members of society.[7] As he said, "the commonest jobbing worker and the finest graduate must at the outset be given the same mental training."[8] He asserted that this approach to education should start in the early years and continue through university. Indeed, he believed that a university education should be "an establishment of general education."[9]

It is important to recognize that his ideas about university education were strikingly consistent with the millennia-old purposes, content, and educational context of education in the tradition of the liberal arts. For example, he asserted that there should be close relations between teachers and students; students should engage in independent research under the tutelage of the teacher[10]; and the curriculum should be open to student exploration rather than involving only a fixed course of study.[11]

It is an irony, then, that while Humboldt is typically described as the educational innovator credited with revolutionizing Prussian (and European) education through a focus on specialization, and he is viewed as the inventor of the modern research university, virtually none of Humboldt's ideas about the liberal arts nature of education or the importance of an engaging approach to education were adopted for Prussian higher education. Indeed, his impact has been described as a myth,[12] as his educational ideas were not rediscovered until a century later. After leading the education ministry for only sixteen months (and actually serving for only nine months—he was on leave for seven months), he was discouraged by the opposition to his plans in the government. Wishing to return to his wife and children, who still lived in Rome, he resigned from the education ministry and resumed his diplomatic duties.

While Humboldt's ideas about liberal education and effective university teaching were rejected, several other ideas of his were adopted. These ideas had a nearly immediate (if largely unintended) impact on all levels of education in Prussia, Europe, and ultimately most of the rest of the world. The first was the belief that specialized study should begin in school several years before beginning higher education. This was a by-product of his belief in the importance of university-level research by both faculty and students, which he viewed as necessary for national progress, as well as an effective pedagogy. For university students to be useful in carrying out research, they needed to specialize in a discipline years before entering the university; students entered the university with a specialization already selected and related course preparation completed. Humboldt's liberal arts idea that higher education involved broader learning and personal growth and development became irrelevant distractions, with an ever-increasing emphasis on developing expertise. Over the decades of the 1800s, the conception developed that the university is a place defined by its research, not because of Humboldt's ideas about it being a tool for effective teaching and learning, but as an end in itself. The idea of the specialization-based research university, in contrast to a teaching university, emerged.

A second major idea of Humboldt's for educational reform was related to teacher quality, which was notoriously poor at the lower levels. To ensure that teachers were well prepared, he instituted a system of professional competency examinations for teachers at all levels, from primary through university.

Third, he advocated for government control of schools—their faculty, curricula, and texts. The combination of these last two ideas—teacher quality exams and state control—resulted in policy changes that have been described as "professionalization from above."[13]

Corresponding in time with a dramatic increase in the bureaucratization of the Prussian state, "universities became increasingly subjected to state bureaucracy, which managed university affairs as part of a national educational policy."[14] Government bureaucrats decided which areas of study were most important because of their contribution to the strength of the state; they decided who qualified for the increasing number of professions by administering complicated and rigorous state exams;[15] and the faculty were state employees. "Eventually, the growth of government bureaucracy and white-collar employees in industry slowly began to shift the careers of university graduates away from the classical liberal professions to public service and business."[16]

Prussian higher education, then, was to have a dramatically different character than education in the tradition of the liberal arts: it was to be "from beginning to end, through and through, a professional school."[17] Its goal was to educate a new kind of elite, who would strengthen, according to the king's highest priorities, the monarchy and the state. Youth were, through position of birth or a winnowing process implemented in elementary and secondary education, tracked either into practical trades or into university-based preparation for professional positions of "superior attainment."

The purpose of a university education, as implemented in Prussia during this time, was first, to "provide educated bureaucrats for the state, and second, to conduct research whose goal was the production of new knowledge."[18] To serve this purpose, the content of higher education, rather than involving the study of the span of human knowledge, now focused entirely on the mastery of information necessary within a particular profession. And finally, the educational context changed from being built on an engaged educational community to being designed to efficiently deliver the information deemed necessary for a particular profession. Large lectures became common, with state exams of information mastery being the definition of the desired learning outcome.

A new university, the University of Berlin (later renamed Humboldt University in honor of Wilhelm von Humboldt and his more famous brother Alexander, a natural scientist), was founded in 1810 to provide an education for bureaucrats and researchers—specialists who would contribute to the success of the king's Prussia. In addition, it refined the methods of the specialized research university through the decades of that century.

With its salutary impact on the needs of the nation-state, this Prussian, specialization-based approach to education was viewed by many (including by many scholars in the United States) as the world's best and adopted by virtually all other European monarchs. Further, because this era—the nineteenth century—corresponded with the imperial empires of the major European powers, this model spread globally through European colonialism to become the standard approach to higher education in essentially all world regions except one: the young United States.

The Yale Report and Renewed Liberal Arts Purpose, Content, and Educational Context

An event occurred near the end of the eighteenth century, just thirty-four years before the founding of the new Prussian specialized universities, which resulted in this approach to higher learning being substantially rejected in the United States. That event was the American Revolution of 1776—which was significant not only for the independence of a people from a colonial power, but also for the creation of an approach to education that distinctly differed from that adopted in Europe and most of the world.

During the decades after the American Revolution, the Cambridge/Oxford approach to higher education in the United States was increasingly threatened. Originally designed for the privileged few of royal England, and adjusted to the circumstances of a royal colony, it needed to adapt to the thinking of a newly independent democratic republic in which leadership was no longer entrusted to a small elite. Echoing Jeffersonian ideas, the emerging American belief was that everyone (except women, slaves, and nonwhites, of course, because they were not allowed to shape society) needed to be educated in ways that serve the higher good. The "everyone" priority and historic liberal arts "higher good" purpose conflicted with the Prussian-European purpose, which was designed to serve the few and advance the goals of the state. With the leading intellectuals of the era working at European institutions and focusing on specialized subjects, interest in the liberal arts was waning.

In response to these challenges, faculty at Yale College (today's Yale University) undertook an exhaustive review and evaluation of higher education. What should be the purpose of higher education, and whom should it serve? With Prussian-based specialized education flourishing and questions being raised about American higher education, it seemed logical to "turn our colleges into German universities."[19] Should an education emphasizing specialized training replace an education designed to prepare thoughtful citizens? The report they wrote, often referred to as the "Yale Report of 1828,"[20] gives tremendous insight into the dynamics of the time: "The Universities on the continent of Europe, especially in Germany, have of late gained the notice and respect of men of information in this country . . . But we doubt whether they are models to be copied in every feature, by our American colleges. We hope at least, that this college may be spared the mortification of a ludicrous attempt to imitate them."

Why shouldn't the European approach be copied? Why would copying European higher education be ludicrous for the United States? The Yale faculty concluded that the purpose of a higher education in the American context—and whom should be served—was fundamentally different than the purpose to be fulfilled in what they called the "Eastern continent" (Europe):

Our republican form of government renders it highly important that
great numbers should enjoy the advantage of a thorough education.
On the Eastern continent, the few who are destined to particular
departments in political life, may be educated for the purpose, while
the mass of the people are left in comparative ignorance. But in this
country, where offices are accessible to all who are qualified for them,
superior intellectual attainments ought not to be confined to any
description of persons. Merchants, manufacturers, and farmers, as well
as professional gentlemen, take their places in our public councils.
A thorough education ought therefore to be extended to all these
classes. It is not sufficient that they be men of sound judgment, who
can decide correctly, and give a silent vote, on great national questions.
Their influence upon the minds of others is needed; an influence to be
produced by extent of knowledge, and the force of eloquence.[21]

In contrast to European elitism and the elitism of higher education in prerevolution America, education in an independent and self-
governing United States was seen to be necessary for every person,
and an education based on a higher, common good was required in
order for a representative form of government to work.*

The Yale Report not only reaffirmed the liberal arts purpose of serving the higher good, it also clearly described both the educational
content and context in ways that were very consistent with the liberal arts ideals developed over earlier millennia. The content of education was "not designed to include professional studies," but rather to

---

*The use of the term "men" and "gentlemen" in the Yale Report was not accidental.
In 1828 "man," not "person," was typically used, and in reality, it meant "white
male"; nonwhites and females didn't have the right to vote, and higher education
for women as well as for nonwhites was uncommon. Nonwhites received the right
to vote in 1870 (though sometimes it was effectively rescinded by state laws), and
women in 1920. Some liberal arts colleges were leaders in this regard through their
inclusive policies: for example, there were black and female graduates at both Ober-
lin College and Antioch College in the decades before the Civil War in the 1860s.
Women are now overrepresented in American higher education (56% female
and 44% male), and whites are only slightly overrepresented (54% of the 18- to
24-year-old population is white, while 56% of undergraduate enrollees are white;
there remain significant disparities across nonwhite groups).

"lay the foundation which is common to them all."[22] Areas of study were to include the full range of human knowledge, from literature to the sciences. The educational goal of study of the full range of knowledge was not the creation of little buckets of specialized knowledge in the student's mind, but rather to involve an understanding of interrelationships among areas of study. Personal and intellectual character was to be balanced: from math comes reasoning, from science comes critical analysis, from literature comes effective communication, from philosophy comes the art of thinking, and so forth.[23]

In describing the context within which education was to occur, the creation of a learning community was viewed as central. Education was to happen in the context of a residential learning community: "Students should be so collected together, as to constitute one family; that the intercourse between them and their instructers [sic] may be frequent and familiar."[24] Effective educational strategies were to be utilized, using techniques ranging from lectures and recitations to informal and extemporaneous discussions to avoid having the student "repose in his seat, and yield a passive hearing to the lecturer, without ever calling into exercise the active powers of his own mind."[25]

So, in deliberate contrast to the specialization approach, a commitment was made to an American approach to higher education—one firmly based on the purposes, content, and context of the liberal arts as it developed over previous millennia. Education was designed to serve the higher good by assuring that all citizens, not just the elite, could become constructive and successful members of society. People, individually and collectively, were to be the beneficiaries of this approach, not simply the state and its rulers.

This renewed and broadened approach to liberal arts education, as championed by Yale faculty, caught fire in the developing United States. With the movement of settlers to the west, and with utopian thinking stimulated by this approach to higher education, "everywhere the mania for founding colleges raged on uncontrolled."[26] Compared to Europe, the number of colleges and universities created was astonishing. For example, in about 1830, "whereas England with a population of 23 million had only four institutions of higher learning, the state of Ohio, with a population of just 3 million . . . was hosting 37."[27] The ratio was one college per millions of people in Europe, compared to one college per tens of thousands of people in the United States. This phenomenon accelerated over time: "From the time of independence (1776) to 1820, a new college opened on average every 18 months . . . This rate was three per year from 1830 to 1845. This rate doubled again in the next 10 years and spurted to 10 new colleges per year in the half decade before the Civil War."[28]

In fact, "once a college had been determined upon, there was likely to be keen competition among towns of the region to have it located in their midst."[29] Land for the college, donations to cover the cost of a college building, and additional funds were typically offered by townspeople: they "sought and welcomed colleges not only as nodes of economic activity but also to fill educational and cultural vacuums."[30]

An illustrative, though humorously convoluted, example of this process was the creation of Hartwick College in New York,[31] where I was honored to be president for more than a decade. The benefactor was John Christopher Hartwick, an itinerant Lutheran preacher who, arriving from Germany in 1746, traveled for fifty years on horseback around northeastern colonial America, preaching in various communities. He was a learned person who accumulated a library of nearly 400 books—astonishingly large for that time, and particularly noteworthy because he spent his clerical life traveling from town to town. While autocratic in his approach to religion and behavior, he was also a utopian—he wanted to create a place where people could live together peaceably and constructively. He purchased large tracts of land from the Native American Mohawks to create an ideal community in which people would live on together and farm the surrounding communal lands. But the irreverent and independent-minded frontierspeople of the time weren't willing to live together in such a utopia, so a rival developer, William Cooper (the founder of Cooperstown, New York), began selling Hartwick's land to settlers without his permission. To cover this illegal action, he schemed to foreclose on a mortgage on Hartwick's land and paid him $33,000 after deducting the mortgage amount[32]—a huge fortune at the time.

Because he lost his land, Hartwick began to think about an alternative possibility: he decided to create an educational institution with these funds, for he believed that education was a critical part of developing a vital and constructive future for humanity. When he died in 1797, his will stipulated he wanted to create a "seminarium"—not a "seminary," as it is used in contemporary English, but a place of higher learning that would be "enabling, preparing, and qualifying proper Persons . . . in Learning or Knowledge of the Instrumental Literature such as generally are taught in the American Colledges [sic]. . . ."[33] The subjects generally taught at that time involved the expanded liberal arts, ranging from classical subjects to some social sciences and sciences.

Because Hartwick kept making additions to his will over a number of years as he journeyed on horseback from town to town, it became a confusing document involving tortuous logic (beginning with his statement that Jesus was to be the recipient of his fortunes before he described his wishes for the seminarium). In competition for access to his funds to create a college, three institutions were simultaneously created upon his death: one in New York City, one in Albany, and one near Cooperstown in his namesake town of Hartwick, New York. Each claimed his estate. The institution in Albany even had Hartwick's body dug up from where it had been buried, far to the south along the Hudson River, and reburied at a church in Albany, believing that it would strengthen their case for claiming the estate.*

---

*Ironically, many years later, with the relocation of city roads in Albany, the cemetery where Hartwick was buried needed to be relocated, and the location of his remains was lost and may well now reside under an Albany street. His tombstone, however, was rescued and later given to Hartwick College.

Eventually, the location in the town of Hartwick won, but that was not the end of the story. A century later, motivated by the dream of a "greater Hartwick," the town fathers of the city of Oneonta (located about twenty miles from Hartwick), who wished to create their own liberal arts college, offered a plot of land on a hillside overlooking the city, including the cost of an impressive college building, if the college was reestablished in this new location. This is exactly what occurred, and a beautiful, valley-view liberal arts college continues to exist there to this day.

An Educational Ecology: The Purpose, Content, and Educational Context of the American Colleges

The purpose of the new American liberal arts colleges as they proliferated during the 1800s was consistent with the principles espoused in the Yale Report of 1828 and was related primarily to the notion of an educated populace being essential to the progress of humanity and society. This idea had particular significance in a developing democracy. For example, "the commitment of the president of the board of trustees for the College of California* was 'to make men more manly, and humanity more humane; to augment the discourse of reason, intelligence and faith, and to kindle the beacon fires of truth on all the summits of existence."[34] (Education for women lagged, though, especially before 1890; although by 1890, 40% of the college's students were women.)[35]

As was the case with Hartwick College, most of the hundreds of colleges founded in this era were "denominational colleges," created as collaborations of local communities and one of the plethora of Christian denominations developing in that era.[36] While

---

*This private college was founded in 1853, and fifteen years later, it merged into a newly formed state institution that became the University of California in 1868.

originally education of the clergy was a priority, the religious focus decreased substantially as a larger interest in higher education grew. "In colonial Harvard and Yale some 70% of graduates went into the ministry; by 1810 it was only 10%."[37] Attendance at these colleges was open to people of all faiths, and "although the education or preparation of ministers was sometimes a consideration, the chief motive was to preserve the community through the sheltered education of laypeople."[38] As the religious emphasis decreased, the purpose of a higher education was refined to be "public service, acculturation of the young, and the civil community"[39]—an education serving a higher, common purpose.

Even religious organizations took this position, as evidenced by this statement of Ohio Baptists in the founding of Denison University: "Our object has been, and is, to build up a useful Institution—suited to the wants, and calculated to promote the welfare of a rapidly growing and free country, where virtuous intelligence, industry, and enterprise are sure to meet quick reward."[40]

Similarly, Presbyterians, in the founding of the College of Wooster, wrote of the higher good: "It is better to give a son a complete education than to give him a farm. He will then be able to earn more in a year than a farm could produce, and he may besides wield a great influence for good."[41] As this statement makes clear, even when personal benefit is acknowledged, the commitment to the public good is fundamental. And this purpose was consistent: "The notion that a college should serve society through the lives of dedicated graduates was not new. As a collegiate purpose it would never disappear."[42]

The content of study at the American colleges evolved over the decades. For many years, the content of the curricula of these colleges always included the classical disciplines, in addition to the broader span of human knowledge in the sciences, mathematics, and social sciences. Students were expected to be able to do their classical work in ancient Greek and Latin, and literacy in Hebrew was also required in some cases. While colleges would have preferred to admit students

with fluency in these languages, they did not use fluency as a crite-
rion for admission (unlike Cambridge and Oxford) because it would
have limited access to college, which would have been contrary to
the "all people" goal of American higher education. As a result, a
very large part of the collegiate curriculum, of necessity, was learning
these languages, and this left less time for the study of the classics
themselves, as well as all the other subjects that educators felt should
be included as essential to higher learning.[43] While generating substantial controversy, to create more time for broader study, English
translations replaced ancient Greek and Latin so that the curriculum
could be expanded more readily as new domains of knowledge developed and areas of study grew. As a result; a much broader range of the
humanities, social sciences, and sciences could be included.

Finally, the educational context, like the purpose, was consistent
over time. Not accidentally, these institutions were called "colleges"—a
word derived from the Latin *collegium,* meaning "community," "society," or "sisterhood/brotherhood." Faculty and students of a variety
of backgrounds and life experiences were brought together into a residential community where they lived and learned together, inside and
outside class. While in part this design was necessitated by the relatively low population density, which required people to travel away
from home to study, it also reflected the belief described in the Yale
Report—that people learn best in an educational community.

This combination of purpose, content, and context characterized
colleges during this era, and as you will learn in the next chapter,
also characterize liberal arts colleges today. But of course, there are
now many types of colleges and universities in the United States,
with a character framed by other significant developments in the
history of American higher education.

Among these significant developments were the Morrill Acts of
1862 and 1890. Establishing "land grant" universities, they had
the purpose of furthering agricultural and mechanical arts, thereby

contributing to the vitality of the newly developing US states. Ultimately, seventy-six universities were founded as a result of these acts—at least one in every state and including many of the premier public universities in the United States today. This dramatically increased the role and availability of higher education and extended the contribution of higher education to regional and national progress. Yet even though this initiative sounds similar to the Prussian approach, it still involved a significant commitment to liberal arts content. As the congressional legislation stated, these institutions were to include classical studies "in order to promote the liberal and practical education of the industrial classes in the several pursuits and professions in life."[44]

A second significant development was the creation of Johns Hopkins University in Baltimore in the 1870s. While often described as bringing the admired German research university to the United States, and its founding president toured European universities as the plans for this institution were developed, he described the plan as follows: "not to follow exclusively any precedent—not to attempt to found a German University nor a French or an English—but to derive from all sources such experience and recommendations as might be adapted to this country and to lead in course of time to an American University based upon our own educational system."[45] Like the European model, it placed value on research at all levels, but in the American tradition, teaching was to remain primary and research was "never allowed—at least in the rationale of the institution—to injure the teaching function."[46]

While the design of the institution evolved somewhat in its early years, claims of similarity to the admired quality of German institutions were apparently made to enhance its credibility. By 1883, it developed a conception of a university in which there was a strong undergraduate "collegiate section" providing liberal arts content (including requirements for foreign language, English composition and literature, logic/ethics, ancient history, and other subjects) and culminating in a bachelor's degree, with specialized education to follow with master's and doctoral degrees.

Therefore, unlike higher education in the Prussian tradition as adopted by most of the rest of the world, in which a student specialized from the beginning, as multidegree universities emerged in the United States, the undergraduate experience typically maintained a focus on liberal arts content, with specialization following through subsequent on-the-job training or by obtaining master's and doctoral education. Thus was born the American comprehensive research university, with both undergraduate liberal arts and graduate specialized degrees—an approach followed by institutions ranging from Princeton and Harvard to flagship state universities.

There have been many other important developments in American higher education since that time, of course, including the elimination of a fixed course of study by Harvard's adoption of the elective system in 1869, which allowed student choice of courses; the development of academic departments to organize faculty and domains of knowledge beginning in the late 1800s; the development of a "student personnel" view in the 1930s, beginning the professionalization of student life; the passage of the GI Bill in 1944, which provided money for college to millions of returning World War II veterans, thereby dramatically increasing the number of college graduates; the growing use of noncampus-based educational experiences, such as study abroad and internships in the 1960s; the Higher Education Act of 1965, providing financial aid to college students; the role of technology in education beginning in the 1970s; and very significantly, the more recent development of a "high impact practices," research-based approach to evaluating the effectiveness of teaching approaches and the development of pedagogical innovation.

But these developments, as well as the contemporary view that the liberal arts is defined by the content of study, do not change the importance of understanding the more complete purpose-content-context framework for viewing the character of liberal arts–based higher education. They also didn't alter the liberal arts commitment to fulfilling a higher, common good through content- and context-based undergraduate education. In the next chapter, we will explore these ideas as they have been implemented in American liberal arts education in recent years. But first, let me make some comments about the underdog status of the liberal arts.

The Frontrunner and the Underdog

Most essentially, what many around the world call "American-style" education, or what some call "distinctively American" education, is distinctive not because Americans invented it. In fact, the essence of this approach was developed and refined over millennia. While saving liberal arts from the trash heap of history, Americans did make a distinctive contribution: unlike its character in earlier millennia (and in contrast to the Prussian/European specialization approach), where higher education was primarily available to the elite, American-style liberal arts was now viewed as necessary for *all* people for society to develop and thrive.

Judging by quantity, whether it is the total number of institutions or the total number of students enrolled, the Prussian specialization model is the global front-runner, and the liberal arts approach the underdog. But does this mean that a specialization approach to higher learning is the better strategy for the advancement of society or the success of the individual? Remember that more people come to the United States than any other nation, seeking this "American-style" approach. Indeed, in other countries, there is a substantial and growing level of interest in American-style or liberal arts education: newspaper articles and opinion pieces advocate for it, ministries of education hold conferences and develop new policies, and the number of liberal arts institutions founded in other countries continues to grow. Recipients of an American-style undergraduate degree are often judged to be more creative and successful over the longer term.

The answer to the question of whether a liberal arts–style or a Prussian-style specialized education is more impactful is testable. If we can clearly identify specific college experiences that characterize liberal arts content and educational context, we can analyze whether any of those experiences are related to the purpose-fulfilling life outcomes that people desire and our society needs. The next several chapters explore this question in detail.

4

Today's Education in the Tradition of the Liberal Arts: Purpose, Content, and Context

Let us think of education as the means of developing our greatest abilities, because in each of us there is a private hope and dream which, fulfilled, can be translated into benefit for everyone and greater strength for our nation
—John F. Kennedy, as quoted in Peters and Woolley, "The American Presidency Project: Proclamation 3422"

While virtually all American colleges and universities include some aspects of the liberal arts—with most institutions preserving at least some portion of the "breadth of content" component—the full liberal arts educational ecology, which fully combines a higher purpose, broader content, and engaging educational context, is today best represented at more traditional liberal arts colleges. As such, in this chapter, we will develop a contemporary understanding of purpose, content, and context through an analysis of these attributes of a higher education at liberal arts institutions.

*   *   *

As described in the previous chapters, education in the tradition of the liberal arts is characterized by a combination of three components:

purpose, content, and educational context. We can think of these three attributes as the "why," "what," and "how" of liberal arts education, as follows:

- *Why* is the *purpose*, which involves the idea that life outcomes should not only benefit the individual, but also should contribute to the well-being of humanity as a whole (the combination of benefit to both the individual and humanity is labeled here as the "common good").
- *What* is learned is its *content*, which involves broad, largely nonspecialized, knowledge that develops understanding and thinking in ways that help people to be effective in their lives and their society.
- *How* is the educational *context*, which involves a community-based, personal, and engaging learning environment.

The essential question is whether the "what" and the "how" have an impact on the "why"—that is, do people who have had particular liberal arts educational experiences live differently than those who did not have those liberal arts educational experiences? If so, what is it about a liberal arts experience that is associated with adult behavior? Are people who have liberal arts experiences, as the skeptics argue, prepared to contribute nothing of value to themselves or society? Or are these the people who are more likely to be life's winners?

To answer these questions, we need to clearly understand what each of the attributes of a liberal arts education involves. The history of the development of the liberal arts describes the purposes served by liberal arts education in the past. For example, in ancient Greece, a person needed to learn to be an effective orator to be successful and contribute to society; in early medieval Europe, students needed to learn Latin to read, study, and communicate effectively in an era lacking a common or dominant language. Obviously, these aren't good indicators of contemporary liberal arts education. What purposes are being fulfilled today, and what educational experiences are intended to fulfill those purposes?

I now present a summary of the three-step process that I used to identify the most frequent contemporary descriptors of a renewed liberal arts education and its outcomes; more detailed information about these steps is presented in the sections that follow.

Step 1: Purpose

Because college mission statements commonly include a description of the purpose—the life outcomes desired—of the education offered by an institution, I collected the mission statements of 241 institutions identified as undergraduate liberal arts colleges. The outcomes goals from the mission statements were compiled (a total of 450, with some institutions having a single stated purpose and some having several), and these were sorted by similarity. A total of 95% of these statements fit into one of six types of purpose. Sorted by frequency, these are:

1. Altruism (contributing to the well-being of others and society)
2. Continued learning (continuing study beyond college, actively seeking new knowledge)
3. Living a fulfilled life (reflective about living a meaningful life)
4. Leadership (in one's daily life and community)
5. Living a personally successful life (individual success and professional achievement)
6. Cultural involvement (interest in culture, music, art, and other creative outlets)

Step 2: Content and Context

To identify the characteristics of a contemporary education in the tradition of the liberal arts, I used the list of descriptions of the liberal arts given in chapter 2. As you may recall, my systematic work to assess the character of liberal arts education included an exhaustive assessment of writings, presentations, and discussions about liberal arts education, including reviews of books and articles on the subject; interviews of educators (college presidents, academic officers, and foundation executives); faculty workshops that asked professors to develop specific descriptions of the means and methods of liberal arts education; and interviews of students at liberal arts colleges, who were asked to describe the liberal arts experience. When I combined the attributes described by these various sources, a long list resulted, including 140 different descriptions—words and phrases—of the content and educational context of liberal arts education.

I sorted these descriptors into two groups: those that described the content of education and those that described the educational context of the liberal arts experience. Within each group, I further subdivided the descriptors into subgroups based on their similarity. Through this process, I identified three aspects of content and three of educational context as being most commonly seen as characteristic of liberal arts education.

Educational content

- Involves nonvocational areas of study
- Develops a comprehensive understanding of the world
- Develops intellectual skills

Educational context

- Involves engaging pedagogy
- Develops larger perspectives
- Involves an authentic learning community

It is important to note that the goal of this process was not to identify every educational attribute that could be considered part of a liberal arts experience. As noted previously, the variety of ideas about liberal arts education is extraordinary, and there is little likelihood that everyone will agree on a single list of salient and distinctive features. So rather than having the goal of including every possible attribute or creating a list that would be acceptable to everyone, the goal was to come up with a list of frequently described educational experiences that might plausibly distinguish a liberal arts education from other approaches to higher education. It is certainly open to debate whether these are the best or the only descriptors of a liberal arts education; for the purposes of this study, however, the question was not one of right or wrong. Rather, the question is whether any of these educational practices are related to the way that graduates live their lives: are there aspects of the liberal arts–based educational experience that are predictive of the ways that people later act as adults?

Step 3: Experiences and Behaviors

While some aspects of a liberal arts education are easy to assess (e.g., whether the study was vocational or nonvocational in nature), other aspects (such as developing larger perspectives) are more difficult to assess. So the final step was to figure out how to know if a person experienced particular aspects of the educational content and context, and whether a person's behavior after graduation as an adult fulfilled any of the six purposes of a liberal arts education (leadership, altruism, continued learning, cultural engagement, fulfillment, and success). A team of educators and researchers* was involved in a multistep iterative process to come up with statements that describe how each aspect is represented in a higher education experience, as well as the types of

*I am grateful to David Strauss, Shanaysha Sauls, and their colleagues at the Art & Science Group of Baltimore for their gifted work and insights in leading this process, and to the following educators for their advice and assistance in sorting through these ideas: Joyce Babyak, Brian Casey, Susan Conner, Grant Cornwell, David Dawson, Sean Decatur, Linda DeMeritt, Michael Frandsen, Gregory Hess, Rock Jones, Joseph Klesner, John Knapp, Gregory Mahler, James Mullen, Carolyn Newton, Gary Phillips, Richard Ray, Lawrence Stimpert, Adam Weinberg, and Eileen Wilson-Oyelaran.

adult behaviors that indicate the purposes are being fulfilled. As part of this process, judgments were made about the saliency of particular concepts (does a word or phrase describe a meaningful aspect of the educational experience?) and distinctiveness (does it differentiate between a liberal arts and a non–liberal arts educational experience?). The final result was the development of one or more "indicator items" for each aspect of the purpose, content, and context of an education in the tradition of the liberal arts. It is important to note that an indicator does not describe the whole liberal arts attribute or purpose; it merely describes an aspect of the attribute or purpose that was a part of a student's education or an adult's behavior.

In the following sections, I describe in greater detail each of these educational attributes and adult behaviors, as well as the development of meaningful indicators.

Why: The Purpose of Higher Learning

The history of the development of liberal arts education makes clear that advancing a higher purpose—the common good, which benefits society as well as oneself—has always been the desired outcome of this form of higher education. This idea is found in the thinking of Greek and Roman philosophers; in the Islamic Golden Age, when humanity was advanced through personal and public enlightenment; and as European education reemerged in the medieval period through the societal advancements derived from liberal arts–educated theologians, lawyers, physicians, and numerous others. And, as described in the Yale Report of 1828 in the United States, a higher education should result in a person who contributes broadly to society:

> But if his thoughts never range on other subjects, if he never looks abroad on the ample domains of literature and science, there will be a narrowness in his habits of thinking, a peculiarity of character, which will be sure to mark him as a man of limited views and attainments . . . He who is not only eminent in professional life

but has also a mind richly stored with general knowledge, has an elevation and dignity of character, which gives him a commanding influence in society, and a widely extended sphere of usefulness.

Is a man to have no other object, than to obtain a living by professional pursuits? Has he not duties to perform to his family, to his fellow citizens, to his country; duties which require various and extensive intellectual furniture?

Is it not desirable that they should be men of superior education, of large and liberal views, of those solid and elegant attainments, which will raise them to a higher distinction, than the mere possession of property and to make such an application of their wealth, as will be most honorable to themselves, and most beneficial to their country?[1]

In a contemporary context, how is this millennia-old idea about the purpose of a higher education represented? As described in the summary at the beginning of this chapter, to answer this question, I compiled the mission statements of 241 undergraduate colleges and the goals—a total of 450 outcomes that they seek to create— and grouped them into six categories based on their similarity.* The categories, ordered by frequency of occurrence and with examples of the types of mission-statement words for each, are the following:[2]

1. Responsible engagement in civic and nonprofit activities (28% of the goals statements)
   - Citizenship
   - Committed service
   - Engage world
   - Solve problems of community
   - Service

---

*These mission statements were all from US colleges and universities classified as four-year arts and sciences institutions by the US Department of Education. The mission statements of seventeen non-US liberal arts–based universities were also analyzed. Similar outcomes, though with differences in emphasis, were found for these institutions. I extend my gratitude to Colleen Smith of the Great Lakes Colleges Association for her help with this process.

2. Continue to be actively involved in acquiring new knowledge and understanding through their lives (22%)

    • Search for truth
    • Critical thinkers
    • Intellectual inquiry
    • Scholar
    • Life of learning

3. Deliberate and thoughtful about choices that create a life of value and fulfillment (21%)

    • Fulfilling and valuable life
    • Live honorably; live responsibly; live with integrity
    • Contribute to well-being of others
    • Life of meaning; satisfying life
    • Life of significance; make difference in the world
    • Reflective life

4. Constructive leadership character (17%)

    • Committed leader
    • Wise leadership
    • Ethical/moral leader
    • Effective leader
    • Leader of character

5. Personally, professionally, and/or financially successful (12%)

    • Flourish professionally
    • Thrive in career
    • Career and professional excellence
    • Competence in their field
    • Fulfilling careers
    • Personal achievement
    • Success

6. Committed to a larger understanding of humanity's cultural achievements (1%)

    • Culturally aware

- Involved with arts
- Involved with humanities

These six categories of goals statements can be sorted into three related groups and labeled as follows:

A Life of Consequence by being a

- Leader (17%)
- Civic Altruist (28%)

A Life of Inquiry by

- Continued Learning (22%)
- Cultural Involvement (1%)

A Life of Accomplishment by living a

- Fulfilled Life (21%)
- Personally Successful Life (12%)

It is easy to see the "common good" nature of this set of goals statements, as they represent a combination of both personal achievements and contributions to the progress of humanity.

What: The Content of Study

Because higher education involves learning, it is not surprising that the content of study—what a student is expected to learn—is one of the characteristics of the liberal arts that we will examine here. It is natural to think of the answer to this question in the same way as we do for elementary or secondary school (involving specific competencies like reading, writing, and arithmetic) or as advocates for job training do (marketable skills such as technical expertise and in-depth knowledge of a type of work). However, as the history makes clear, an education in the tradition of the liberal arts, unlike the specialization model developed in Prussia in the 1800s, has always focused on the development of an effective mind and productive behavior rather than on the mastery of specific areas of expertise. A liberal arts education is viewed as the higher learning that is needed before one specializes, and regardless of whether one subsequently specializes, that is necessary in professional, social, and personal life.

We will consider three aspects of content here: the degree to which the education is not specialized or vocational in nature, involves study across the span of knowledge, and develops essential intellectual skills.

Content 1: Nonvocational

Education in the tradition of the liberal arts has always involved the development of broader competencies; specialization and specific preparation for a profession or career were avoided, not because it wasn't feasible to focus the curriculum narrowly, but because it was viewed as contradictory to the goals of getting a first higher education degree.* Remember the Yale Report of 1828, which stated that this approach to education was to avoid narrowness or specialization: "The course of instruction which is given to the undergraduates in the college, is not designed to include professional studies. Our object is not to teach that which is peculiar to any one of the professions; but to lay the foundation which is common to them all."[3]

The idea of an undergraduate college major—another American invention of the late 1800s—has grown in importance such that

---

*In principle, professional programs need not exclude the liberal arts, so the potential value of the liberal arts could still be realized for those studying for a particular job or profession. In practice, what typically happens, even at those institutions where liberal arts study is a component of professional program requirements, is that the liberal arts plays only a minor role. This is often an unintended consequence of the fact that professional programs, in their quest to ensure that their graduates have mastered all aspects of their discipline, leave little time for broader study. For example, you will learn later in this book that two aspects of liberal arts study with substantial impact are taking more than half of one's courses outside one's major and considering the ethical or philosophical implications of what one is studying in most classes. Both of these experiences could be part of professional program requirements, but for practical reasons rarely are.

study in depth (the college major), in addition to study in breadth, became a curricular requirement at virtually every American college. Yet within a liberal arts framework, a college major was never intended to be preparation for a profession per se, but rather to provide the foundation for greater life and professional success through subsequent study and experience.

As such, an indicator of vocational versus nonvocational education today is whether the college major is in a professional field such as business, accounting, engineering, education, and nursing, as opposed to a major in the humanities, social sciences, or math and sciences.

Content 2: Span of Study

The study of a diverse range of subjects has long been a characteristic of the liberal arts. As the range of human knowledge grew, especially during the Islamic Golden Age and later through the Renaissance and beyond, the areas of study increased. The use of the word "span" here is deliberate because of its two different meanings. First, it describes the full range of something from end to end. In the case of learning, study must involve the full span of human knowledge, ranging from the humanities to the social sciences and sciences. As described earlier, while liberal arts study cannot exclude the humanities, it also cannot include only the humanities. Without studying the full range of human knowledge, learning in the tradition of the liberal arts will not occur. When Harvard was founded in 1636, its charter stated that higher education was for "the advancement of all good literature, artes, and Sciences"[4]— clearly emphasizing this idea.

The second meaning of "span" is something that functions to link or connect separated places (i.e., a bridge span). In the case of learning, while understanding the full range of knowledge is essential, its value is limited unless one also understands connections among areas of knowledge. Inherent in this concept is the idea that learning should be multidisciplinary or interdisciplinary.* For example, education in the tradition of the liberal arts celebrates the study of philosophy and the study of biology equally; but learning in these domains without also considering how they interrelate is insufficient. That is, an understanding of the implications for humanity of manipulating chromosomes requires knowledge of both these disciplines, and a liberal arts education must be deliberate in helping students make linkages among the many areas that they will study. Each component (discipline) must be understood as part of a whole—they are interrelated—with essential insights coming from an understanding of how domains of knowledge are connected.

Through understanding of the full span of human knowledge combined with insight into how they interrelate, a person is better able, over a lifetime, to continue learning and to understand the implications of the many choices that need to be made in a continually changing living and working environment. In an American context, the Yale Report makes many statements related to this idea:[5]

> Two great points to be gained in intellectual culture, are the discipline and the furniture of the mind; expanding its powers and storing it with knowledge. The former of these is, perhaps, the more important of the two.
> In laying the foundation of a thorough education, it is necessary that all the important mental faculties be brought into exercise.

The importance of this approach to the content of learning—one that focuses on the mental capacities that various areas of study

---

*In recent decades, interdisciplinary study, in which two or more disciplines are deliberately linked through faculty collaboration, has become quite common. Interdisciplinarity is not, in fact, a new idea—it was represented in ancient Greek philosophy, in which various domains of knowledge were synthesized to develop a broader or deeper understanding, and this conceptual approach continued as a feature of the liberal arts through the years. Its current importance derives from the ever-increasing narrowness of specialized disciplines and the need to link separate areas of study to better understand phenomena (e.g., economics and social psychology to understand political behavior, or biology and chemistry to understand disease).

uniquely contribute to a larger understanding—is stated in the Yale Report as follows:[6]

> He is acquainted with the region where he is, acts more understandingly in what he undertakes, and is found, in consequence of his knowledge, to be, in all his transactions, a more practical man . . . Educated in this way, besides the advantages of mental discipline which have been already mentioned, he enlarges the circle of his thoughts, finds in his superior information, new means of benefiting or influencing others, and his mind is thus far liberalized by liberal knowledge.

These ideas remain in the thinking of today's educators whom I interviewed for this book. They frequently stated how a liberal arts education must include breadth (e.g., courses in sciences and mathematics, social sciences, humanities, histories, languages, and arts), involve the development of an understanding of the interrelatedness of knowledge, and develop broader perspectives (e.g., engage in the big questions and ethical dilemmas, both contemporary and enduring).

How can one know whether a student's education is broad and diverse and involves developing an understanding of how domains of knowledge interrelate and inform one another? The best approach, of course, would be to examine college transcripts and course syllabi, although this would likely give little insight into the degree to which interrelationships were examined. Short of this level of analysis, are there actual experiences that a person can describe—not just opinions about a college experience—indicating that their course of study involved the span of knowledge and the ways that areas are interrelated? Based on in-depth discussions among educators and social scientists, the following types of experiences, taken together, are contemporary indicators that a person experienced the span of study while in college:

- The number of courses completed unrelated to one's major or similar fields
- The number of courses taken in the humanities (for nonhumanities majors)

- Discussion of philosophical, ethical, and literary perspectives on the human condition in most classes

Content 3: Development of Intellectual Skills

Educators and employers alike treasure people who can think critically and reason effectively. Precisely what this means has been an area of controversy that can be traced to ancient Greece: "Beginning in Greece in the fifth and fourth centuries B.C., the debate commenced as to whether the arts of reason or the arts of speech and language should take precedence in this education for the liberal (free) citizen."[7] Logic was central to the development of the Islamic Golden Age,[8] although as the Golden Age came to an end, its purpose became to confirm doctrines of faith[9] (as was subsequently the case in Christian Europe). But in the Yale Report of 1828, the needs of a representative democracy placed a premium on educating people who could reason and think critically:

> Fixing the attention, directing the train of thought, analyzing a subject proposed for investigation; following, with accurate discrimination, the course of argument; balancing nicely the evidence presented to the judgment; awakening, elevating, and controlling the imagination; arranging, with skill, the treasures which memory gathers; rousing and guiding the powers of genius.

> A liberal education . . . is best calculated . . . to strengthen and enlarge the faculties of the mind, and to familiarize it with the leading principles of the great objects of human investigation and knowledge. A liberal is obviously distinct from a professional education. The former is conversant with those topics . . . necessary or convenient, in any situation of life, the latter, with those which qualify the individual for a particular station, business or employment.[10]

How can we know if the methods of instruction being used develop the intellectual habits and skills of reasoning and critical thinking? From the in-depth discussions among educators and social scientists, contemporary college experiences identified as likely indicators of reasoning and critical thinking include the following:

- Professors who encourage the examination of strengths and weaknesses of one's own views
- Coursework that frequently emphasizes discussions of questions to which there is not necessarily a right answer
- Being required to write papers for most courses

It is important to note that in the context of the liberal arts, these indicators are (or should be) equally applicable in all disciplines; study in the sciences and social sciences, as well as in the humanities, can involve these experiences. That is, if a consideration of the impact of one's own assumptions, discussing enigmatic issues, or writing is consigned only to humanities courses, then a liberal arts education will not, in fact, be occurring. While it may be outside the comfort zone of some faculty in nonhumanities disciplines to include some of these types of learning experiences in their teaching, it is precisely what needs to happen if one wishes to follow the liberal arts approach to education.

In summary, then, what a student studies and learns in college—its content—involves three components: whether it is nonvocational, whether it involves a span of knowledge that includes (but is not limited to) the humanities, and whether it develops essential intellectual skills.

How: The Context of Study

It seems that nearly everyone—educators, students, parents, historians of the liberal arts, legislators, journalists, and more—routinely describe the liberal arts solely in terms of its content. People defend or attack the value of the liberal arts based on the real or perceived value of the subjects taught (e.g., the humanities) or the lack of professional specialization. When the educational environment is considered (e.g., class size, interaction among faculty and students, residential character), these features are often described in amenity-like terms. That is, such attributes are seen as creating a pleasant atmosphere, perhaps more akin to a country club, which make a college a nicer place to be but are not essential to the value or impact of education.

But a more careful reading of the millennia-long history of education in the tradition of the liberal arts suggests that there has always been an attempt to create a personally involving, community-based, educational environment as an essential characteristic of this approach to higher learning. Indeed, ancient educators seemed to know what learning researchers and neuroscientists have recently demonstrated empirically: the ways in which human interaction is constructed can dramatically enhance learning by adding behavioral and affective dimensions to the learning environment (there will be more on this subject in chapter 9).

I will now consider three aspects of the educational context: the degree to which the educational experience uses teaching approaches that have been demonstrated to engage the student, encourages the development of larger perspectives, and involves an authentic learning community.

Context 1: Engaging Pedagogy

The first context attribute of an education in the tradition of the liberal arts relates to the methods of teaching that are utilized. Among today's college and university educators, there is the sense that a concern about effective pedagogies is a new development. Indeed, there is a great deal of recent research on "high-impact" teaching strategies, and yet placing a priority on student learning has characterized liberal arts education since its inception. History is replete with statements about the importance of pedagogies that deeply engage students in the learning and thinking process, ranging from individual tutorials and discussions to methods of creating compelling lectures. As described in chapter 2, Plato advocated for the active engagement of students in learning; in the Islamic Golden Age, students were encouraged to debate their teachers and challenge their statements; and in medieval Europe, requirements were listed for effective lecturing.

In the American context, the Yale Report makes similar statements about the importance of engaging pedagogy:[11]

> Opportunity is given, however, to our classes, for a full investigation and discussion of particular subjects, in the written and extemporaneous disputes, which constitute an important part of our course of exercises . . . It is to secure the unceasing and strenuous exercise of the intellectual powers, that the responsibility of the student is made so constant and particular.
>
> By a due proportion of professors and tutors, we may unite the advantages of experience, with ardor and activity; of profound investigation, with minute attention to elementary principles; of personal attachment and individual responsibility, with such an adjustment of the different parts of the system, as will give unity and symmetry to the whole.

In a contemporary context, liberal arts educators emphasize the importance of student learning engagement, with indicators including the following:*

- Students taking a large role in class discussions in most classes
- Taking classes with thirty students or fewer during the first year at college
- Seminars involving discussion as a critical part of the learning process, especially in the first two years at college

Context 2: Development of Larger Perspectives

In ancient Greece, education was meant to engage "the whole man, body and soul, sense and reason, character and mind."[12] During the

---

*There is a substantial body of literature on teaching methods that involve high-impact practices. While some aspects of these teaching methods are included in the questions listed, the current list of high-impact practices was not used because we were interviewing people who graduated before some of these methods were developed and many of the associated terms were in use (e.g., first-year seminars and service learning).

Islamic Golden Age, ideas from Europe, the Middle East, and Asia were sought out and brought together with the explicit goal of broadening understanding and challenging narrow thinking. And this multiplicity of perspectives was brought into medieval Europe, deliberately broadening knowledge and contributing to the Renaissance. In the context of the American experience, the Yale Report speaks eloquently of the needs for the kinds of learning that will make people effective when contributing to the society of their time:[13]

> Has he not duties to perform to his family, to his fellow citizens, to his country; duties which require various and extensive intellectual furniture?
> He ought to be allowed time to settle his own opinion on every important point, by the slow process of comparing and balancing the various and conflicting opinions of others.

In a contemporary context, educators and social scientists identify the following experiences as indicators of the development of broader perspectives and sensibilities in a college education:

- Learning about people from other cultures as an important part of college education
- Having frequent serious conversations with others who are very different in terms of their religious beliefs, political opinions, or personal values
- Discussing issues such as peace, justice, human rights, equality, and race relations with other students

Context 3: Authentically Involving the Learning Community

Americans often take for granted the idea that a college campus amounts to more than just classrooms. But the fact that students live on or near a campus with facilities for both work and play is very different from the European approach, in which the university is a place where students go to take classes and exams; the rest of their student lives occur elsewhere, with student clubs, sports teams, and other organizations existing outside the university context. The idea of a learning community is rarely seen as a centrally important factor necessary to create an effective educational experience.

Yet education in the context of community has deep roots. In ancient Greece and Rome, the educational context was created by a tutor who traveled to homes or other community locations where they typically worked with small groups of students. During the Islamic Golden Age, "Circle Schools" brought students and teachers together into very personal interactions, and the first universities were fully residential and involved in- and out-of-class relations among faculty and students. In the early medieval era in Europe, the education was organized around the creation and support of residential educational communities because students from dozens of nations joined together to live and study. This community-based approach was particularly important because books and written documents were rare, and well-educated scholars even rarer.

In the new American colonies, the founders of Harvard sought to replicate the "college as community" model, and the institutions subsequently founded followed this pattern as well. By 1828, the Yale Report formalized the importance of the learning community:

> A most important feature in the colleges of this country is, that the students are generally of an age which requires, that a substitute be provided for parental superintendence. When removed from under the roof of their parents, and exposed to the untried scenes of temptation, it is necessary that some faithful and affectionate guardian take them by the hand, and guide their steps. . . . The parental character of college government, requires that the students should be so collected together, as to constitute one family; that the intercourse between them and their instructers [sic] may be frequent and familiar.[14]

So the prototypical American college or university, whether small or large, has a campus with not only classrooms and libraries, but also residences, student centers, sports and recreation facilities, and more. While current competition among colleges to have the most attractive and extensive facilities can be strong—often described as an amenities war, fueled by the desire to create a country club atmosphere—this relatively recent and costly development is a perversion of the importance of having an authentic educational community for impactful liberal arts education.

Yet merely having attractive campus facilities does not mean that an authentically involving learning community exists; indeed, a campus with extensive amenities and popular sports activities may not have an authentic learning community, and an authentically involving learning community can exist with only modest campus facilities. Enthusiasm can come from football games, activity can come from going to the fitness center, thinking can come from spending time in the library—but in the context of education in the liberal arts tradition, these are not the types of experiences that create an authentic learning community. The idea of "authenticity" is that faculty, students, and staff interact with one another in intellectually and personally meaningful ways, informally and formally, not only in the class but outside the class as well.

And, of course, the hundreds of residential colleges created in the 1800s in small and large towns in the developing United States were nearly invariably residential in character, with the lives of faculty and students centered around a residential living and learning community. In this educational context, faculty, students, and staff worked with and knew each other inside and outside of class in personally significant ways. The practice of having such a deliberate learning community has continued to be a key attribute of a liberal arts–style education in the United States.

How can one know whether an authentic learning community is characteristic of a student's time outside of class? What kinds of actual experiences—not just opinions about a college experience—could indicate that an authentic learning community exists? Based on discussions among educators and social scientists, the following were identified as indicators of the presence of a personal and involving educational experience:

- Professors knowing students' first names
- Talking with faculty about academic subjects outside class
- Talking with faculty about nonacademic subjects outside class
- Having a mentor or mentors who have a lasting impact on goals, intellectual growth, or personal growth
- Living either on campus or in college- or university-sponsored housing
- Participating actively in college- or university-based clubs or organizations
- Leading campus organizations
- Participating in athletics
- Campus activism

Again, none of these questions defines what an authentic learning community is; rather, these elements are seen as *indicators* that such an educational community exists.

In summary, then, the *how* of an education in the liberal arts tradition—its context—involves three attributes: the use of personally engaging pedagogy, the development of larger perspectives, and learning in an authentic learning community.

An Educational Ecology of the Why, What, and How of Education

It is clear that the *why* of education in the tradition of the liberal arts—its purpose—has been consistent since its inception. Its purpose has been, and continues to be, the higher, common good. The *what* of liberal arts education—its content—has always been about foundational preparation for life impact, including the nonvocational development of ways of thinking and an understanding of the span of human knowledge. As the span of human knowledge has increased, so has the areas of study included in the liberal arts. *How* this education is experienced—the educational context—has consistently involved pedagogy, people of different backgrounds and life experiences, and a personally engaging educational community.

This approach to education—its purpose, content, and context—stands in marked contrast to the Prussian-based approach adopted throughout the world, in which people are tracked into trades or professions even before entering college. In most other nations, those selected for higher education are admitted into a particular specialty designed to develop relatively narrow areas of expertise. In contrast, an American-style liberal arts education is intended to be available to every person from any strata of society and regardless of future personal or professional goals. The son of a farmer may choose to be a farmer and should be valued for his choice, and the daughter of a tradesperson may choose to be a tradesperson and should be valued for her choice. We have always needed farmers and tradespeople—and today also need plumbers, electricians, child care, and other essential workers—but in the American approach to a higher education, every person should have the opportunity to develop their passions and abilities in the ways that best serve their dreams and a shared future of humanity, whether as farmer, tradesperson, specialist, or college-educated professional.

The Yale Report of 1828 became a remarkable, lasting template that, even today, recognizably describes the distinctive content, context, and purpose of an American-style liberal arts education—an approach to higher education that is considered the best in the world. In contrast to the Prussian purpose of higher education, this method of education is designed to serve a larger, unselfish goal: the advancement of both humanity and the individual.

With six characteristics of a liberal arts education—three relating to content and three to context—have we completed our understanding of liberal arts education? Can we stop at this point, satisfied with our new way of describing liberal arts education? The answer is no: if we stop, we will have done nothing more than create yet one more description of liberal arts education to add to the hundreds of such descriptions that already exist.

We must consider the essential question of impact. Regardless of the degree to which one may feel passionate about a particular educational attribute—whether it be vocational preparation or the value of an authentic learning community—if the attribute has no impact on the way that people live their lives, then what value does it have? Do the content and educational context of a liberal arts education actually make a difference in the ways that people live their lives? It is to this question that we now turn.

5

Understanding the Impact of College Experiences on Adult Life: The Research Approach

> It's oversimplistic to say it's just getting a job with a certain salary. There are things about citizenship, broad knowledge, and deep understanding of the world, that we should have in mind. And, those are very difficult to measure.
> —Bill Gates, "The Future of College"

With the content and context of study in the tradition of the liberal arts itemized, how can we learn whether any of the specific attributes of this approach to education have an impact on the way that people live their lives as adults? To accomplish this, we carried out objective analyses of liberal arts–related educational experiences and the adult behaviors of 1,000 graduates of a wide variety of types of colleges and universities, and statistically assessed the relationship between specific college experiences and adult behaviors. To provide first-person examples of the statistical findings, in this chapter I have also included the narratives of a number of liberal arts college graduates. In this chapter, I describe this research approach in detail.

*   *   *

We know that graduating from college is an important predictor of many aspects of adult life; college graduates are more likely to succeed professionally, live longer, higher incomes, and other life advantages.[1] All these are outcomes mostly benefit the individual—they are "selfish outcomes." In contrast, liberal arts education is committed to furthering the common good, which includes benefit to humanity as well as the individual: living a life of consequence as a leader and altruist, living a life of inquiry through continued learning and cultural involvement, and living a life of accomplishment by having a fulfilled and a personally successful life. Is an education in the tradition of the liberal arts related to these more magnanimous outcomes? Or, to state it succinctly: are any of the aspects of the content or context of liberal arts education associated with particular, purpose-fulfilling life outcomes?

This is an important way of framing the question about liberal arts education and its impact; the goal is not merely to say, "Isn't the liberal arts wonderful?" (or not), but "What is it about an education in the tradition of the liberal arts that is associated with life impact?" Unless we know whether, for example, nonspecialization appears important or educational community appears important (or any of the other content and context attributes), we have no way of knowing which educational features need attention and which do not.

So, is there evidence that any of the six identified liberal arts educational experiences have a relationship with any of the six life outcomes? This question is represented in figure 5.1.

If there are relationships between any of the six identified attributes of a liberal arts educational experience and adult behavior, then we will have learned something valuable; we will have gained important new insights into what it is about an education in the liberal arts tradition that is associated with life outcomes. It also will give us new information about what actually matters about this approach to education.

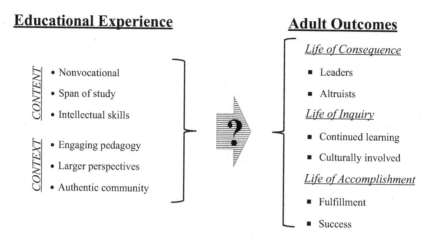

Figure 5.1
Relationship between educational experience and adult outcomes

So, do any of these attributes of an American-style higher education bear a significant relationship to the ways that adults live their lives after college? Answering this question objectively requires, rather than arguments or opinions, carrying out research on specific college experiences and testing their relationship to adult behaviors.

The Research Approach: Life Outcomes

When in life should liberal arts–valued behavior be assessed? There are, quite literally, thousands of studies on college impact, but in general, they look at effects that occur either while a student is in college or shortly after graduation. In addition, they typically have a narrow focus, involving simple-to-answer questions about impact (such as the income that one gets from one's first job), and opinions about college and its effects, rather than objective assessments of actual behaviors.

What we really want to know is how college graduates behave over their lifetime and compare those behaviors to the character of the college education they received. From the point of view of being able to prove cause and effect, the ideal strategy would be to randomly assign a large number of high school graduates to different colleges, and also randomly assign each of them to various types of experiences while in college. And then, for each of those people, wait for ten, twenty, thirty, or forty years to examine their adult behaviors—after all, adulthood continues for many decades—as the meaningful indicators of a person's life outcomes may not emerge until well past middle age. With this approach, we could have our answers by the year 2060, but by then, the information will probably be irrelevant—and I certainly won't be around to learn the outcome.

Instead of giving up on developing insights into the aspects of a liberal arts education related to adult behaviors—or losing any opportunity to influence current thinking about the implications of various educational choices—I adopted a different research approach. Rather than following the same people for decades, we interviewed college graduates of different ages (i.e., one, two, and four decades after graduation) from a variety of types of colleges and universities (ranging from liberal arts colleges to major research universities). Specific, objective questions about their college experiences and their behavior as adults* were asked of each graduate. In addition, eighty-five graduates of liberal arts colleges were asked to write narratives describing what they believed to be important aspects of their college experiences. Excerpts from these narratives provide first-person examples of the research findings from the objective interviews.

------

*In research parlance, this is a cross-sectional design rather than a longitudinal design. Any research design that does not involve random assignment (e.g., randomly assigning people to the college they will attend, which is a very impractical idea in the case of college enrollment) raises questions about causation. A cross-sectional design introduces factors that weaken conclusions about cause and effect. In this research, these factors are addressed in part through subsequent analyses that match individual characteristics at the time of college entry. More important, however, the degree to which the results to be reported here are consistent with the findings of other observational and experiment-based research on collegiate learning, and is also consistent with neuroscience research, strengthens confidence in the results reported here. These issues and analyses are presented in chapter 9 and in appendixes 1 and 3.

Interview Research

Method

How should we study the impact of college experiences on adult behaviors? There are many opinion studies about what matters in college, in which people make assertions about how they think that college, or some part of college, influenced them. In contrast, this study involved interviews of 1,000 college graduates in one of three adult life stages:

- A younger group of relatively recent graduates between twenty-five and thirty-five years old; these are people who are beyond searching for their first postcollege jobs or life choices (e.g., going to graduate school, remaining at their parent's home) though are likely to still be figuring out their own life courses
- A middle group of alumni between thirty-six and forty-five years old; these are individuals who likely are reasonably established in their life choices, both professionally and personally
- An older group of people between fifty-five and sixty-five years old who are well established in their lives and jobs and likely at the peak of their professions

Rather than rely on questionnaires or e-mails (to which people often don't respond fully), we chose to use individual telephone conversations carried out by expertly trained interviewers who have the ability to establish sufficient rapport that responses would be both candid and complete. For consistency in the information gathered, a structured interview schedule was used.

The research program was implemented in a series of steps. Preliminary interview questions were developed, pilot-tested, and refined. A first draft of the interview schedule was then developed, pilot-tested, and refined. A final interview schedule was then developed, consisting of about 100 questions ranging from demographic information to the indicators of a liberal arts educational experience and adult life behaviors.* Interviews of 1,000 adults were completed over a period of several months. The interview responses were coded and entered into a data file so that the relationship between college experiences and adult behaviors could be statistically explored.

Who?

Whose college experience and adult behavior should be studied? As described earlier, the focus of this study was to understand the impact of an American-style liberal arts approach versus other approaches to college education—not the impact of college versus no college. Thus, only college graduates participated in this project. Second, because the goal of this research was to assess the impact of liberal arts practices, our sample needed to include some people who experienced few liberal arts practices and others who experienced many liberal arts practices. Remembering that some of the attributes of a liberal arts education could occur to a lesser or greater degree at any institution—small or large, exclusively liberal arts or comprehensive—participants needed to be recruited from a broad cross section of types of institutions. To create this diverse group of people to interview, some with extensive experience with one or more of the six attributes associated with a liberal arts education and others without, we utilized a two-step process.†

First, a cohort of adult college graduates of varying ages who attended a diverse range of types of colleges and universities was developed. Using a nationally representative panel sample,‡

---

*The Art & Science Group of Baltimore was responsible for developing the interview schedule and pilot testing and managed the full interview and data coding process.
†The entire representative sampling process was developed and managed by the Art & Science Group.
‡Panels are developed by national polling organizations as an alternative to other methods of selecting people to participate in polls such as random telephone number dialing, in which many people don't answer a call or refuse to participate. A panel consists of a demographically nationally representative group of individuals who have agreed to be interviewed; for any research project, participants are randomly selected from this very large group.

individuals who were college graduates and in the desired age groups (i.e., twenty-five to thirty-five, thirty-six to forty-five, and fifty-five to sixty-five) were randomly selected to participate. What was important about the use of this panel sample is that it allowed us to include graduates of all kinds of institutions—public/private, large/small, research/undergraduate, selective/nonselective, and liberal arts/non–liberal arts. As such, our research findings are not, as is often the case in higher education research, limited to the one or few colleges involved in this particular project.

While virtually every American college and university includes some aspects of liberal arts–based education—for example, requirements for study outside the major, use of effective teaching methods, and extensive extracurricular programs—most graduates of the typical university or college today will have had a modest number of these experiences.* As such, college graduates randomly drawn from a nationally representative sample will include only a small number of people who are likely to have had a relatively complete liberal arts education (involving more extensive experience with all six educational attributes). To ensure that the full range of liberal arts experiences were represented in this study, we implemented a second sampling step by randomly selecting participants from a list of 84,400 graduates of liberal arts colleges.† It is important to emphasize that the purpose of this added sample was *not* to oversample liberal arts colleges per se, but rather to increase the number and range of liberal arts practices that could be analyzed through this

---

*Approximately 90% of adults who have been college graduates over the past four decades graduated from non–liberal arts institutions (it is more than 95% today).

†The list of 84,000 graduates was the complete living alumni body of twelve quality colleges that have maintained an educational experience that is characteristic of American-style liberal arts education. My thanks to the following liberal arts colleges for their participation: Albion College, Allegheny College, Antioch College, Denison University, DePauw University, Earlham College, Hope College, Kalamazoo College, Kenyon College, Ohio Wesleyan University, Wabash College, and the College of Wooster.

research. The analyses reported in the study are not based on institution type, but rather on specific educational experiences regardless of institution type. (As reported in appendix 3, it is important to note that liberal arts educational practices are significant and substantial within both groups when they are analyzed separately.)

It is also worth noting while there is often the perception that students who attend liberal arts colleges are wealthy, this is often not the case due to the high amount of financial aid offered by liberal arts colleges. The percentage of Pell Grant (federal aid for families with high financial need) recipients for the liberal arts colleges included in this study in 2019 was 29.8%,[2] as opposed to the national average for all undergraduates (32%).[3]

Interview calls were made to randomly selected members of the nationally representative panel until a total of 600 interviews were completed and calls were made to randomly selected members of the liberal arts group until a total of 400 interviews were completed.

With a total of 1,000 individuals interviewed, the respondents had a range of backgrounds (family socioeconomic status, test scores) and attended a variety of institution types (public/private, small/large, lower/higher quality.) Appendix 2 presents a report of these characteristics, and appendix 3 examines the implications of the over-representation of liberal arts colleges in this study. As described in the previous section, one-third of the participants were twenty-five to thirty-five years old, one-third were thirty-six and forty-five years old, and one-third were between fifty-five and sixty-five years old.

Questions

What college experiences are related to what kinds of adult behavior? It is impractical to ask about every aspect of a person's college experience and about everything they do as adults. Our challenge is somewhat simplified because we only want to learn about six categories of educational experience and the six types of adult behavior.

This doesn't mean that there may not be other attributes of education or behavior that might be important, but for the purpose of this project, we limited our interviews and analyses to this set.

In chapter 4, indicators of liberal arts life outcomes, content, and context were listed. These indicators were carefully developed into questions that would be distinguishing indications of people's educational and life experiences. For example, the question "How many hours each week did you study?" does not indicate a distinguishing feature of a liberal arts education because any type of college education could include this attribute. Similarly, questions related to problem solving or critical thinking, while frequently described as central attributes of a liberal arts education, are difficult to use as differentiators because professional and specialized programs often focus on this as well. Can you imagine an effective engineering or marketing major that did not involve critical thinking and problem solving? On the other hand, discussing philosophical, ethical, or literary perspectives on the human condition in most classes, or a student frequently speaking with faculty about nonacademic subjects outside of class, would be distinguishing; these aspects are strongly liberal arts in character.

It is important to note that the indicator questions asked in this study are about behavior—that is, they are meant to elicit statements about actual experiences (what a person did), not opinions about what matters or what respondents liked. This is critical because in the research reported here, the focus is not on what people think matters (e.g., "I think talking to faculty outside of class time helped me to become a more capable leader as an adult"), but rather on what actually happened (e.g., there is a significant relationship between the frequency with which people spoke to faculty outside of class time and their exercise of leadership as adults). What people think matters is not of interest here; reports of educational experiences and adult behavior is the focus.

Of course, as noted earlier, this is a cross-sectional study of individuals who graduated between one and four decades ago. As such, the responses to the questions about college behavior are based on respondents' memories of an earlier time, and responses to questions about current behavior are self-reports that may not reflect actual behavior. There is a rich and complex body of research literature on the accuracy of self-reported information, and suffice it to say that many factors influence the accuracy of such studies, ranging from the tendency of individuals to give socially desirable responses to issues involved in the reconstruction of memories of past events. While we took care while developing and pilot-testing our questions and used consistent and concrete interview questions about experiences that could be easily remembered, it remains the case that self-reports of current and remembered events are imperfect indicators of reality.

As a final note, these indicators of college experience and adult behavior also had to be appropriate for people of varying adult ages. For example, queries about college teaching approaches could not include questions about the use of technology or involvement in service learning (community service for course credit) because they would not be meaningful for the older people included in this study, whose college experience happened before computers were commonplace or service-learning methods were used.

Understanding the Relationship between College Experiences and Adult Behavior

What is the relationship between various attributes of a college experience and the way that a person behaves as an adult? To establish an empirical relationship between college experiences and adult behaviors,[4] the first step was to code the responses to each interview question as "lower" or "higher"—meaning that, relative to the other people interviewed, the frequency of the behavior asked about placed them in the "less frequent" group or the "more frequent" group.*

The next step was to create a single overall score for each of the six categories of educational experience and each of the six categories of adult behavior. Recall that no single question was designed to assess the presence or absence of an experience or outcome; rather, each question was designed as an indicator of the presence or absence of an attribute. Therefore, responses to all the questions related to each category were combined into a single composite score. For example, nine questions were asked about the attributes of an authentic learning community. The scores on the responses to each of these questions were combined into a single "lower" or "higher" score through a median split of the total—the idea being that this single score gives an overall indication of the degree to which a person experienced these aspects of community. This process was completed for each of the six attributes of educational experience and the six categories of adult behavior.

The number of people who scored lower or higher for each educational experience attribute was then compared to the number of people who were low or high on each category of adult behavior. For example, of those who reported higher levels of adult leadership, 67% reported having experienced a lower level of involvement with their college community, and 84% reported having experienced a higher level. The statistical significance of this difference was tested using a chi-square test. However, statistical significance (meaning that effects could happen by chance less than 5% of the time) was not sufficient for it to be included in the results to be reported. Relationships needed to be substantial, as determined by the following three criteria:

---

*See appendix 4 for detail on the data and analytic approach.

1. They are statistically reliable.*

2. They involve larger effects (those effects for which there is at least a 20% increase in frequency for one group).†

3. The pattern of results is not significantly different within the three age groups separately.

These three criteria encourage us to focus on those attributes of a college education that are likely to be most consistently meaningful.‡ (Other findings from the study raise more nuanced questions and will be subsequently addressed in articles in specialized journals.)

It is important to reemphasize that, unlike much research related to the liberal arts, this project included graduates of all types of institutions. The analyses reported do not compare liberal arts colleges with non–liberal arts colleges. Instead, because most American colleges, regardless of type, use at least some liberal arts practices, comparisons are made between graduates who experienced relatively more or less of each of the six types of liberal arts–related experiences, regardless of the kind of institution attended. As such, the usual critique—that those who choose to attend liberal arts colleges are different kinds of people and thus act differently as adults—is not the case with these research results. (This issue is explored

---

*All results are significant at the $p < .05$ level two-tail (most were $p < .001$). Appendix 5 presents the complete results of the analyses.

†Given a statistically significant effect, the magnitude of the difference between two groups is calculated using an "incident risk ratio," which is the ratio is the probability of an adult behavior among the group that had a high level of a particular liberal arts experience divided by the probability of the adult behavior for those who had a low level of that experience. While requiring both a statistical significance and a relatively larger difference means that some statistically significant results are not reported, by considering only larger effects, our attention is focused on those attributes that make a bigger difference and thus might be considered more meaningful. Appendix 5 presents more complete information on this statistic.

‡Given that this research is cross-sectional in design, appendix 1 presents a consideration of the question of causation—that is, whether there a causal relationship between the college experience and the adult behavior.

statistically in appendix 3, in which analyses that do not include any liberal arts college students are reported.)

As will be discussed in chapter 11, a person who desires to get liberal arts experiences and the associated life outcomes is far more likely to find them at liberal arts colleges, but with diligence and care, it is possible to find particular liberal arts experiences at other types of institutions as well. It is also worth pointing out that there is reason for confidence in the work reported in this book: as described in appendix 1, the results are very consistent with the findings of related research on college outcomes, and chapter 9 provides a theory- and research-based rationale for these significant effects.

Narrative Reports

At the same time as the research project described here was being implemented the Council of Independent Colleges undertook an initiative to develop informative narratives describing the character of a liberal arts education. Eighty-five graduates from forty-nine different liberal arts colleges wrote open-ended descriptions of their undergraduate education, including whatever experiences and outcomes they found most salient. Excerpts from their narratives are used in chapters 6, 7, and 8 to illustrate, through these first-person accounts, the statistically important findings from analyses of the interview research.

6

Research Outcomes: Lives of Consequence as Leaders and Altruists

Liberal education matters far beyond the university because it increases our capacity to understand the world, contribute to it, and reshape ourselves. When it works it never ends.
—Michael S. Roth, *Beyond the University: Why Liberal Education Matters*, 195

We now begin an examination of the relationships between the six types of liberal arts educational experiences and the aspects of adult behavior identified in the history of the liberal arts, as reported in earlier chapters. In this chapter, the focus is on the relationship between a liberal arts education and living a life of consequence through leadership and altruism.

How does a higher education—an education in the tradition of the liberal arts—help prepare a person to contribute to the lives of others? Some people enter college wanting to make this kind of difference but feel that there are insurmountable barriers to accomplishing this goal. One college graduate, Theressa, describes her youth as follows: "Since a child, I wanted to become a doctor, but many were not supportive. Repeatedly, I heard, 'You are black, poor, and a girl. Being a doctor doesn't happen to people like you.'" She then states that her liberal arts educational experience

> empowered, prepared, and transformed me . . . exploring diverse concepts, thoughts, and ideas on varied topics; and appreciating the importance of discipline in behavior, integrity in action, and respect for all. The active learning, inter- and intra-personal communication skills and leadership obtained from my extracurricular college experiences prepared me for many roles and responsibilities that are invaluable in both my personal and professional life. After college, it was eleven years before I could start medical school. But a well-rounded liberal arts education prepared and enabled me to quickly adapt and transition to other career options. In short, my liberal arts education . . . paved the way for me to sustain and ultimately become a physician and travel the world as a contributor to the global medical community . . . a far cry from the "poor black girl from the inner city."

John, another liberal arts college graduate whose life has been committed to public service as a state senator, member of Congress, and presidential appointee, emphasizes the importance of the nature of the educational community in his assessment of the liberal arts impact:

> From small classrooms that created an intimate learning environment to the support and mentorship of inspired administrators, caring staff, good teachers, and motivated faculty . . . college provided more than a degree—it provided me with knowledge, purpose, and a sense of civic responsibility. . . . For me, that well-rounded education better prepared me for the challenges and opportunities I faced throughout my career, and I continue to benefit from the knowledge, lessons, and opportunities that began with a bedrock liberal arts education.

While Theressa, working in public health, and John, working in state and national governance, are contemporary examples of societal involvement—as leaders and contributors to society—what it means to be a leader and civically engaged person has changed with time as societies evolved and forms of government transformed.

In ancient Greece and Rome, leadership and civic responsibility involved participation in decision-making assemblies by free men. In medieval and colonial Europe, as well as in colonized North America, leaders were an elite (and nearly always men) who served and protected royal privilege. But the American Revolution changed this, with the critical need for *every* person to be engaged in society.

Recall from chapters 2 and 3 that before the American Revolution, a liberal arts education was designed to protect society *from* the everyday person, with governance restricted to the ruling class that served the monarchy. In contrast, in the postrevolutionary United States, in which "our republican form of government renders it highly important that great numbers should enjoy the advantage of a thorough education,"[1] the liberal arts was reconceived as an education *for* people who would be constructively involved in society. This was a new, and distinctly American, contribution to the liberal arts tradition. The Yale Report of 1828 eloquently describes the need for the kinds of people who will be effective leaders and contributors to American society, saying that "he who is not only eminent in professional life, but has also a mind richly stored with general knowledge, has an elevation and dignity of character, which gives him a commanding influence in society, and a widely extended sphere of usefulness."[2]

Like Theressa and John, Bernadette, a research scientist whose work involves endangered species, emphasizes the importance of the liberal arts educational context in shaping her life:

> During my four years in residence on campus, I was surrounded by students from seven different countries and was myself a foreign student. Exploring life's big questions became a global experience for me. It raised my awareness of the benefits of diversity and the importance of sharing experiences. Whether in or out of class, my peers were always welcoming and informative. Although a biology major, I also took courses in philosophy, theology, ethics, music, and art history, among others. I not only enjoyed my learning

experience but developed the ability to think critically, make sound judgments, and awaken my creative imagination. The broader my learning experience, the more connected topics seemed. Faculty members played an important role in my college experience. The only science course I had in high school was biology, and I had to be tutored in math, chemistry, and physics. My professors were patient and gave unstintingly of their time, tutoring me so that I could pursue my desired major. Their dedication and example instilled in me the determination to do the same for others who need help.

How do these alumni narratives align with the findings from analyses of the responses of 1,000 college graduates? *As you will learn, the research findings indicate it is the liberal arts educational context—the development of larger perspectives and experiencing an authentic learning community—that has a strong connection to living a life of consequence. On the other hand, the content of study is not substantially related to either leadership or altruism.*

Educational Experience, Leadership, and Altruism

Theressa, John, and Bernadette describe the educational experiences that they feel shaped them into societal leaders who would engage in work of benefit to society. The experiences they cite include exploring diverse concepts, developing respect, active learning, learning communication skills, leadership experiences, having small classes, mentorship, involvement with diverse students, exploring life's big questions, developing critical thinking, and dedicated professors. This is not a surprising list, as these are the kinds of ideas frequently expressed as the experiences that students have at liberal arts institutions; it is noteworthy that the emphasis is on the educational context as opposed to the content of the education.

The question is whether these subjective reports are supported by systematic research involving a large cross section of college graduates. The findings reported here, then, are based on the interview responses of 1,000 graduates of a wide range of types of colleges and universities (see appendix 2 for a description of this group). As described in chapter 5, six aspects of the educational experience and six dimensions of adult behavior were assessed and statistically analyzed. In this chapter, we examine the relationships among all six aspects of the educational experience and the first dimension of adult behavior on the right: living a life of consequence through leadership and altruistic civic involvement. This analysis is represented in figure 6.1.

As described in chapter 5, the relationships among the six types of educational experience on the left of figure 6.1 and indicators of both leadership and altruism are tested statistically for significance and then assessed for magnitude. Chapter 4 included a description of the questions relating to the educational experience, and the indicators of leadership and altruism are described next. I label those relationships that are both statistically significant and of larger magnitude as "substantial" effects and are described in this

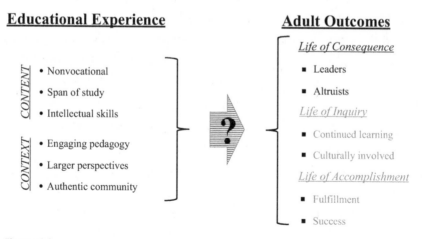

Figure 6.1
Relationship between educational experience and living a life of consequence

chapter.* The analyses of the relationship between the educational experience and continued learning are presented first, followed by the analyses of cultural involvement.

Leadership

How do we know if an adult is a leader? Of course, we could just pose the simple question: "Are you a leader?" But in this research, we aren't interested in soliciting opinions—we want to know what people actually do, just as, in the case of describing their college experiences, we wanted people to describe what happened in college, not merely their opinions or fallible memories about college and its impacts. Thus, what kinds of things do adults actually do if they are leaders? A person elected president of their nation is a leader by definition, and a respected community leader is another kind of leader. But these are not leadership behaviors that most people can exhibit, especially the younger adults in our study. What are the kinds of behavior that almost anyone can display if they are exhibiting leadership as adults?

As indicators of leadership, our research design team identified the kinds of behavior characteristic of leaders: being chosen by others to lead the work of various kinds of organizations and being sought by others to provide counsel or direction. As such, the following questions were asked of the participants in this research project:

- Other than positions at work, have you been elected or appointed to a top-level leadership position in a social, cultural, professional, or political committee, board, or group?
- How often do people come to you for advice about matters outside your area of expertise?
- How often do you mentor less-experienced individuals?

---

*A complete description of this analytical approach is given in full in chapter 5 and appendix 4, assumptions about causation are reported in appendix 1, and the full statistical results are presented in appendix 5.

To reiterate a point made earlier: these questions are not designed to define what leadership *is*; rather, they are *indicators* of the kinds of behavior that could be characteristic of twenty-five-year-old to sixty-five-year-old leaders in contemporary society. The responses to these three questions were combined into a single indicator of leadership, with individuals classified as exhibiting either a lower or higher degree of leadership.

Indeed, the graduates quoted earlier in this chapter could respond affirmatively to one or more of these questions: Theressa is a globally respected physician, John has been an appointed and elected government official, and Bernadette is an influential scientist.

Leadership Research Findings   Based on the statistical analysis of our data from 1,000 interviews of graduates of a broad range of colleges and universities, what types of college experiences are related to adult leadership? As shown in figure 6.2, we find that only the educational context has a substantial relationship with leadership. Specifically, *those who developed larger perspectives during college and who experienced an authentic learning community were 25–28% more likely to act as leaders as adults.*

What specific college experiences did these adults have in college related to the development of larger perspectives and the experience of educational community?*

Larger Perspectives Experiences   Two of the indicators of developing a larger perspective are substantially related to adult leadership, as shown in figure 6.3. *Those who had substantial discussions with other students about issues of significance to humanity, or had frequent discussions with people of differing beliefs and views, had a 26–27% greater likelihood of acting as leaders as adults.*

---

*Demographic analyses are presented in appendix 4. While it does not satisfy the statistical criteria described in this book as meaningful, nor is it a predictive covariate, socioeconomic status of the family while in high school has a very weak relationship to leadership, with $p = .04$, but a relative effect of only 8%.

Increase in probability of leadership for those who experienced:

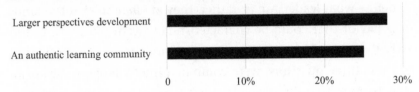

Figure 6.2
The relationship between educational context and leadership

Increase in probability of leadership for those who:

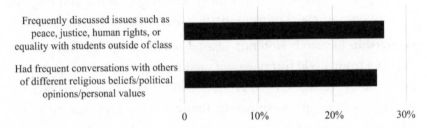

Figure 6.3
Developing larger perspectives and leadership

Increase in probability of leadership for those who:

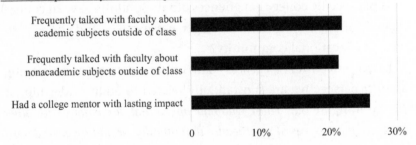

Figure 6.4
The connection between authentic educational community and leadership

Authentic Learning Community   Three of the indicators of educational community are substantially related to adult leadership, as shown in figure 6.4. *Those who had a mentor, or who frequently talked with faculty outside of class time about both academic and nonacademic matters, were 21–26% more likely to act as leaders as adults.*

Summary of Leadership Findings   Adult leaders are those who, in college, did the following:

- Developed larger perspectives through out-of-class discussions with other students about issues of significance to humanity and engaged in discussions with other students of differing beliefs, values, and life experiences
- Experienced an authentic educational community through close out-of-class relationships with faculty and mentors

Thus, this research demonstrates that it is the educational *context* that is related to adult leadership. The analysis found *no* significant overall relationship between leadership and the content of study, including having a particular vocational or nonvocational major, developing intellectual skills, or having a broader span of study.

The relationship between leadership and educational experience is graphically summarized in figure 6.5.

As interviewees in their narratives said, they were "able to get the one-on-one education," be "stretched in every way possible," and "learned to interact with students of all socioeconomic, racial, and ethnic backgrounds." David, a respected civic and nonprofit leader as well as a state legislator, emphasizes the importance of the relationships of students with faculty and staff in his description of his educational experience: "Each student has value; students are not just a number. The faculty and staff get to know you by name. Even years after graduation, I still see staff members that call me by name in the community. They really value their students and their students' education and success."

Altruism

What types of behavior benefit society? What are behaviors that virtually anyone can exhibit that indicate an altruistic involvement with society? Our research design team identified three kinds of behavior indicative of altruistic involvement, which almost anyone can do: making financial contributions to nonprofit organizations,

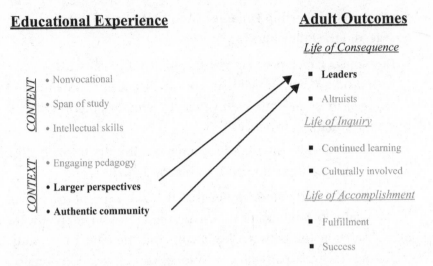

Figure 6.5
Relationship between educational experience and leadership

voting, and volunteering. As such, a number of questions were asked of the participants in this research project:

- Do you make charitable donations to any organizations or causes?
- What percent of your income do you donate each year?
- Do you vote in presidential elections?
- Do you vote in off-year elections?
- How often do you spend time each month in volunteer work?
- How many hours do you spend in volunteer work each week (or month)?

The responses to questions about voting, donating, and volunteering were combined into a single indicator of altruism, with individuals classified as exhibiting either a lower or higher degree of altruistic behavior.

How does one's college experience relate to altruistic adult behavior? Michele, the founder of a nonprofit serving families and children and who obviously allocates her own time and resources to this endeavor, states: "Liberal arts colleges offer a type of learning that encompasses all aspects of life. Combining the residential experience with a commitment to extracurricular interests, and a challenging curriculum that seeks to present a well-balanced young adult ready to take on the world, liberal arts colleges afford students the opportunity to not have all of the answers straight away, but still be able to succeed in our modern world." Is her viewpoint supported by systematic research involving a large group of college graduates who attended many types of institutions?

Altruism Research Findings   What college experiences are found to be statistically related to altruistic adult behavior in the analysis of the responses of the 1,000 college graduates? As indicated in figure 6.6, the analyses show that adult altruism is associated with only one aspect of the educational context.* Specifically, *those who experienced an education in an authentic learning community were 26% more likely to report altruistic behavior as adults.*

Authentic Learning Community   What types of college learning community experiences are substantially related to adult altruism? Five of the indicators of educational community are substantially related to adult leadership, as shown in figure 6.7. *Those who frequently spoke with faculty about nonacademic matters, had a mentor, and were active in or led campus organizations had a 20–30% greater likelihood of behaving altruistically as adults.*

Three types of adult behavior were used as indicators of adult altruistic involvement in society: donating to nonprofits, volunteering, and voting. Does the experience of being educated in an authentic educational community relate to all three of these adult behaviors? It turns out that voting is not related to experiencing college

---

*The respondents' ethnicity was also statistically associated with altruism (see appendix 4). Because the direction of the effect was the same and the magnitude of the effect virtually identical (26% for whites and 30% for persons of color), results separated by ethnicity are not being presented here. The full analysis of the data may be found in appendixes 4 and 5.

Increase in probability of altruism for those who experienced:

Figure 6.6
The connection between educational context and altruism

Increase in probability of altruism for those who:

Frequently talked with faculty about
nonacademic subjects outside of class

Had a college mentor with lasting impact

Lived in college housing

Actively participated in college or university
organizations

Led a college or university organization

```
0        10%       20%       30%
```

Figure 6.7
Relationship between an authentic learning community experience and altruism

community, but both donating and volunteering are. Indeed, as shown in figure 6.8, those who experienced *an authentic educational community had a 56% higher probability of contributing a larger percentage of their income.* More specifically, those with a *closer relationship with faculty or had a mentor or were more involved on campus had a 38–62% greater likelihood of donating a larger percentage of their income.*

In addition, those with nonvocational majors were 35% more likely to donate a larger percentage of their income as adults.

There is a similar pattern regarding experiencing an authentic learning community as it relates to spending more time volunteering, as shown in figure 6.9. Overall, those who experienced an *authentic educational community were 42% more likely to report*

Increase in probability of altruism for those who experienced:

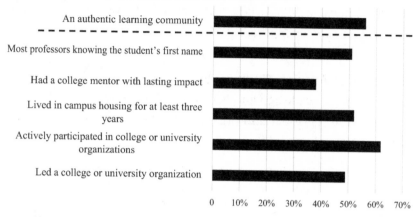

Figure 6.8

Connection between donating a larger percentage of income and being in an authentic learning community

Increase in probability of altruism for those who experienced:

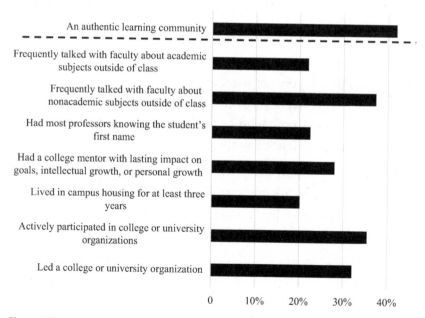

Figure 6.9

Connection between spending more time volunteering and experiencing an authentic learning community

volunteering more hours as an adult. And again, it is *those who had a closer relationship with faculty, had a mentor, or were more active and involved on campus that had a 20–37% higher likelihood of spending more time volunteering.*

Summary of Altruism Findings   Bo, who graduated from a liberal arts college a decade ago and is now involved with an organization that provides personal and organizational development programs, says the following:

> It was important to me to have the freedom to pursue a variety of both academic and social interests, to develop strong new relationships, to question the things that did not make sense to me, and to look for answers to those questions. I wanted to have the support of a university faculty and campus atmosphere that encouraged individuality . . . I have asked myself over the years if maybe I should have studied something more practical during my college years, but the truth is that I would never trade my Spanish and international studies degrees for other degrees because they have given me the freedom to take advantage of incredible experiences as an adult that I only dreamed about when I was younger.

His description is very consistent with the findings from the analyses of the 1,000 interviews of college graduates, which indicate that adult altruists are those who experienced an authentic educational community, as evidenced by the following:

- Close out-of-class relationships with faculty, including both academic and nonacademic matters
- Active involvement in the extracurricular program by living on campus and being involved in and even leading campus organizations

Insofar as adult altruism is concerned, only the educational *context* is related to adult behavior. Although majors in professional areas reported lower rates of donating, there were *no* substantial overall relationships between altruism and the content of study, nor the other aspects of the educational context.

Figure 6.10
Relationship between educational experience and altruism

This overall relationship between adult altruism and educational experience for the graduates interviewed may be graphically summarized as shown in figure 6.10.

Lives of Consequence as Leaders and Altruists

In analyzing the educational experience and life outcomes of the 1,000 college graduates, who attended a broad range of types of institutions, three essential insights emerge:

1. The importance of educational context. Those who shape society as leaders and altruists are consistently those who have experienced an undergraduate education in the context of a personal and authentically involving learning community. Specifically, those living a life of consequence had a substantially higher probability of experiences such as

   • Frequently talking with faculty outside of class about both academic and nonacademic subjects

- Having professors who know the student's first name
- Having a mentor with a lasting impact
- Leading or participating in college or university clubs and organizations
- Living on campus for at least three years

2. In addition, those who are leaders had a substantially higher probability of experiences that develop broader perspectives:

- Frequently discussing issues such as peace, justice, human rights, or equality with students outside of class
- Having frequent conversations with others of different religious beliefs, political opinions, and personal values

3. There is no substantial impact for the content of study on leadership or altruism. In this research, other than the fact that professional majors donated a smaller percentage of their income, questions asking about college major, course of study, or developing particular intellectual capabilities are unrelated to adult leadership and altruism.

The educational context, then, rather than the content of study, is the powerful framework associated with those who live a life of consequence. As a mentor to students at a medical school where she is the director of surgical residency as well as a trauma surgeon, Angela describes the importance of both the educational community and the impact of students of different backgrounds on her liberal arts experience:

> In addition to the obvious benefits of small class size, the professors were accessible and could share valuable insights. They also recognized my passion for medicine, so they directed me toward appropriate research opportunities and work experiences. By the time I took the medical school entrance exam, I was well prepared for my next academic challenge. . . . Outside of academics, campus life should be one of the most important considerations when choosing a college. In retrospect, I probably developed most of my leadership and crisis management skills as a dorm resident assistant.

Living in the dorm also allowed me to establish my independence and interact with students from other academic disciplines, backgrounds, and countries.

Hers is a life of consequence through leadership and altruism—an exemplar of a long-held purpose of education in the tradition of the liberal arts.

Next, we turn to the second type of adult outcome: living a life of inquiry through continued learning and cultural engagement.

7

Research Outcomes: Lives of Inquiry through Continued Learning and Cultural Involvement

Anyone who keeps learning stays young. The greatest thing in life is to keep your mind young.
—Henry Ford, as quoted in Seldes, *The Great Thoughts*, 139

While, as I described in earlier chapters, the specific content of what should be studied in an education in the tradition of the liberal arts has evolved, the notion that such study should be designed to develop people who value the cultural achievements of humanity and continue to learn over their lifetimes has remained constant. Robert, a professor and former college president, says that when he first visited colleges as a high school student-athlete, the coaches "tried to impress me with fancy weight rooms, special dining facilities, and players who had 'made it' in the NFL." But at one liberal arts college, the coach instead asked about his life goals—what he wanted to do after graduation. He chose to attend that college, and he describes his educational experience and the life that he has lived in this way:

> A young faculty member in the chemistry department . . . told me
> that my science and mathematics course selections were appropriate
> for either science or premed, but then spent time urging me to
> apply for admission to a high-powered European history course

and a writing-intensive English literature course. I took both of those courses. The professors broadened my horizons and have enriched my life ever since. As my advisor for four years . . . [he] continued to guide me not only in science and mathematics, but also in fields such as philosophy, psychology, sociology, and art. The four years . . . were like being a kid in a candy store; there was so much to choose from and so many talented faculty willing and able to help you.

The liberal arts education . . . gave me the skills that I need at every stage of my career. In addition, it enriched my family life, my social life, and my involvement as a citizen in my communities. My wife and I share reading interests in history and spend hours together in art museums. We are constantly sending and receiving books in numerous fields with our five children and now are starting to do so with our grandchildren. A liberal arts education continually renews and enlivens all stages of your life.

This description is very consistent with the ancient Greek educational ideal that schooling "prepared the mind for the more advanced stages of education and culture."[1] This preparatory goal has persisted through the millennia, based on the belief that by gaining an understanding of essential areas of human culture and knowledge, a person is prepared to continue to grow and develop throughout life.

As described by the Yale Report of 1828, an American-style liberal arts education is intended to create the learning person, from literature through science:

When a man has entered upon the practice of his profession, the energies of his mind must be given, principally, to its appropriate duties. But if his thoughts never range on other subjects, if he never looks abroad on the ample domains of literature and science, there will be a narrowness in his habits of thinking, a peculiarity of character, which will be sure to mark him as a man of limited views and attainments. Should he be distinguished in his profession, his ignorance on other subjects, and the defects of his education, will be the more exposed to public observation. On the other hand, he who is not only eminent in professional life, but has also a mind richly stored with general knowledge, has an elevation and dignity of character, which gives him a commanding influence in society, and a widely extended sphere of usefulness.[2]

Susan, a physician, not only credits her professors for telling her to "not just to memorize the facts, but to ask why and how," but also gives a somewhat humorous description of the value of the Yale Report's "mind richly stored" by telling the following story:

> I was obligated to take certain subjects outside of my major.
> I remember complaining to my advisor especially about having to take a fine arts course, which required memorizing multiple paintings and artists. He replied that someday, perhaps at a cocktail party, I would be happy to have this knowledge. The moment actually occurred on a trip with close friends to Italy. I walked into the art museum and immediately recognized a painting. "Ah, my favorite Botticelli, *Man with a Medal*." The look of amazement on the faces of my friends, and even the guide, made the course worth the effort. Susan the science nerd knew something about art!

But she also goes on to report, in a more serious tone, that she is "now a frequent visitor to art museums and never tires of revisiting those old paintings and learning about new ones," and that she has "developed a passion for history and am glad for the solid introduction I received at school."

How do the alumni narratives align with the findings from the analyses of the responses of 1,000 college graduates from a diversity of colleges and universities? *As the results reported here show, continued learners and those who are culturally involved are those who experienced all aspects of a liberal arts education—both the content of study and the educational context.*

Educational Experience, Continued Learning, and Cultural Involvement

In this chapter, we examine the relationship of the content of study and the character of the educational context with adult behavior related to living a life of inquiry through continued learning and cultural engagement. This analysis is represented in figure 7.1.

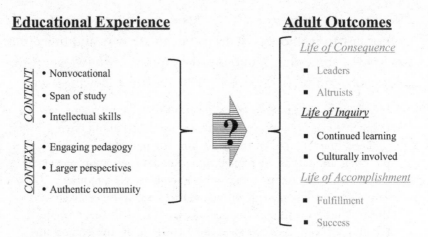

Figure 7.1
Relationship between educational experience and life of inquiry

As described in chapter 5, the relationship among the six types of educational experience on the left of figure 7.1 and indicators of both continued learning and cultural involvement on the right are tested statistically for significance and then assessed for magnitude. Chapter 4 included a description of the questions relating to the educational experience, and the indicators of continued learning and cultural involvement are described next. I label those relationships that are both statistically significant and of larger magnitude as "substantial" effects.* The analyses of the relationship between the educational experience and continued learning are presented first, followed by the analyses of cultural involvement.

Continued Learning

How do we know if an adult is engaged in continuing learning? What kinds of adult behavior indicate this outcome? Using the

___

*A complete description of this analytical approach is given in chapter 5, assumptions about causation are reported in appendix 1, and the full statistical results are presented in appendix 5.

same methods as those described in chapter 6 regarding leadership, the following questions were developed:

- In the typical day, how many hours do you spend listening to, reading, watching, or discussing social, environmental, or humanitarian issues?

- In the typical day, how many hours do you spend listening to, reading, watching, or discussing technology?

- Thinking about a typical day, about how much time, in hours, would you say you spend altogether listening to, watching, and reading the news online, in print, on TV, or on the radio—or do you not do any of those things on a daily basis?

- What is the highest level of education you have completed?

Reiterating a point made in the last chapter, these questions are not designed to describe what a continuing learner *is*; rather they are *indicators* of the kinds of behavior that may be characteristic of those who are continuing to be learners—to be intellectually involved—as twenty-five-year-olds to sixty-five-year-olds. The responses to these questions were combined into a single indicator of continued learning, with individuals classified as exhibiting either a lower or higher degree of continued learning.

As Pilar, a liberal arts graduate who founded a microfinance organization providing mentoring and financial support for low-income people, says: "My college experience, from the first day, became one of constant discovery about myself, the world we live in, and how one can use one's education to work for changes that improve the lives of others."

Are Pilar's thoughts consistent with the research findings?

Continued Learning Research Findings What college experiences are related to continued learning in adulthood? The analyses of the interviews of the 1,000 college graduates in this study show, as indicated in figure 7.2, those who demonstrate continued learning in adulthood experienced all the content and context characteristics of an education in the tradition of the liberal arts. *Those who became continuing learners were 29–37% more likely to have also experienced the full liberal arts content of education: a nonvocational major, broader span of study, and intellectual skills development. In addition, continuing learners were 29–42% more likely to report having experienced the full liberal arts context of education: experiencing engaging pedagogy, developing broader perspectives, and education in an authentic learning community.*

What specific college experiences did these adults have in college that related to continued learning?* We can examine the experiences substantially related to continued learning for each of the aspects in figure 7.2.

Nonvocational Majors As shown in figure 7.3, within the nonvocational majors the greatest impact (positive or negative) appeared to be with *business/accounting majors, who were 29% less likely to be continuing learners, and social science majors, who had a 36% greater probability of being continuing learners.* Humanities majors, as well as math and science majors, were not significantly more likely to be continuing learners than other majors.

Span of Study As indicated in figure 7.4, *continuing learners had a 20% higher probability of having studied broadly outside their major, as well as a 29% higher probability of having integrated humanities issues into most of their classes, regardless of their major field.* It is worth noting that being a humanities major did not relate specifically to continued learning; it is bringing the questions of primary concern to the humanities into other disciplines that resulted in significant effects.

Intellectual Skills All three experiences that are indicative of intellectual skills development are related to continued learning, as indicated in figure 7.5. *Continued learners had a 25–37% greater*

---

*Demographic analyses are presented in appendix 4. While not satisfying the statistical criteria described in this book to be considered meaningful, gender has a very weak relationship to continued learning, with a marginal $p = .06$ and a small impact (11% relative effect).

Increase in probability of continued learning for those who experienced:

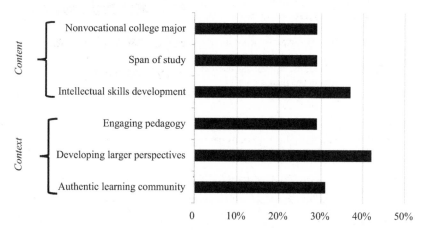

Figure 7.2
The connection between educational content and context and continued learning

Increase in probability of continued learning for those who were:

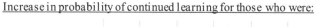
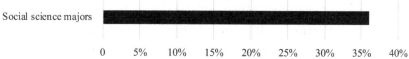

Figure 7.3
Relationship between nonvocational majors and continued learning

Increase in probability of continued learning for those who:

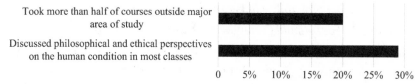

Figure 7.4
Relationship between span of study and continued learning

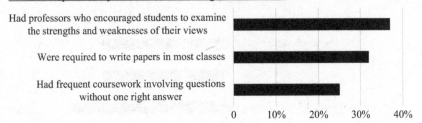

Figure 7.5
Connection between intellectual skills development and continued learning

probability of taking classes in which professors challenged the thinking of students, required papers, and assigned topics for which there is not necessarily one right answer.

Engaging Pedagogy   Two of the indicators of teaching methods that actively involve students in learning are substantially associated with continuing learning in adulthood, as indicated in figure 7.6. *Those who took seminar or smaller courses early in their college experience had a 23–25% higher probability of becoming continuing learners as adults.*

Larger Perspectives   All three indicators of students developing broader perspectives in their education are substantially associated with continued learning, as shown in figure 7.7. *Those who frequently discussed issues of significance to humanity outside of class, who had frequent conversations with students of different values and life experiences, or who learned about other cultures while in college had a 29–56% higher probability of becoming continuing learners.*

Authentic Educational Community   Indicators of close relationships with faculty or mentors, as well as campus activism, are related to continuing learning, as shown in figure 7.8. Specifically, those that were *more involved with faculty outside of class time, had faculty who knew their first names, had a mentor, or were involved in campus activism were 23–32% more likely to also continue learning as adults.*

Continued Learning and Earning an Advanced Degree   The adult outcome of continued education combines the responses to questions

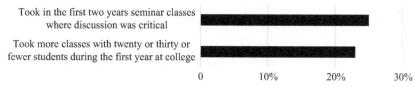

Figure 7.6

Relationship between engaging pedagogy and continued learning

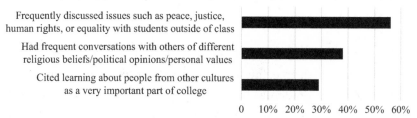

Figure 7.7

Relationship between larger perspectives and continued learning

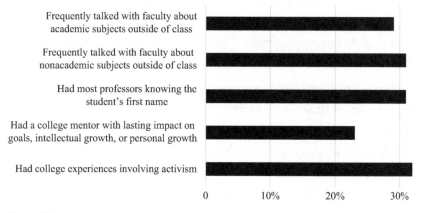

Figure 7.8

Relationship between authentic community and continued learning

Increase in probability of earning an advanced degree for:

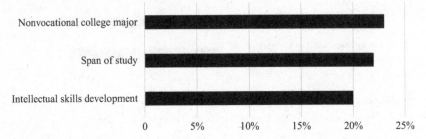

Figure 7.9
Connection between earning an advanced degree and educational content and context

about listening to, reading, watching, or discussing news and earning an advanced degree. It is interesting to look separately at the question of whether graduates have subsequently earned a master's or a doctoral degree. The indicators of graduate study alone turn out to be a subset of the indicators described previously. Specifically, as shown in figure 7.9, *those with a nonvocational major, who undertook a broader range of study, or who had their intellectual skills developed in coursework had a 20–23% higher probability of earning an advanced degree.*

Within the nonvocational category, *business or accounting majors had a 37% lower probability, and math or science majors had a 27% higher probability, of earning an advanced degree.*

Summary of Continued Learning Findings   It is striking that every dimension of the college experience is related to continued learning in adulthood—both content and context attributes. Those who continue to be actively involved in learning after graduation through reading, study, or discussion were substantially more likely to have done the following:

• Obtained a nonvocational major
• Studied a broader range of subjects in college
• Developed intellectual skills in their coursework
• Experienced more engaging teaching

- Had a greater level of meaningful out-of-class involvement and discussion with students of different backgrounds, values, and life experiences
- Had closer out-of-class relationships with faculty and active involvement on campus

A graphical representation of this set of relationships between educational experience and continued learning is shown in figure 7.10.

Steve, a successful actor—a profession involving constant learning about times, places, cultures, and people—says that both the content of study and the educational context are important: "I got to study the sciences while also jumping into the theater. I got to write my thesis on religion while studying abroad in the U.K. I was surrounded by an eclectic mix of peers who pushed me and exposed me to experience so many different cultures and ideologies." And, he goes on to say, this results in continuing learners in all kinds of professions, by noting that among his college friends: "We have a surgeon, a lawyer who works for a high-profile judge, a tech executive, a business owner, a radiologist, and somehow, an actor."

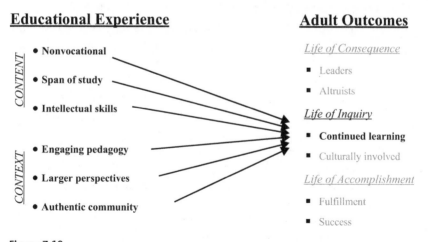

Educational Experience   ## Adult Outcomes

CONTENT
- **Nonvocational**
- **Span of study**
- **Intellectual skills**

CONTEXT
- **Engaging pedagogy**
- **Larger perspectives**
- **Authentic community**

Life of Consequence
- Leaders
- Altruists

Life of Inquiry
- **Continued learning**
- Culturally involved

Life of Accomplishment
- Fulfillment
- Success

Figure 7.10
Relationship between educational experience and continued learning

Cultural Involvement

How do we know if an adult is engaged in continuing learning and involvement in humanity's cultural wisdom? What are the kinds of adult behaviors that indicate these life behaviors? Using the same methods as those described in the last chapter regarding leadership, the following questions indicative of involvement in cultural activities were developed:

- About how often do you attend concerts, the theater, or museum exhibits?
- In the typical day, how many hours do you spend listening to, reading, watching, or discussing literature, theater arts, and/or music?
- In the typical day, how many hours do you spend listening to, reading, watching, or discussing pop culture and entertainment news?

As described earlier, these questions do not *define* cultural involvement; they are behaviors *indicative of* cultural involvement. The responses to these questions were combined into a single indicator of cultural involvement, with individuals classified as exhibiting either a lower or higher degree of cultural involvement.

Cultural Involvement Research Findings   What college experiences are related to cultural involvement? Larry, a liberal arts college graduate and now a professor of language and culture, describes his experience in this way:

> The faculty members with whom I interacted nurtured in me a true love for the world of ideas. The small classes, the expectation of intellectual engagement, and the scholarly mentoring kindled within me an appreciation for the liberal arts and an intellectual curiosity that I had no idea I possessed. Not only did I receive a remarkable academic experience, but I built a durable relationship network that remains central in my life today, as I approach the date of my forty-year reunion. My experience as a student leader, resident assistant, and student-athlete exposed me to caring professionals outside the classroom who helped me to understand the crucial role all campus agents play in the growth, development, and success of students.

Does this narrative description align with the statistically supported findings of our research on the adult behavior of college graduates? As was the case with continued learning, culturally involved adults are those who experienced all aspects of a liberal arts education—both the content of study and the educational context. As shown in figure 7.11, *those who are culturally involved had a 36–42% higher probability of experiencing the full liberal arts content of education: a nonvocational major, broader span of study, and intellectual skills development. In addition, continuing learners had a 22–40% higher probability of experiencing the complete liberal arts context of education: experiencing engaging pedagogy, developing broader perspectives, and education in an authentic learning community.*

What specific college experiences did these adults have related to each of these attributes of a liberal arts education?* All of these are explored in the following sections.

Nonvocational Major   Overall, nonvocational majors had a higher probability of cultural involvement, as shown in figure 7.12. This effect is most substantially because *humanities majors had a 45% higher probability of being culturally involved, whereas business majors had a 39% lower probability and math and science majors had a 26% lower probability of cultural involvement.*

Span of Study   Figure 7.13 shows that two of the indicators of breadth of study are substantially related to cultural involvement. *Those who studied more broadly—taking many courses in the humanities and whose courses, regardless of major area, included the discussion of issues of significance to humanity—had a 30–47% higher probability of being culturally involved as adults.*

Intellectual Skills   As indicated in figure 7.14, *those who were required to write papers in most classes and having assignments for which*

---

*Demographic analyses are presented in appendix 4. While it does not satisfy the statistical criteria described in this book as meaningful, nor is it a predictive covariate, socioeconomic status of the family while in high school has a weak relationship to cultural engagement, with $p = .03$, and a relative effect of only 15%.

Increased probability of cultural involvement for those who experienced:

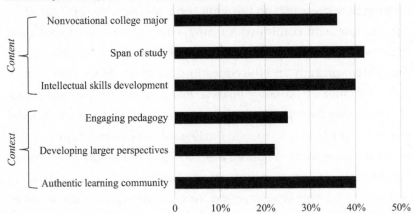

Figure 7.11
Connection between educational content and context and cultural involvement

Change in probability of cultural involvement for:

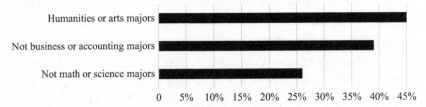

Figure 7.12
Connection between nonvocational major and cultural involvement

Increase in probability of cultural involvement for those who:

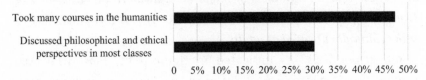

Figure 7.13
Relationship between span of study and cultural involvement

there was not necessarily a right answer had a 37–49% higher probability of being culturally involved as adults.

Engaging Pedagogy   As shown in figure 7.15, *those who experienced a more student-involving education through classes that involved discussion and taking seminars had a 37–47% higher probability of being culturally involved in adulthood.*

Develop Larger Perspectives   All three indicators of the development of larger perspectives are substantially associated with cultural involvement, as shown in figure 7.16. *Those who frequently discussed issues of significance to humanity, frequently interacted with people of different values and life experiences, and who learned about people of other cultures were 26–39% more likely to be culturally involved as adults.*

Authentic Educational Community   As shown in figure 7.17, indicators of close relations with faculty or mentors and campus involvement are related to continuing learning. Specifically, those that were *more involved with faculty outside of class time, had a mentor, or*

Increase in probability of cultural involvement for those who:

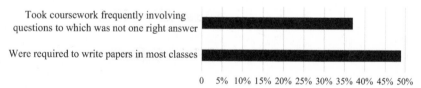

Took coursework frequently involving
questions to which was not one right answer

Were required to write papers in most classes

0   5% 10% 15% 20% 25% 30% 35% 40% 45% 50%

Figure 7.14
Relationship between intellectual skills development and cultural involvement

Increase in probability of cultural involvement for those who:

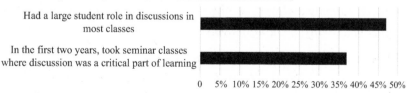

Had a large student role in discussions in
most classes

In the first two years, took seminar classes
where discussion was a critical part of learning

0   5% 10% 15% 20% 25% 30% 35% 40% 45% 50%

Figure 7.15
Connection between engaging pedagogy and cultural involvement

Increase in probability of cultural involvement for those who:

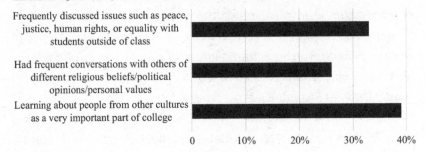

Figure 7.16
Connection between larger perspectives and cultural involvement

Increase in probability of cultural involvement for those who:

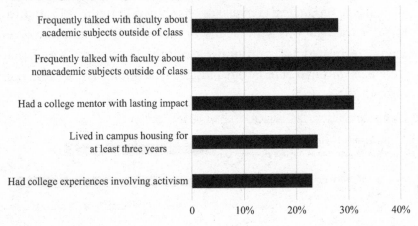

Figure 7.17
Connection between authentic learning community experience and cultural involvement

lived on campus and were involved in campus activism had a 23–39% higher probability of cultural involvement as adults.

Summary of Cultural Involvement Findings   As was the case with continued learning, all six attributes of the educational experience—content and context—are related to cultural involvement in adulthood. Those who are culturally involved adults, as indicated by attendance at concerts, theater, museum exhibits, or studying or discussing the arts are substantially more likely to have done the following:

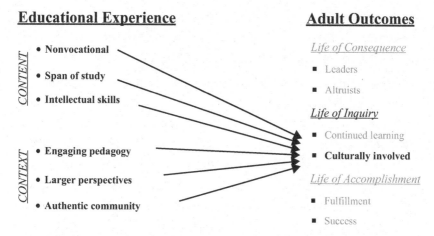

Figure 7.18
Relationship between educational experience and cultural involvement

- Had a nonvocational major
- Studied a broader range of subjects in college
- Developed intellectual skills in their coursework
- Experienced more engaging teaching
- Had a greater level of meaningful out-of-class involvement and discussion with students of different backgrounds, values, and life experiences
- Had closer out-of-class relationships with faculty and active involvement on campus

A graphical representation of this set of relationships between educational experience and cultural involvement is shown in figure 7.18.

Living Lives of Inquiry through Continued Learning and Cultural Involvement

Three overall insights emerge from the analysis of the relationship between the educational experiences and life outcomes of the 1,000 graduates of the range of colleges and universities involved in this study:

- All six aspects of the liberal arts educational experience—three of content and three of context—are related to the six aspects of adult behavior associated with liberal arts outcomes.

- Perhaps this result, in which both the content and context of education is significant, should not be surprising, in that this chapter's consideration of "lives of inquiry" focuses on the life of the mind, whereas the last chapter, on leadership and altruism, focused on actions relating to other people. As such, it seems reasonable that the educational content—what is studied—should be significantly related to the outcomes reported here.

- Nonetheless, it is significant that a life of inquiry—an active life of the mind—is also consistently related to the educational context, including the nature of relationships and degree of involvement with faculty and other students outside of the classroom. An active adult mind is not simply associated with coursework or material mastered; it is equally associated with the character of the educational environment.

In a narrative about her college experience, Anne, who as a professional musician and music teacher is a lifelong learner and culturally involved, describes the character of her educational experience as follows:

> I learned from upper classmen who guided me through example.
> We shared family stories, hardships, and thoughts on values, religion, education, and where our futures might lead us. I have fond memories of our teamwork as we put on productions, supported the women's field hockey team, and motivated one another to practice and study. We were not just a community but were more like a family. I learned from my mentors, and I too became a leader. My professors were articulate and well read. They, in turn guided us in how to practice, read with discernment, and find balance. Classes such as philosophy, psychology, and religion enlightened us and allowed us to think more deeply about values, morals, and purpose, as well as understanding humanity with a clearer mind. My professors . . . inspired me through asking questions, listening, teaching, and sharing specific

techniques, telling personal experiences, and making something difficult into something accessible.

That is an apt description of the significance of both the content and context of study—a life of the mind associated with the full spectrum of liberal arts educational experience.

In the next chapter, we turn our attention to the educational experiences related to a life of accomplishment.

8

Research Outcomes: Lives of Accomplishment through a Fulfilled and Successful Life

Human felicity is produc'd not so much by great pieces of good fortune that seldom happen, as by little advantages that occur every day.

—Benjamin Franklin, *The Autobiography of Benjamin Franklin*, 238

What is the relationship between college experiences and living lives of accomplishment, both personally and professionally? One college graduate, Clayton, who is the founder of several significant nonprofit organizations, a mentor to many, and chief executive officer (CEO) of a well-known corporation, highlights the significance of having one's thinking opened wide through both coursework and out-of-class experience, especially because he came from a small community. He says:

> Being from a farming area, I hadn't had such a breadth of exposure to different courses and disciplines. The social sciences and humanities—philosophy, literature, public speaking, sociology, psychology, economics, and foreign language—were most important to me . . . The ability to take those classes and to be involved with a diverse group of students from all different kinds of places

and economic backgrounds opened up a broad and rewarding world for me . . . My liberal arts education still helps me to successfully navigate uncharted territories as an entrepreneur and a philanthropist. It can do the same for countless others.

In describing her college experience, Virginia—who originally thought that she would become a veterinarian, so she studied the sciences heavily—instead pursued graduate degrees in animal science, entered the business world, and ultimately became the president of a company providing veterinary services. Noting that "college was a stepping stone into life," she said that, more important than specialized training, college "educates the whole person for life—not just a wedge of the mind in science and math for a few years. I learned to appreciate different cultures and religions, which served me in my career as I interacted with Japanese, Middle Eastern, and Native American customers." Further, she noted that there is more to life accomplishment than economic success; fulfillment is also key, and one's college education can make an important contribution to this life outcome: "Personal happiness and acceptance do not just happen at a certain age. Learning who you are, enjoying where you are, and identifying noncareer areas of interest start in a liberal arts college system and continue to grow in well-rounded, happy people."

The idea that life fulfillment—living a meaningful life—is an important purpose of a higher education traces its roots to ancient Greece, when ideas about a life well lived were expressed. With Plato and Aristotle as early advocates, the underlying Greek ideal of "virtue" was passed on from generation to generation through the centuries. By the time of revolutionary America, the notion of living a thoughtful, virtuous life was inherent in the writing and thinking of many influential people of the time, including the prolific writer, statesman, and US founder Benjamin Franklin,[1] whose many writings included frequent advice on how to live a good and fulfilled life. Franklin hoped "that some of my descendants may follow the example and reap the benefit."[2]

Nearly forty years after Franklin's death, the Yale Report of 1828 reflected these values, saying: "The great object of a collegiate education, preparatory to the study of a profession, is to give that expansion and balance of the mental powers, those liberal and comprehensive views, and those fine proportions of character, which are not to be found in him whose ideas are always confined to one particular channel."[3]

In addition to the long-standing emphasis of the liberal arts on living a life of value and fulfillment, the second outcome that we are considering in this chapter is personal success. This life outcome is less directly related to long-held liberal arts purposes. That is to say, while the purpose of a liberal arts education is to serve the advancement of both the individual and humanity more broadly, the liberal arts perspective is that individual success should not be just for selfish purposes, but also as a contribution to a greater good. In some sense, of course, we take the success of the educated individual for granted. After all, from its earliest roots involving the training of people to defend the city-state, success was assumed (after all, an unsuccessful warrior was a dead warrior—not useful at all).

In the later development of the liberal arts, the outcome of a higher education was to give people the knowledge essential for success in the Greco-Roman era; the ability of the individual to be effective in governance and public discourse was prized. Although such individual achievement was part of the result, it was valued because it also contributed to a higher purpose—the public good. Indeed, the knife in Julius Caesar's back could have been a reflection of the fact that he was too personally, selfishly successful.

Through much of history (including in Europe and in colonial America), only the elite—people from families of money and power—were eligible for higher education, so the contribution of an education in the tradition of the liberal arts to personal success (in contrast to societal success) was not obvious. Indeed, the Yale Report not only fails to describe personal success as an outcome of the education it proposed, but also cautions that people's accumulated wealth should be used in a way that "will be most honorable to themselves, and most beneficial to their country."[4] American-style liberal arts education grew based on the outcomes contributing to the broader good, of making "humanity more humane."[5] So, with that caveat—that personal success should not be for selfish purposes—I will explore in this chapter personal success, as well as living a fulfilled life, as two aspects of living a life of accomplishment.

One liberal arts graduate named Bill, who completed college more than four decades ago, described himself when entering college as like some young people today: not thinking that he needed much other than money, adventure, and a good job. But his college experience shaped him in ways that he believes helped him to become personally successful, while also contributing to the public good:

> The residential community of students, faculty, and even the highest-level administrators were interested in me, on a personal level, and that made an enormous difference. Professors and administrators were available; they engaged with their students individually to help us filter new experiences, opportunities, and options at our relatively naive stage of life. I was curious, and that curiosity was encouraged. I received a broad, liberal arts exposure to several disciplines that fed my natural curiosity—some I thought I might be interested in, but failed to excel in, others that I hadn't originally been attracted to but did excel in . . . [providing] set up for success in my career—as well as in a wide range of interests beyond that career . . . What was important to me then, and continues to be now, was the ability to explore widely and to absorb things that were of little use until later in my career—when they suddenly were.

So, studying broadly, being deeply involved in a college community, and developing a range of interests—"from clueless to clued in," as Bill says—led him to not only to professional success as a broadcast executive, but also to deep involvement in public-serving work.

How do Bill's conclusions about college impact, and the ideas expressed by Clayton and Virginia at the beginning of this chapter, compare to the objective analyses of college experiences and life outcomes of the 1,000 graduates of a wide range of types of institutions whom we interviewed for this research? *As you will learn in the following sections, those who report living a more fulfilled life studied a broader range of subjects, developed intellectual skills, and were nonvocational majors. In addition, their courses were engaging, and they had more extensive out-of-class involvement with faculty, mentors, and peers. Those who are more personally successful, with greater incomes and higher positions, report a very different college experience: despite the first job advantage of vocational preparation, greater success over the longer term accrues to those who study more broadly and are more involved with faculty and mentors outside of class; college major is unrelated to longer-term success.*

Educational Experience, Personal Fulfillment, and Success

In this chapter, we examine the relationship of the content of study and the character of the educational context with adult behaviors related to living a life of accomplishment—a fulfilled and successful life. This analysis can be represented as shown in figure 8.1.

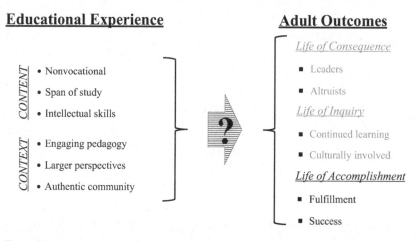

Figure 8.1
Relationship between educational experience and life of accomplishment

As described in chapter 5, the relationships among the six types of educational experience on the left side of figure 8.1 and indicators of both fulfillment and personal success on the right side are tested statistically for significance and then assessed for magnitude. Chapter 4 included a description of the questions relating to the educational experience, and the indicators of fulfillment and personal success are described next. I label those relationships that are both statistically significant and of larger magnitude as "substantial" effects.* The analyses of the relationship between the educational experience and continued learning are presented first, followed by the analyses of cultural involvement.

Life Fulfillment

As Annis, a liberal arts graduate and the successful author of over twenty books, says: "Although earning a degree was satisfying, benefits that I had not foreseen were even more fulfilling: a heightened awareness of the world outside family, friends, and community; a connection with the past through the study of ancient literature and philosophy; and a sense of continuity to the future as I began to understand the true purpose of education for the first time."

How do we know if an adult is living a life of fulfillment? Using the same methods as described in previous chapters, we developed questions about behaviors that were indicative of living a fulfilled life. Participants were asked the following:

- How much time do you spend reading, discussing, and thinking about how you should live your life?
- How much time do you spend reading, discussing, and thinking about the impact of the way you live your life?
- Do you tend to just live life without analyzing it?[6]

---

*A complete description of this analytical approach is described in full in chapter 5, assumptions about causation are reported in appendix 1, and the full statistical results are presented in appendix 5.

- How satisfied are you with your career path in general?
- How satisfied are you with the specific job you have right now?
- How satisfied are you with your personal and family life in general?

To repeat a point made in previous chapters, these questions are not designed to define what personal fulfillment *is*; rather, they are *indicators* of the kinds of thoughts and actions that a more fulfilled twenty-five-year-old to sixty-five-year-old might exhibit. The responses to these questions were combined into a single indicator of fulfillment, with individuals classified as exhibiting either a lower or higher degree of fulfillment.

Fulfillment Research Findings   What do our analyses of the descriptions of college experience and life outcome of the 1,000 college graduates interviewed for this study tell us? Five of the six aspects of a liberal arts education are substantially related to living a fulfilled life, as shown in figure 8.2. *For the content of study, those who had a college major in a nonvocational field, studied more broadly, and developed intellectual skills in coursework had a 44–66% higher probability of living a fulfilled life. For the educational context, those who took courses in which the teaching was more involving of students and experienced an*

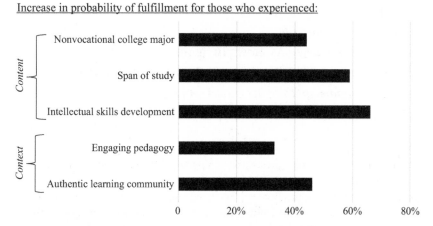

Increase in probability of fulfillment for those who experienced:

Figure 8.2
Relationship of educational content and context to fulfillment

authentic learning community had a 33–66% higher probability of living a fulfilled life.

What specific experiences are related to each of these overall findings?*

Nonvocational Major   What types of college major are most significantly associated with the finding of nonvocational majors living a more fulfilled life? As shown in figure 8.3, humanities and social science majors sit at one end of the continuum and business and accounting majors at the other. Specifically, *humanities and social science majors were 31– 42% more likely to report behaviors associated with living a fulfilled life, whereas business and accounting majors had a 40% lower probability of living a fulfilled life.*

Span of Study   As shown in figure 8.4, those living a more fulfilled life had a *41% higher probability of having taken many courses in the humanities and a 59% higher probability of having integrated humanities issues into most of their classes, regardless of their major.*

Intellectual Skills Development   Coursework emphasizing the development of intellectual skills is powerfully related to living a fulfilled life, as shown in figure 8.5. Specifically, those whose *professors required students to write papers, gave assignments on topics for which there is not a single right answer, or made students examine the strengths and weaknesses of their own arguments had a 51–149% higher probability of living a fulfilled life.*

Engaging Pedagogy   As shown in figure 8.6, those who experienced *teaching methods that directly engaged students in learning—more discussion, seminars, and smaller classes—had a 20–61% higher likelihood of living a fulfilled life.*

---

*Demographic analyses are presented in appendix 4. While it does not satisfy the statistical criteria described in this book as meaningful, nor are they predictive covariates, gender has a marginal $p = .06$ relationship to fulfillment, with only a 12% relative effect, and SES of the family while in high school has a weak relationship to fulfillment, with $p = .013$ with a relative effect of only 18%.

Increase in probability of fulfillment for those who were:

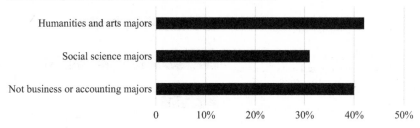

Figure 8.3
Relationship between nonvocational major and fulfillment

Increase in probability of fulfillment for those who:

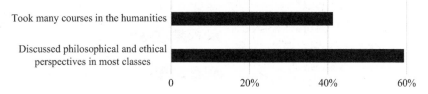

Figure 8.4
Relationship between span of study and fulfillment

Increase in probability of fulfillment for those who:

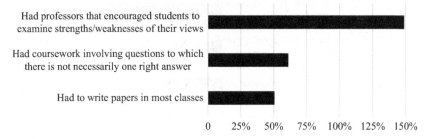

Figure 8.5
Relationship between intellectual skills and fulfillment

Increase in probability of fulfillment for those who:

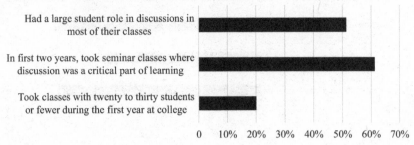

Figure 8.6
Relationship between engaging pedagogy and fulfillment

Increase in probability of fulfillment for those who:

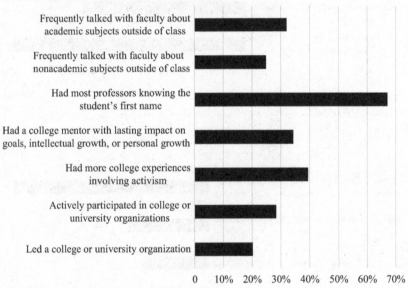

Figure 8.7
Relationship between learning community and fulfillment

Authentic Learning Community   As shown in figure 8.7, *those who had closer relationships with faculty (featuring out-of-class conversations about both academic and nonacademic matters and had faculty who knew their first name), had a mentor, or were more involved in campus activities (as an activist or being involved in or leading campus organizations) were 20–67% more likely to report living a more fulfilled life as adults.*

Summary of Life Fulfillment Findings   For those who report living a more fulfilled life, the following is true:

• The content of college study matters, with those who studied more broadly (including the humanities and considering issues of significance to humanity in most classes), developed intellectual skills in coursework (including examining the strengths and weaknesses of one's beliefs, dealing with issues without a single right answer, and writing papers), and had a nonvocational major (especially not a business or accounting major) had a higher probability of living a fulfilled life.

• The context within which education occurs is essential, including experiencing student-involving pedagogies (involving smaller classes and more discussion) and high levels of out-of-class academic and nonacademic involvement with faculty and other students had a higher probability of living a fulfilled life.

Similar to the findings for adults who continue to learn and are culturally involved, those who live fulfilled lives are those who have experienced both the intellectual and the experiential aspects of a liberal arts education. Thus, the relationship between the educational experience and living a fulfilled life may be represented as shown in figure 8.8.

In her narrative, college graduate Alison, a successful journalist, nicely summarizes how her liberal arts education relates to life fulfillment:

> I did not major in music. But in the four years I spent at [college] I sang with both the school's premier touring group and its jazz ensemble. . . . My experience with the choral program exemplifies the value of my liberal arts education. The administrators and faculty . . . understood I wasn't attending college simply to pursue a career, but also to develop my interests and talents. They worked to teach the whole person, not just the journalist I would become.

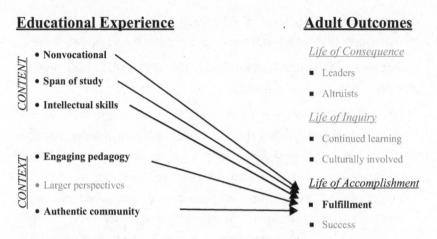

Figure 8.8
Relationship between educational experience and fulfillment

The lessons I learned through my participation in the college's choral program weren't limited to notes and rhythms. When I served as president of my choir, I learned how to manage a group of people who didn't always want to listen to me and how to plan fundraising events. I learned how to balance the work I needed to do for my classes with my rehearsal schedule. And I learned what it means to make time to pursue your passions. I now am employed full time as a reporter for a newspaper, and every day I use the skills my four years . . . taught me. I routinely speak with people who aren't happy to hear from me, but I've figured out how to work with them anyway. And because I'm consistently juggling several stories at once and have to find time to fit in interviews, research and writing, it's helpful that I've had practice managing a busy schedule. Perhaps most importantly, I've remembered to carry the liberal arts mindset into my adult life . . . to cultivate a life that is full, happy, and not solely career-driven.

Personal Success

In common usage, there are many ways to define success, but in this analysis, we focus specifically on outcomes of direct benefit to the individual. This is in contrast to the types of other-serving successes represented in the earlier analyses of leadership and altruism. What indicators of personal success were used in this study? Our research design team identified two key questions indicative of individual achievement in contemporary society:

- What is your position level at your current job? (classified as entry, midlevel, upper level, and president/owner/CEO)
- What is your total current annual household income?

In addition, questions were asked about the respondents' position and income immediately after graduation.

As described earlier, these questions do not define personal success; they are life outcomes that are indicative of the success of twenty-five-year-old to sixty-five-year-old graduates. The responses to these questions were combined into a single indicator of success, with individuals classified as exhibiting either a lower or higher degree of personal success.

Success Research Findings   For the first time, the overall analyses show that none of the six categories of the educational content or context was substantially related to the measure of personal success, as indicated by combining position and income; the liberal arts had neither a positive nor a negative effect. Also, for the first time, three demographic characteristics of the respondents are directly related to an adult outcome: with success assessed by salary and position, males are 24%, whites are 43%, and those coming from families of higher socioeconomic status (SES) are 26% more likely to report being successful as adults. When the two aspects of the success outcome—income and level of position—are analyzed separately, gender is significantly and substantially related to position level (males are 39% more likely to be in a higher position), and ethnicity and family SES are related to having a greater income (77% in favor of whites, and 31% in favor of higher SES). For position achieved, only gender is significant and substantial, with males 39% more likely to be in a higher position.

There is an intriguing result related to aspects of liberal arts study, however. As shown in figure 8.9, *those who studied more broadly by*

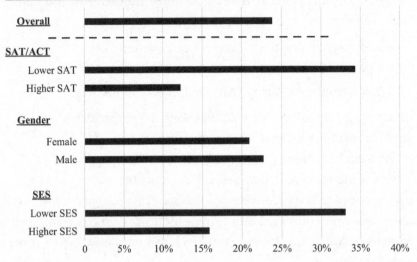

Figure 8.9
Relationship between various demographic characteristics and taking more than half of courses outside the major

taking more than half of their courses outside their major were 24% more likely to report a higher income as adults. Analyses within the personal attribute categories indicate that this effect was more substantial for those with lower SAT/ACT scores (34%) and those of lower family SES (33%). The effect was roughly equivalent for males and females.

Longer-Term Success   The findings reported here were those that were characteristic of people regardless of age, including those who graduated ten, twenty, or forty years ago. However, of course, both income and position commonly change with age. The description of the career progression of Deborah, a senior officer of a major corporation, exemplifies this idea:

> How could someone with an interdisciplinary studies major
> combining sociology, Spanish, and Latin American studies go on
> to have this career? The answer is that my liberal arts education
> did not prepare me for one particular job or profession; it prepared

me for any that I would choose once I truly found my passion. . . .
faculty devoted to teaching each student both as an individual and as
a team player taught me three critical things that have made all the
difference: How to Learn, How to Think, and How to Communicate.
The broad-based perspective and agility that support problem-
solving and characterize any successful career, with all of its twists
and turns, its challenges and opportunities. Significantly, it was from
this foundation that I built the capacity to become a leader in my
profession and community . . . Those who know how to collaborate
effectively with diverse individuals and teams, learn quickly in new
circumstances, think creatively in reaction to ever-changing realities,
and communicate in a way that reaches people who are bombarded
with information. Although initially daunting, it is exciting to live in
this world and to have the opportunity to contribute.

This narrative suggests that looking separately at the older, well-
established cohort of college graduates may provide insight into how
a liberal arts education is linked to position and income over one's
career. So analyses were carried out on the responses of the 326 college graduates between fifty-five and sixty-five years old—those who
are well established in their lives and jobs and likely at the peak of
their profession. There are several instructive findings from the analyses of the experiences of these older college graduates that replicate and extend the findings reported here for all graduates.

Within this well-established group, the effects of gender and
ethnicity on overall success disappear; however, one's SES while in
high school continues to be significant and substantial, with those
having a higher SES also 20% more likely to report a higher income
as adults. The question, then, is whether there are any liberal arts
educational experiences associated with success for those who grew
up in lower- as well as higher-SES families. Indeed, there are two.

First, as shown in figure 8.10, the single liberal arts attribute that
is significantly and substantially associated with success is experiencing a college education in an authentic learning community,
with a 32% higher probability of reporting later life success.

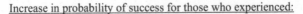

Increase in probability of success for those who experienced:

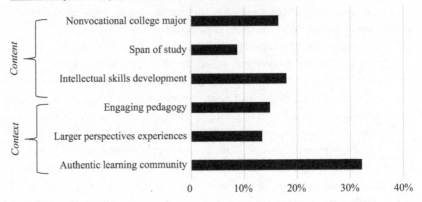

Figure 8.10
Relationship of educational content and context to success

However, given the significant effect of family SES, this result must be examined within the context of that demographic variable. It turns out that having experienced an authentic learning community is positively related to adult success, regardless of one's youthful SES, with that experience being far more substantial for lower-SES respondents (64%) than for higher-SES respondents (20%).

When examining the specific experiences associated with this overall effect, as shown in figure 8.11, it turns out that out-of-class relationships are the significant contributors: more frequently talking with faculty about academic (39%) and nonacademic matters (25%) outside of class and having a mentor (24%) were both associated with more substantial success outcomes. Another very important point is that all these effects are far more substantial for those who came from a lower-SES family than those who came from a higher-SES family.

The second finding of interest relates to the finding reported here on the breadth of study. Taking more than half of one's courses outside one's major turns out to be especially thought-provoking when it comes to its relationship to long-term success. As shown in figure 8.12, for these established respondents, those who reported taking more

Increase in probability of success for those who experienced:

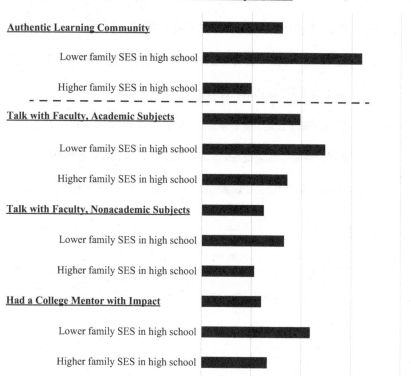

Figure 8.11
Relationship of authentic learning community experience to success

than half their classes outside their major reported a higher incidence of overall success (20%), with higher income being the major component of this finding. While this effect occurred regardless of SES, it was particularly substantial for those who grew up in a lower-SES family: namely, higher reported overall success (72%) and income.

Summary of Personal Success Findings   For life success (income and position), the liberal arts had neither a positive nor a negative effect. However, as might be expected, males, whites, and those from wealthier families are advantaged when it comes to earning a higher income and reaching a higher position. But that is not the end of

Increase in probability for those who took more courses unrelated to the major:

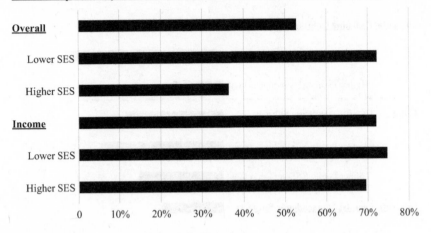

Figure 8.12
Courses unrelated to the major: Effect on success and income

the story insofar as liberal arts–related educational experiences are concerned.

Over the long term, the significant effects of both gender and race/ethnicity disappeared in this research, with only family SES when in high school remaining as a significant factor. However, liberal arts educational experiences ultimately become significant: those who experienced a more authentic educational community involving closer out-of-class relationships with faculty and a mentor report greater long-term success, regardless of socioeconomic position. This effect is especially strong for those who came from families of lower SES. Further, it is striking that the relationship between taking more courses outside of one's major is substantially associated with success—especially income—and again, this effect is stronger for those who grew up in families of lower SES.

A graphical representation of this set of relationships between educational experience and success is shown in figure 8.13.

Educational Experience   Adult Outcomes

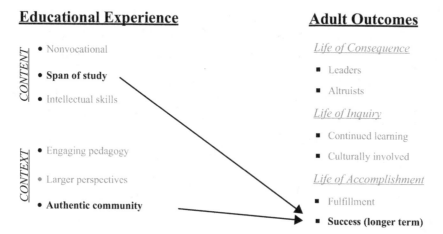

Figure 8.13
Relationship between educational experience and success

Lives of Accomplishment through Fulfilled and Successful Lives

David, an accomplished physician, describes the importance of both the content of study and the educational context in his reflections about his college experience:

> The variety of experiences I embraced at college made me fearless to attempt new endeavors, even when the odds of success were low. Its small size afforded me the liberty to participate . . . without concern for failure. The absence of constraints on my course selection stimulated an intense intellectual curiosity and nurtured a capacity to hear different viewpoints without prejudgment, to reject none without due consideration, and to ponder unconventional thought. It was this inquisitiveness and freedom from fear of failure that challenged me to leave behind a career in the military and start medical school at age forty-two.

In support of David's observations, as demonstrated by the analyses of the college experiences and life outcomes of the 1,000 graduates involved in this study, life fulfillment is related to having experienced the full scope of the liberal arts—both the content of study and its educational context. Having a nonvocational major, a broader span of study, and intellectual skill development in the context of engaging pedagogy and an authentic educational community all matter.

Yet the experiences associated with life fulfillment and life success are not identical. Indeed, the renowned investor Warren Buffett clearly differentiates between money matters and meaning. In a report to his shareholders, he succinctly stated: "Price is what you pay; value is what you get."[7] For the measures of success used in this study (income and position), liberal arts practices had neither a positive nor a negative effect; initially, it is what the student brings to college that matters most—gender, race/ethnicity, and family SES. Yet there are two important caveats to this finding. First, those who took more than half their courses outside their major were more likely to report a higher income as adults, and this effect was particularly powerful for those with lower SAT/ACT scores and those of lower family SES. Second, over the long term, not only is a broader span of study related to success, but having experienced an education in an authentic educational community (out-of-class engagement with faculty, mentorship) is also associated with success. The fact that these effects are particularly powerful for those who grew up in a lower-SES family is particularly striking.

The idea that there is no substantial relationship between having a vocation-oriented major and longer-term success is interesting, given that people, ranging from students and parents to politicians and policymakers, have become increasingly concerned that college should result in a good job. Yet specialized study is not the predictor of longer-term success; our research findings emphasize the importance of breadth of study for all, especially for those who enter college from less economically advantaged families.

These findings are a valuable endorsement of education in the tradition of the liberal arts as it relates to living a life of fulfillment, as well as longer-term personal success. In this era of rapid change, people hold many different jobs over their career: the Bureau of Labor Statistics reports that "individuals born in the latter years of the baby boom (1957–1964) held an average of 12.3 jobs from age 18 to age 52."[8] For a fulfilling and successful life in a time of continuing change, it is clearly advantageous to be well prepared to learn anew and think creatively through an education that is broad in character and involves learning to work and live effectively with others.

9

The Brain and Impact Education

Nothing great was ever achieved without enthusiasm.
—Ralph Waldo Emerson, *Select Writings of Ralph Waldo Emerson*, 96

The research reported in the previous three chapters has revealed that the more social or human interaction–based aspects of a liberal arts education are more consistently related to life impact than is the content of college study. Oscar-winning film producer and author Brian Grazer wouldn't be surprised by this finding: "We are all human beings. We all have emotions. We all have something to share. We are made for connection. It is the source of growth, discovery, joy, and meaning in our short, sweet time here on Earth."[1]

Why might this be the case? It turns out that contemporary cognitive neuroscience research gives insights into the powerful impact of social and emotional influences on learning.

*   *   *

Our research findings yields an important insight: in examining life outcomes, there are more frequently substantial relationships between adult behavior and the educational *context* (authentic educational community, development of larger perspectives, engaging pedagogy) than for the *content* of education (major, span of study, development of intellectual skills). This phenomenon is clear when examining the frequency with which various educational experiences are related to all six life outcomes assessed in this research. Figure 9.1 lists college experiences, with those at the top generally related more frequently to substantial life impact than those at the bottom.

	Educational context	Educational content
Higher frequency	Frequently talked with faculty about nonacademic and academic subjects outside of class	
	Had a college mentor with lasting impact	
	Discussed issues such as peace, justice, human rights, or equality with students outside of class	
		More than half of courses taken outside one's major
	Most professors know the student's first name	
	Actively participated in college or university organizations	
		Coursework frequently involved questions to which there is not necessarily one right answer
	Classes where discussion was a critical part of learning	
	College experiences involving activism	
	Lived in campus housing for at least three years	
		Discussed philosophical and ethical perspectives on the human condition in most classes
		Required to write papers in most classes
Moderate frequency	Frequent serious conversations with others of very different religious beliefs, political opinions, or personal values	
	Led a college or university organization	

Figure 9.1
Frequency of educational experiences related to life outcomes

What this chart makes clear is that, while both context and content are related to life impact, experiences related to the educational context are more frequently related to substantial adult outcomes than is the content of study. Substantive out-of-class involvement with people at the college (both faculty and students), including the exploration of issues of significance to humanity and diverse perspectives, describes the types of college experiences that generally are more frequently related to life impact. The content of study also matters, with span of study and the development of intellectual competencies and experiences being more frequently related to life impact.

It is also useful to note what is *not* listed on this chart, and two of these stand out. First, study for a particular career and college major are rarely related to long-term life impact. Second, while it is frequently asserted that participation in athletics develops leadership and life success competencies, it actually was not found to have any substantial effects on any of the life outcomes analyzed. On the other hand, involvement in, including leadership of, college organizations is frequently related to positive life outcomes.

So why does educational context more often relate to life outcomes than the content of study? The economist Bryan Kaplan, citing volumes of social science research, makes the case that higher education is a waste because people remember little of what they study—the content, especially the specialized content, is quickly forgotten.[2] While the assertion that students forget most of what they study seems impertinent, a candid teacher will often lament the lack of recollection of material "learned" by their graduates, or even last year's students in this year's course. Among other things, Kaplan concludes higher education should, therefore, become vocational, although he acknowledges that merely graduating from college still has value to employers because it is a social endorsement.

The effects reported in this research provide some support for Kaplan's findings about the lack of value of the content of study generally. But the overall research findings dispute his conclusions. First, vocational education has no long-term relationship to long-term success and has a negative relationship to a number of other life outcomes. But, more important, his assumption that a lack of student ability to remember factual content means that college study is a waste is a fundamentally wrong. We have learned that not only do the more general aspects of content learning matter for a number of important life outcomes, but also the educational context of study is particularly impactful.

Most people tend to think of learning as a rather objective and rational process, in which knowledge is transferred from a teacher or book (or the Internet) into the mind of the student. Some call this the "empty vessel" approach (an empty brain, into which information is poured), and some describe it as a "vacuum cleaner" methodology (the student mind sucks up all the information presented). Many of us carry in our mind's eye the movie image of a severe schoolmaster or schoolmistress having students memorize facts in cadence with the beat of a ruler on a desk. In the 1980s, the Harvard psychologist Howard Gardner described this mechanistic, rational approach (without the beat of the ruler) as gaining considerable force at the time that the computer revolution occurred: human cognition was "orderly, precise, step-by-step."[3] Yet even at that time, he expressed reservations about this view, asserting that "the community surrounding a cognizing individual is critical"[4]—a view that has guided his pioneering work on learning since then.

Indeed, two decades after Gardner's assertion about community, a remarkable compendium of three decades of research on how college affects students by noted researchers Ernest Pascarella and Patrick Terenzini reports that "critical thinking, analytic competences, and general intellectual development thrive in college environments that emphasize close relationships and frequent interaction between faculty and students as well as faculty concern about student growth and development."[5]

Why is this? Contemporary research on human cognition—"the process of obtaining knowledge and understanding"[6]—consistently finds that the social context of learning is critical. This effect is associated with the role of emotion in learning. Think of the teacher who, in your experience, had the greatest impact on you—the one who made you most interested, most intrigued, and most motivated to learn. How would you describe this person? Was this teacher a calm and objective transmitter of facts or an individual whose passion and excitement for a subject was captivating? How did this person relate to you? Were you a container into which the teacher poured information, expecting you to vacuum up everything presented? Or did this teacher treat you as a person whose life and thinking were of value and importance?

Objective research indicates that it is not, in fact, the teacher who most efficiently fills the empty vessel, who is best at fostering learning. As one report says, "Effective teachers are typically described as those who develop relationships with students that are emotionally close, safe, and trusting, that provide access to instrumental help, and that foster a more general ethos of community and caring in classrooms."[7] The persistent problem of high dropout rates for online courses[8] may well relate to the lack of this type of relationship.

The field of affective social neuroscience now embodies the nexus of our understanding of how humans learn: based on extensive neuroscience research, we now know that "it is literally neurobiologically impossible to build memories, engage complex thoughts, or make meaningful decisions without emotion," and that "learning is dynamic, social, and context dependent . . . emotions form a critical piece of how, what, when, and why people think, remember, and learn."[9]

This is the case, it turns out, because social relationships, emotion, and learning all involve the same brain systems—they do not happen independent of one another, in separate portions of the brain. Emotions affect all aspects of cognition, including how much attention one pays, the process of storing information in memory, and creative thinking and problem solving.[10] And this effect is not limited to situations in which passions may normally be aroused; even in what most people view as highly empirical and objective sciences—math and engineering—deeper understanding requires emotion to make learning work.[11] Think of the ways that gifted interpreters of science weave emotion—humor, suspense, surprise, joy—into the ways that they teach science (examples include Carl Sagan, Neil Degrasse Tyson, and Bill Nye). Their use of emotion is not accidental; it is a deliberate, powerful approach to pedagogy.

In the founding days of liberal arts education, the ancient Greeks understood this—for them, "advanced education involved a deep and absolutely personal bond between teacher and pupil, a bond in which . . . emotion, if not passion" was essential.[12] In recent years, this relationship of social and emotional factors to learning in college has been demonstrated in experimental studies. For example, students vary in the degree to which they feel they "fit in" at a particular college—that they are a part of the learning community—and lack of a feeling of fit can be a particular challenge for minority students. In one study, students were randomly assigned to groups in which some experienced a simple training exercise designed to have them develop the belief that they were like other students at their college—that they belonged. Those who entered college with a lower level of social belonging and who also received this training had higher grades, better health (as assessed by frequency of doctor visits), and a more positive sense of well-being. This effect lasted over the three years that the students spent in college after the training.[13] The impact of this sense of being a part of a learning community has been repeatedly shown to have numerous positive effects on academic achievement, as well as a range of other constructive college activities.[14] Indeed, there are literally hundreds of social psychological research studies that document the amazing power of social learning, beginning in childhood and continuing throughout life.

So the association between learning and emotion in relationship-based education is well documented through social psychological and neuroscience research—learning does not happen in a mechanistic way via a focus on the mastery of facts. It happens when social and emotional dynamics are harnessed in an educational environment. Nearly 400 years ago, the founders of Harvard, without the benefit of current research in social neuroscience, believed that the historic educational practices of the liberal arts they were emulating was the best way to learn:

> Book learning alone might be got by lectures and reading, but it was only by studying and disputing, eating and drinking, playing and praying as members of the same collegiate community, in close and constant association with each other and their tutors, that the priceless gift of character could be imparted.[15]

10

The Question of Value: Impact Education

We do not look inside of ourselves enough to understand our strengths and weaknesses, and we do not look around enough—at the world, in history—to ask the deepest and broadest questions. The solution surely is that, even now, we could all use a little bit more of liberal education.
—Fareed Zakaria, *In Defense of a Liberal Education*, 169

This book began by describing the confusion that exists regarding the meaning of study in the tradition of the liberal arts. The public perception is often that this approach to collegiate learning involves studying things that are "impractical" or "useless." Critics justify this view by asserting that liberal arts study—which they often understand to be limited to humanities subjects such as art, philosophy, music, and history—have little connection to getting a job or earning a living. As reported earlier in this book, although employers and academics alike have argued that liberal arts–based education is valuable in the workplace, it is hard to convince skeptics that it is more valuable than professional majors. Indeed, opposition to the liberal arts has sometimes been perversely strengthened by humanities academics who, in their efforts to defend humanities disciplines from elimination, argue that the sole definition of liberal arts should be studying in the humanities, or that "liberal arts" and "humanities" mean the same thing.

Even those who have not limited the definition of the liberal arts to the humanities have a seemingly insurmountable challenge: with literally hundreds of descriptions of the liberal arts, and different portrayals used by different colleges, we have no clear or consistent way of characterizing the essence of this approach to education. Without this clarity, it is impossible to document its value. It is clear what it means to get a business degree or an engineering degree—there are agreed-upon standards for program content—but it isn't clear what it means to get a degree in the tradition of the liberal arts.

We are suffering from a "forest and trees" problem: with so many trees (the hundreds of current definitions of the liberal arts and widely varying requirements), we have a hard time seeing the liberal arts forest (getting a more cohesive view of what it is). Just as stepping back from the trees helps us see the forest, the approach used in the project reported in this book has been to step back from the details of the liberal arts by looking at it from a millennia-long perspective. Over many centuries, during which education in the tradition of the liberal arts has existed and innovatively evolved, can we detect consistent educational attributes?

So, we began by asking two questions: "What are the kinds of learning and experiences that characterize liberal arts study?" and "What kinds of outcomes have liberal arts educators tried to create?" The idea was that by finding answers to these questions, we could focus on the question of impact: Are any of the characteristics of liberal arts education related to particular life outcomes? If some of these characteristics are related to one or more desired outcomes, we have a basis to assert that some features are essential components of the liberal arts. And presumably we can either ignore attributes without impact or figure out how to make them impactful.

What did we learn about the relationship between liberal arts education and life outcomes, as reported in previous chapters? I have summarized these extensive relationships in figure 10.1. Every bubble indicates that there is a statistically significant and substantial relationship between an aspect of the liberal arts educational experience (listed along the left side) and a life outcome (listed across the top).

This graphic shows that the educational *context*—the bottom half of the chart—is related to all three categories of liberal arts–based adult outcomes assessed in this study: lives of consequence, inquiry, and accomplishment. Educational *content* is related to two of the three: lives of inquiry and lives of accomplishment. The liberal arts attribute that is most consistently related to all three aspects of adult life is an education in an authentic and personally involving educational community. The behavioral indicators of

		Adult Behavioral Outcomes					
		Life of Consequence		Life of Inquiry		Life of Accomplishment	
		Leaders	Altruists	Continued learning	Culturally involved	Fulfillment	Personal success (longer term)
Content	Nonvocational			●	●	●	
Content	Span of study			●	●	●	●
Content	Intellectual skills			●	●	●	
Context	Engaging pedagogy			●	●	●	
Context	Larger perspectives	●		●	●		
Context	Authentic community	●	●	●	●	●	●

Figure 10.1
Relationship between educational experience and life outcomes

community used in this study most often substantially related to life impact include frequently talking with faculty outside of class time about nonacademic as well as academic matters; professors knowing students' first names; students having a mentor who had lasting impact; discussing issues of significance to humanity with other students outside of class time; and being actively involved with (or even leading) campus organizations. It is important to note that no particular one of these experiences defines the concept of "educational community"—rather, all of them are indicators of the kinds of experiences that a student might have if an authentic educational community exists. The notion that these types of experience are impactful is supported by extensive research in recent years, which finds, for example, that "support and challenge from faculty bolster academic self-concept, leadership, political and civic engagement, and moral character."[1]

It is noteworthy that span of study—especially taking more than half of one's courses outside one's major—is related to more life outcomes than the other aspects of the content of study. Life fulfillment, longer-term personal success, continued learning, and cultural involvement are all associated with this educational experience.

It is also interesting to note that the full range of liberal arts experiences is consistently associated with lives of inquiry, as well as fulfillment—outcomes that we might view as being more "of the mind." On the other hand, for those aspects of adult life that are more behavioral—lives of consequence as well as personal success—it is having experienced an authentic educational community that is most associated with this outcome. Also important is the fact that long-term success relates closely to having a broader span of study while in college.

The issue of nonvocational study demands note. In this research, not only is having a vocational major—one that prepares a person for a particular job or profession—unrelated to personal success in the long term (e.g., income, position achieved), but it actually is negatively related to living a fulfilled, culturally involved, and learning life. In fact, longer-term income and position at work are more related to essential aspects of a liberal arts education, such as taking more than half of courses outside one's major area of study and closer out-of-class relationships with faculty and a mentor; further, this effect is especially strong for those who came from families of lower socioeconomic status (SES).

Finally, by showing that different aspects of liberal arts education are associated with different types of life outcomes, important information is now available. For example, a student whose priority goal relates to leadership development may want to focus particularly on colleges that develop larger perspectives and are characterized by an authentic learning community. Or a college most committed to developing cultural engagement will want to ensure that all aspects of study in the tradition of the liberal arts are fully supported. These types of implications are explored more fully in chapter 11.

It is now important to comment on the findings as they relate to three questions:

- Do particular liberal arts experiences guarantee life outcomes?
- Are these results true for all people and all colleges?
- To what degree can we be confident that it is the liberal arts practices that actually account for the different life outcomes?

Probabilities, Not Destiny

The fact that such relationships exist across the 1,000 people in this research does not mean they will be true for every person. Some adults, for example, are not interested in art and museums regardless of their undergraduate education; some people are personally successful without a college education of any type. Or, to state it the other way around, it is not the case that a person who doesn't have these educational experiences cannot be a leader, or altruistic, or live a fulfilled life. The findings do not describe certainties, but rather statistically significant relationships between the nature of the college experience—the essential attributes of a liberal arts education—and adult life. So, while having liberal arts–type experiences certainly does not guarantee how a person will come out as an adult, it is apparent that it increases the likelihood of positive outcomes for lives of consequence, inquiry, and accomplishment. As an analogy, if an investor (or a gambler) had the opportunity to invest (or bet) on outcomes where they could consistently find an advantage of even a few percentage points, they certainly would believe that an investment (or bet) was warranted. And the effects associated with liberal arts education are many times stronger than that. Indeed, the liberal arts is valuable when it comes to increasing the likelihood of positive life outcomes.

Generalizability of Findings

While we can now objectively document that liberal arts education is associated with important, positive life outcomes, it would be problematic if the effects were different for some types of institutions or particular types of people. Do these results occur at different places and for different people?

The issue of whether these findings occur for different types of colleges and universities is explored in appendixes 2 and 3. First, remember that people from all types of colleges and universities— large and small, liberal arts and research universities, highly ranked and not—are included in this study. Thus, the analyses of the impact of liberal arts educational practices are true across a wide variety of types of institutions. But also remember that, because the purpose of this research was to assess the impact of liberal arts practices (not the type of institution), it was important to ensure that all liberal arts practices were adequately represented. Because only a small percentage of the nationally representative sample of college graduates attended a liberal arts college, an additional sample of graduates of liberal arts colleges was added so that we could be confident that the full range of liberal arts experiences is included in the study. But that fact raises the possibility that the results are due only to the overrepresentation of liberal arts graduates—that the results really were due to the institution type rather than the type of educational experience. To test this idea, the same analyses reported in the book were repeated using only the data from the 537 respondents that did *not* attend a liberal arts college. The results demonstrate that, while less common at non–liberal arts institutions, liberal arts educational experiences have the same type of long-term life effects, regardless of the type of institution attended.*

Do these effects occur for different types of people? What about differences for women, or nonwhites, or students who do not test well, or children of differing socioeconomic background? To examine this question, I completed further analyses on various subgroups; appendix 4 provides a summary of these results, and appendix 4 offers more detailed information. The impact of the liberal arts educational experience on life outcomes holds regardless of demographic differences. For life success (income and position), where liberal arts practices had neither a positive nor a negative effect, individual differences (gender, race/ethnicity, and SES) are initially significant factors. However, over the long term, only family SES continues to have a relationship with success, and even this effect is conditioned by the liberal arts experience. Specifically, while a broader span of study (e.g., taking more than half of one's courses outside one's major)

---

*Although the pattern of outcomes is the same, liberal arts colleges are twice as likely to include the full range of liberal arts educational experiences. Or, stated the other way around, a student attending a liberal arts college is twice as likely to encounter liberal arts educational practices.

continues to be predictive of long-term success for all students, it is particularly advantageous for those who come from a family of lower SES.

What is important about these analyses is that, while particular liberal arts experiences may have a stronger or weaker relationship for some graduates than others, the nature of the relationships between college experiences and life outcome is broadly consistent across all groups and for all institution types. Regardless of differences between students, the impact of education in the tradition of the liberal arts is substantially and consistently related to their going on to live lives of consequence, inquiry, and accomplishment.

Cause and Effect

Do liberal arts experiences actually cause the reported effects on adult behavior? Or are people who are more likely to live lives of consequence, inquiry, and accomplishment also more likely to choose to have liberal arts experiences? That is, are these effects reported because people who are predisposed—or predestined—to be consequential, inquiring, and accomplished adults also happen to prefer liberal arts experiences as students? If this were the case, then it is something about innate differences in type of person rather than in the nature of the educational experience that matters. Appendixes 1 and 3 explore this question in some detail. In the briefest summary, while there can be no completely definitive answer to this question, the available evidence suggests that liberal arts educational experiences indeed have a real impact on the ways that people live the rest of their lives. It is not that those destined to be more impactful and successful as adults choose liberal arts collegiate study and that four or more years of college education have no effect; it is that an education in the tradition of the liberal arts contributes to adult life impact and success.

11

Capturing Impact: Implications and Value

The more that you read, the more things you will know.
The more that you learn, the more places you'll go.
—Dr. Seuss, *I Can Read with My Eyes Shut!*

The implications of the insights reported in previous chapters about the nature of higher education are legion. This chapter will review a number of them, including how to find and acquire an impactful education; institutional policies and priorities; the role that diversity, equity, and inclusion play in social justice; the use of information technology (IT); the future of higher education in a postpandemic and disrupted era; the role of faculty; the place of study in the humanities; how colleges should be assessed and marketed; government policies; college costs; and the value of higher education to the future of the individual and society.

*   *   *

The means and methods of liberal arts education—innovatively developed, tested, and revised over millennia—are indeed powerful. Those who live a life of consequence, a life of inquiry, and a life of accomplishment are those who have also experienced an education with a common good *purpose* that comprises the *content* of study and the educational *context* of higher education in the tradition of the liberal arts. It is also reassuring to learn that those who have studied a broader span of human knowledge are likely to be more personally successful over the long term.

The importance of the educational context (in contrast to the content of study) is especially noteworthy. It is conventional to think of out-of-class time—at least the time not spent in the library or doing homework—as wasted. Indeed, many students spend a great deal of time not directly involved with coursework: recent research indicates that today's student, over a typical week, spends an average of 57% of each day socializing, recreating, working, volunteering, and/or involved with student clubs.[1] While it is undoubtedly the case that a great deal of time can be "wasted" by college students (assuming that the goal is to have college students spend their time learning things with lasting value), the out-of-class context of education does matter.

Indeed, the beginning of the 2020s, an era shaped by pandemic shutdowns of many aspects of life (including school), is particularly instructive regarding the essential character of higher education. Although it seemed obvious that closing schools for young children would be problematic because of the challenges involved for working parents—which certainly turned out to be the case—many initially assumed that remote education approaches would be perfectly fine for college and university education. Advocates of this approach have suggested the long-anticipated technology-based revolution of pedagogy would finally occur, obviating the need for expensive campuses and face-to-face education. After all, given the predominant societal perspective that higher education means mastering higher levels of content, it is clear this could be accomplished with distance-education methods. On a very short timeline, colleges and universities invested heavily in the kinds of technology necessary to support this approach. While most faculty quickly put in their best (and sometimes heroic) efforts to shift to remote pedagogy, their expressions of concern were often dismissed as an unwillingness to embrace change. It turned out that the students were ultimately more convincing, with responses ranging from protest to lawsuits: they argued that a college education without a face-to-face college experience was not what they wanted.

At first, it was easy to dismiss student concerns as meritless—as merely a desire for largely unsupervised time to play and party (wasted time). But underlying the view of many students, as well as faculty, was the belief that the nature of the experience does make a difference in the value of education, and from this research, we now have evidence supporting this idea. Lifelong leaders, altruists, continuing learners, and culturally involved people who live a fulfilled and successful life are those who spent their out-of-class time talking with professors or mentors about nonacademic as well as academic matters; they are people who, while in college, spent time talking with other students outside of class about issues of significance to humanity; they were actively involved in college activities and organizations; and they had conversations with students from different backgrounds, with different values. We now know that these, as well as other out-of-class college experiences related to being involved in an authentic educational community and developing larger perspectives, can be powerful learning experiences. Rather than wasted time, these activities can be educationally significant.

This same point was a central conclusion of a study of 100 students at Hamilton College reported in an insightful book titled *How College Works*. It involved interviews of these students beginning in their first year of college and continuing annually for the six years after graduation. The researchers found that effective college learning *required* strong personal relationships, and that social belonging is essential. As they state in their conclusion: "Knowledge and skills count, but so do relationships, attitudes, standards and habits of work and thinking, and membership in broader communities, all less easily acquired in later life."[2] What we now know from our research is that the importance of educational context is true not only for the graduates of this one liberal arts institution, but also for the graduates of many types of colleges and universities, and that this impact lasts not merely for a decade, but for a lifetime. Meaningful interactions with faculty, mentors, and other students outside of class are especially impactful, regardless of the type of college attended.

Because impactful learning occurs through the study of content in a significant educational context, we have the opportunity to be deliberate in thinking about the full character of the educational experience, and not merely react to the preferences and pressures of the moment. If one believes that the college experience should be designed to have lifelong impact, what insights do we have of possible importance to students, colleges and universities and their faculty, and government and society? In each of the following discussions of the implications of the findings for higher education, it shouldn't be surprising that the often-overlooked importance of the educational context, as well as breadth of learning and experience, are emphasized.

Finding an Impactful Higher Education:
The Liberal Arts Ideal

Nonvocational education, studying a broad span of knowledge, growing intellectual skills, experiencing engaging pedagogy, developing larger perspectives, and learning in an authentic community have each been found to have an impact on later adult life; together, they represent a liberal arts educational ecology. It is important to note that the results reported—the relationships between the attributes of the education itself and life impact—were based on graduates of all types of schools: large and small, liberal arts colleges and research universities, higher quality and lower quality, and so on.

So, when the findings reported in earlier chapters indicated that, for example, those who are leaders are 41% more likely to have experienced an authentic learning community and 36% more likely to have developed larger perspectives in college, those effects were true across all the types of colleges and universities where these attributes were strongly present.

While some liberal arts–based practices may be found at many colleges and universities, if a person wants to maximize the likelihood of obtaining an education that includes these impactful experiences, in wanting to become a consequential, wise, and accomplished adult, what kind of college or university should they attend? Not all colleges are equal; a student is not equally likely to have these experiences anywhere. In a recent study of 30,000 college graduates, only 14% of students had a mentor who encouraged them, a professor who cared about them as a person, and at least one professor who made them excited about learning. When having been active in campus organizations and having an internship are added to these educational community experiences, this study finds that only 3% of college graduates will have had all of these—and these people feel that all of these are the aspects of their college education that were most important.[3] Further, college size is strongly related to this issue. In a recent Gallup-Strada national study of all institution types, 45% of those who attended colleges with an enrollment under 5,000 reported that "my professors care about me as a person," whereas only 24% of those attending larger institutions made this same statement.[4]

It is the undergraduate liberal arts college that provides an education characterized by close outside-of-class relationships among faculty and students, as well as the other experiences found in the research to have life impact: a nonvocational education, a broader span of study, and an education that grows intellectual skills, uses engaging pedagogy, and develops larger perspectives. The advantage of these institutions in providing the six impactful educational experiences is substantial; this research indicates that they are, on average, twice as likely to provide them.* This is not surprising, in that these are the places that have maintained a deep commitment to education in the tradition of the liberal arts, without the competing needs of graduate students, faculty whose futures are determined more by their scholarly fame than their undergraduate teaching, or the national prominence of their football teams. Further, because many of these impactful educational experiences are associated with close and personal relationships among faculty and students, institutions of smaller scale are far more likely to be able to deliver on them. While students and parents are sometimes concerned about the fact that there are fewer choices of college major at these institutions than at large places, this characteristic is also consistent with the research finding that specialized study makes little long-term difference.

Thus, whereas a student may be able to experience some liberal arts practices at any institution, the odds of having these experiences with a long-term life impact is far higher at the smaller liberal arts college.

Implications for Student College Choice

The factors that students use most often in college choice are cost and aid,[†] majors offered, location, employability of graduates, and the average starting salaries of graduates.[5] Further, three-quarters of college-bound students believe that college rankings—typically heavily influenced by perceptions of prestige—give useful information about college attributes and outcomes.[6] According to the results of

---

*For more, see the analyses reported in appendix 3.

[†]The question of cost is a confusing issue, in that today's financial aid policies frequently make schools with high listed tuitions actually the cheapest to attend; those colleges that are believed to be the most expensive often turn out to be the most affordable because of the financial aid provided.

our research, should these be the kinds of factors considered in college choice by students and parents?

From the perspective of the research findings, rather than prestige or tuition or majors offered, the first question that students should consider is their purpose for attending college. Is it only to maximize first job income, or does it include longer-term outcomes such as leadership, accomplishment, involvement, and fulfillment? First job income is frequently associated with vocational or professional degrees. While the majors with the highest salaries change over the years based on supply (the number of graduates with a particular vocational or professional degree) and demand (positions available), with a little lucky foresight, a good choice can be made. A decade or two ago, the highest starting salaries were for business and accounting degrees; currently the majors with the highest starting salaries are several types of engineering (electrical, chemical, computer, and mechanical) and software design.[7] There's no good way to predict which professions will receive high first job incomes tomorrow, although fate is sometimes generous.

In this research, we learned that if one's goal is to maximize success (income and position achieved), then vocational or professional degrees may not be the best long-term choice. By the time a person reaches the age of thirty-two, on average, an individual will have worked in four different jobs,[8] and on average, people hold ten to fifteen different jobs over a career, with a job change every 4.2 years.[9] Those who will be more accomplished are those who have developed larger perspectives while in college and have experienced an authentic college learning community. In addition, those who took more than half their courses outside their major area of study have higher salaries in the long term. Given an era of rapid change and newly emerging opportunities, this effect is not surprising: people with these educational experiences are better prepared to be effective, as jobs and opportunities continuously change, and those who have had more experience working constructively with others are more accomplished as adults. Indeed, Richard Arum and Josipa Roksa have documented the fact that students studying in nonvocational liberal arts fields (social sciences, humanities, sciences, and math) perform higher on attributes likely to be very valuable in a changing world of work: critical thinking, complex reasoning, and writing.[10]

There are now a plethora of articles in the business press and newspapers, and scores of books as well, about the relationship between liberal arts study and professional success. None describe it more completely than George Anders's book with the instructive title *You Can Do Anything—The Surprising Power of a "Useless" Liberal Arts Education.*[11] But there are many others as well, including *A Practical Education— Why Liberal Arts Majors Make Great Employees*[12] and *The Fuzzy and the Techie—Why the Liberal Arts Will Rule the Digital World.*[13] As described in the first chapter of this book, Steve Jobs credits liberal arts courses that he took for his success at Apple. Suffice it to say, choosing a professional or specialized major or program of study may not be the best route to a life of achievement.

In its recent analysis titled "Jobs for Tomorrow," the World Economic Forum states that "the transition to the new world of work will be both human- and tech-centric"[14] and involve general (cross-functional) skills that "are typically non-cognitive capabilities which are needed across all professions," including "Leadership, Communication, Negotiation, Creativity and Problem-Solving."[15] In their summary regarding employment and the skill sets needed by successful professionals, they further state that[16]

> there is a coming together of digital and human tasks best tackled by people with a broader, more holistic mindset. Traditionally, we have seen this pan out in the context of talent with liberal arts backgrounds. Often viewed as generalists, compared to hires with technical or STEM [science, technology, engineering, and math] backgrounds, their breadth of exposure often gives them a distinct advantage. Those qualified in the liberal arts are also attuned to learning many new and disparate topics—another plus in an age that demands lifelong learning.

So, instead of thinking solely about a specialized major simply with the hope of receiving a higher income in one's first job, this research indicates that a prospective student might consider salary and achievement over the longer term and the value of living a life involving leadership, making contributions to society, continuing to learn, or being culturally involved, and/or living with a sense of fulfillment. If these types of life outcomes matter, then the criteria for selecting a college change dramatically. College experiences associated with these outcomes are not usually represented in college guides; they are related to liberal arts–based educational practices. These involve the educational context associated within the authentic community: professors knowing students' first names; faculty interacting with students outside of the classroom about academic and nonacademic matters; having few adjunct professors who aren't around outside of class time; students having a significant mentor or mentors; professors actively engaging students in their learning; and learning relating to understanding different perspectives through involvement in campus clubs and organizations and experience with others who have different life experiences and values.

Of course, in addition to this description of the impactful educational context, the content of education matters. But the key issues here relate not to the practical or professional character of the major, but whether the course of study encourages studying in breadth and helps the student understand how different areas of knowledge interrelate, and whether students are encouraged to develop their own intellectual capabilities through written papers and professors who challenge each student's thinking. Indeed, every student, including those enrolling in professional programs, should take as many courses outside their major field as possible, for it is clear that breadth of study is associated with long-term fulfillment and success.

These key educational content and context attributes are most frequently and fully found in smaller and often less famous institutions, where a more personalized education can occur—institutions that still provide an education in the tradition of the liberal arts. While college guides don't provide systematic information on educational content and context, the interested student (or parent) can derive good questions from those asked in the interviews reported in earlier chapters, as well as in the following sections of this chapter.

Implications for College or University Purpose and Priorities

There are many types of universities in the United States, and every institution establishes its own priorities for the outcomes it intends. For those institutions where the learning outcomes assessed in this study—those with the goals of having graduates be leaders, altruists, continuing learners, culturally involved, fulfilled, and successful—this research has a number of clear implications.

The first of these relates to the mission and goals of the college or university. Some have the purpose of directly contributing to society through the research carried out by faculty; others by the services they provide to the economic development of their region; and still others by a focus on preparing students for a productive life. For those seeking to educate undergraduate students, the question is whether the common good is being advanced by educating them for lives of consequence, inquiry, and accomplishment. Fulfilling these liberal arts purposes requires a clear linkage between this mission and the priorities, programs, and actions of the institution, as well as the educational experience and graduation requirements for students. As Tim Clydesdale put it, "To call on purpose is not to ask colleges and universities to go beyond their core mission; it is to ask that they *intentionally and systematically* implement their already existing pledge—to produce purposeful, globally engaged citizens and to do so with broader inclusivity than they may ever have done before."[17]

Not only must the institution's mission be clear as to what outcomes are desired (and many college mission statements are unclear about intended outcomes), but resources also must be allocated to support those aspects of the educational experience that are associated with the goals identified. To have an authentic learning community does not, for example, merely require that there be student activities or football games at which to cheer, but that the faculty and staff have the time to be directly involved in the life and development of each student. Similar questions may be asked about other aspects of an impactful educational experience.

Second, given clarity of purpose, resources need to be allocated toward those educational practices that are associated with the desired outcome. As the bubble chart shown in figure 10.1 in chapter 10 makes clear, different aspects of the educational experience are associated with different life outcomes. For example, if a college seeks, more than anything else, to educate students who will place a life priority on serving others, then creating and supporting an authentic community should take precedence over other aspects of the college experience. If long-term success in income and position is a priority, then not only should an authentic community be supported, but also graduation requirements should include a substantial span of study outside the major. Alternatively, if continued learning is the institution's goal, then all aspects of a liberal arts experience are important. Or, if other types of life impact are essential institutional goals—leadership, cultural engagement, life fulfillment, success, or something else—then resources must be allocated to those aspects of the educational content and context that have been found to be associated with those outcomes.

Third is the issue of vocational and professional undergraduate majors. In recent years, an enormous priority has been placed on providing specialized education. This pressure comes from students, parents, and legislators who believe (incorrectly) that specialization in a particular area of undergraduate study is required to have a useful and successful life. In addition, pressure can come from the academic disciplines and professions themselves, as new areas of specialization develop and attention turns toward adding professors and courses to teach those subspecialties. While the development of specialization has many benefits, it should not be represented in the first higher education degree; specialization should come later, whether through on-the-job experience or further graduate study. For those colleges and universities committed to undergraduates, an ever-increasing number of specialized courses should not be added, nor new faculty hired as new subdisciplines develop. Institutions and their faculty must focus on creating opportunities for the kinds of breadth of study that allow students to develop an understanding of how the many aspects of the physical and living environment interrelate, as well as of the difficult issues to consider when making important decisions. Indeed, rather than focusing on coursework within disciplines, interdisciplinary, multidisciplinary, or transdisciplinary education should be emphasized.

Fourth, and closely associated with the last point about specialization, the graduation requirements should match the educational experiences that have the intended life outcomes on graduates. Part of this need is straightforward (e.g., limiting the number of courses that can be taken in one's major field so that a large portion of courses are taken in other disciplines). Another important part of this need is challenging but accomplishable—for example, ensuring that many courses in all disciplines include a consideration of the significant issues facing humanity or a consideration of how content in one field is related to another. Yet another part of this may be more difficult to do, and even more difficult to assess—for example, ensuring that students don't just spend time hanging out with those with similar life experiences (as is the case with most social groups), but also that they have serious conversations with other students who are very different in terms of their religious beliefs, political opinions, personal values, and/or life experiences.

Fifth, faculty and the many staff who are also a part of the larger educational experience need to receive support in the development of the capabilities that are associated with long-term impact on students. Included in this category are new faculty and staff orientations that include learning about impactful educational practices, programs, or offices that enhance effective and engaging teaching approaches and showcasing of best learning practices. In addition, academic advisors need to develop a deeper understanding of the importance of study outside their own area of expertise so they can be effective in their guidance of students' course of study.

Sixth, the reward system associated with evaluating faculty and staff for promotion, salary increases, and recognition should be consistent with impactful practices. While most teaching-oriented institutions place first priority on an evaluation of teaching, they often also require faculty to be active researchers and published writers and to serve on university committees. This may not be inappropriate, but given that each responsibility is time-consuming, professional expectations should match the intended educational outcomes. Further, whereas it is simple to count a professor's number of publications or how many committees they serve on, methods to assess impactful work, which is more difficult to measure, need development (e.g., time spent in meaningful nonacademic interaction with students outside of class time or the use of engaging pedagogy).

And finally, as described in the section titled "Implications for the Use of Part-Time Faculty," later in this chapter, institutions must realize that choosing to increase the use of contingent faculty may well constitute a decision to decrease the impact that they want to have on the way their graduates live their lives.

Implications for Diversity, Equity, Inclusion, and Social Justice

As described in the history presented in the first three chapters of this book, the liberal arts approach to higher education has always had the purpose of fulfilling a higher good—the common good—namely, an education benefiting both society and the individual. Of course, what specific common good that society and individuals need to serve has changed over time and place. A current substantive issue for the United States relates to those who have been most excluded from opportunities in our society's wealth and leadership-building mechanisms, including higher education. While this general concern is not new—it has carried a number of different labels in recent decades—the current renewed focus most often carries the label "diversity, equity, and inclusion" or the related term "social justice."*

While a liberal arts education does not have to commit itself to these particular issues—a different common good may be chosen—if an institution chooses an aspect of social justice, it is describing a key purpose of the education it is providing. That is, the outcome of the education should contribute to the full and equal participation of all people in a mutually beneficial society. If an institution adopts "diversity, equity, and inclusion," it is deciding that the educational content and context should meaningfully involve the full range of people and ideas (i.e., background; life experience; race, ethnicity, and culture; beliefs; perspectives; and/or knowledge). Diversity, equity, and inclusion may be intended to contribute to the common good outcome of social justice or to a particular societal priority such as "black lives matter," or they may be intended to serve other purposes, such as meeting the needs and priorities of

---

*In times past, it was clear that higher education practiced exclusion in the types of people who were allowed access (by race, religion, gender, and class), as well as in the content of study (even breadth of study often constrained participants by including only traditionally acceptable American or European, white male–dominated teaching materials and thinkers). Today, de facto exclusion barriers remain, principally associated with race and socioeconomic status (SES)—namely, affordability, quality of precollegiate education, and family experience with and knowledge of higher education. Breadth of study in many disciplines—particularly the humanities—is now much less constrained, though much progress remains to be made.

the nearby community or ensuring the survival of the institution in an era of demographic change.

The first implication of a liberal arts view of this topic is that purpose, content, and context must be aligned. If social justice is the purpose, then ensuring that the content and context of education are diverse and inclusive may be part of the approach, but that is not likely to be sufficient to achieve the long-term outcome (e.g., see the description of the importance of "fit" in chapter 9). If meeting the needs of those in the nearby community is the purpose, the approach to changing the content and context of education needs to begin with a bottom-up analysis of the needs and interests of those being served, rather than the more typical process, which begins with campus committees. If institutional survival is the purpose (which is not a liberal arts goal, but it may allow a liberal arts education to continue), then a careful market analysis of what will both attract and retain a more diverse student population needs to be the starting point.

Of course, these (or other) purposes are not necessarily mutually exclusive, but the implications for the content and context of education are likely to be very different. Unless purpose and educational content and context are carefully and fully aligned—to wit, that the content and context of the educational experience directly serve the intended purpose—an institution will likely be ineffective in fulfilling any useful purpose.

What about the liberal arts content and context of the education itself if an institution commits to this educational priority? Several findings are suggestive. We know that breadth of study is related to living a life of inquiry and a life of accomplishment. For these issues, breadth of study must be characterized not only by the inclusion of a range of disciplines, but also by the inclusion of diverse sources of knowledge within those disciplines (e.g., the contributions of persons of color, females, or other cultures). But changing the content of study is not, by itself, enough; the educational context is powerful.

The development of larger perspectives is related to adult leadership and a life of inquiry; indeed, the ability to engage constructively with those who bring different perspectives and life experiences is an urgent need of contemporary society. This involves out-of-class engagement, such as having frequent serious conversations with others who are very different in terms of their religious beliefs, political opinions, personal values, or life experience, and discussing issues such as peace, justice, human rights, equality, and race with other students outside of class. As such, recruitment strategies will need to be implemented and responsive retention strategies developed to have a college environment that is not homogeneous in background, life experience, and beliefs. Further, in appropriately shaping the educational context to provide broader perspectives, the organization's leadership and staff also need to reflect and include people from a diversity of backgrounds and life experiences; institutions need to be willing to grow and evolve to reflect diversity at all levels.*

In addition, we also learned that being involved in an authentic community is powerful, with outcomes associated with lives of consequence, inquiry, and accomplishment. Students need to be able to say, "I frequently talk to faculty outside of class time about both academic and nonacademic matters"; "Outside of class, I talk with other students about issues such as peace, human rights, and equality"; "Most professors know my name"; and "I'm involved in campus organizations." It's not that any one of these describes what an authentic learning community is, but they are indicators of the kinds of experiences that students will have if they are a part of the type of educational community associated with important life outcomes. Disagreement or protest won't be (and shouldn't be) eliminated in such a community, but differences in perspective can

---

*Imagine if throughout the development of the United States, those in power used wheelchairs? Wouldn't you think that there always would have been ramps everywhere?

be appreciated and exchanged respectfully, with the goal of further-ing understanding. The research described in chapter 9 affirms this point: those who entered college with a lower level of social belong-ing (students of color) but who received training to help them develop a sense of belonging had higher grades, better health, and a more positive sense of well-being.[18] Numerous other studies affirm the power of community belonging.[19]

Implications for the Role of Technology in Higher Education

In this age of technology, there have been many initiatives designed to replace face-to-face educational methods with computer- and network-based education. The belief is that learning, including in higher education, can be more effective and less expensive by replac-ing human teaching with machine-provided teaching. There is undoubtedly no organization that has spent more to develop and support this approach than the Gates Foundation. The foundation's creator, Microsoft founder Bill Gates, is understandably an advocate of this idea, and his speeches sometimes have something of an anti–liberal arts theme. That is, with the purpose of increased efficiency, the emphasis is on the mastery of specific content, and the technology context means that learning through human interaction is replaced by learning through machine action.

However, while Gates's speeches often advocate the use of technol-ogy to replace people in the learning experience for content mastery and to improve efficiency, when questioned, his views are less nar-row. He believes there are larger purposes that need to be fulfilled—purposes that very much have a liberal arts character and that are prominent in his own philanthropic work. Microsoft's current pres-ident, Brad Smith, and executive vice president, Harry Shum, take the same view in talking about the necessary content of a higher education, adding that this is as true for the success of newly emerging technology fields as it is for more traditional fields: "Languages, art, history, economics, ethics, philosophy, psychology, and human development courses can teach critical, philosophical and ethics-based skills that will be instrumental in the development and management of AI solutions."[20]

So, is education in the tradition of the liberal arts fully endorsed by these influential, technology-savvy, societal, and corporate leaders? Insofar as content is concerned, the answer is "yes." But what about the liberal arts context of education? In response to a question at an event where he advocated for content-based and technology-provided education, Gates affirmed the importance of a liberal arts educational context: "There is an unsolved piece that is absolutely critical. I still believe in physical places of learning for a fairly significant part of what goes on." He went on to say that this "unsolved piece" had something to do with "social and relational" elements. What he does not seem to know—which liberal arts educators, as well as neuroscientists, do know—is that these social and relational elements are fundamental aspects of learning in the liberal arts tradition. They constitute the powerful context that create learning. From the research reported in this book, its impact is clear, and there is nothing secret nor unsolved about the power of socially based learning to make education truly effective: neurological research demonstrates why it has such an important impact.

Indeed, Google's digital evangelist, Jaime Casap, asserts that an effective higher education is much more liberal arts–like than technical. It should teach students to be knowledge seekers ("Where education is a commodity that students can find on their own . . . the question you guys need to ask them is, 'what do you need to know to solve the problem?'") and learning needs to happen in a social context ("Education [is] set up as an individual sport, but the digitized world requires collaboration—it is a team-based sport.")[21]

The implication then, is that technology should not be used to replace the socially rich educational community. However, there may be opportunities to increase the impact of technology-supported learning by developing effective ways to broaden the learning experience (e.g., to develop understandings of the interrelationship of knowledge or to develop intellectual skills) and identifying ways to enhance interpersonal interaction to increase the power of the social context in learning.

Implications for Higher Learning in a Disrupted, Pandemic, and Postpandemic Era

The issues related to teaching and learning in a disrupted era in which people cannot gather face-to-face* build upon the ideas described in the previous section regarding the use of technology in teaching. From our research, we know that a socially rich learning environment is essential to educational impact, an idea also affirmed by technology leaders and visionaries.

Much has been written about strategies that can be used to increase the role of meaningful interaction among students and with faculty in remote learning environments: having students study course content with assignments before class and using joint meeting time for discussion and debate; ensuring that everyone can hear and see each other (a common problem with conferencing software, or even when speaking with masks and/or in a socially distanced environment); using multiple small-group chat sessions to encourage the participation of everyone in class; having students

---

*Because I am working on edits to this chapter in the depths of the COVID-19 pandemic, in which many colleges in the United States and around the world are closed to in-person education and remote methods are being used, the challenges to continuing the personal approaches to education that our research has found to be impactful are likely to be greater than ever.

participate in the design and redesign of the course over the term to address the challenges involved in less traditional approaches to education; ensuring that the course design is one in which the professor doesn't need to talk too much; professors sending individualized or personal messages to students; scheduling sufficient advising time; and much more. The use of conferencing applications such as Zoom has certainly been a positive development, in that it increases opportunities for person-to-person engagement that is very different from the more traditional machine-based provision of content.

But the broader question in the case of major disruptions of our customary approaches to education is how the interconnected educational ecology comprising the liberal arts, which includes interpersonal interactions outside of class, can be provided when people are not allowed to gather together. Outside-of-class interaction among students and faculty are impactful, including the interactions among students of different backgrounds and life experiences; students discussing issues of significance to the future of humanity; substantial out-of-class time in which the students talk with faculty about both academic and nonacademic matters; mentoring relationships; faculty being attentive to student backgrounds and preparation such that they use individually engaging approaches to pedagogy; and student involvement in campus organizations and activities.

The list of ideas for addressing these contextual priorities is much shorter than is the case with content learning: having students still live together (perhaps in pods so that interaction occurs only among smaller groups), even while taking classes using remote or distanced methods; ensuring that every student has a designated mentor or advisor with whom they have time to interact individually (whether by videoconferencing or socially distanced face-to-face meetings); assigning preclass or postclass questions for face-to-face or distance discussions in small groups; and developing and supporting ongoing convenings of student groups and organizations in which relationships can be developed, whether electronically or in person. There are undoubtedly other very good ideas that can be developed if educators and students devote as much time and attention to creating an effective and interpersonally engaging educational context as has been spent on content learning. Both time and attention are essential to developing and implementing these and other strategies, and this requires deliberate policy and resource decisions in what is already a time- and resource-strapped era. Faculty are already consumed with efforts to redesign courses to work in a distanced environment, often needing to have both in-person and technology-based approaches simultaneously available. And because out-of-class interactions among students and faculty have always happened without substantial planning, it is hard to imagine how, in a deliberately calculating manner, one can create opportunities for distanced but engaging interpersonal relationships.

But there is another, ultimately more important question. The sudden and extreme changes in higher education that have resulted from the 2020 pandemic have given us the opportunity to rethink what really matters for higher learning. Rather than merely looking for a future where everything returns to normal, or perhaps to contemplating a future in which technology-based tools take a more prominent role in higher education, we can pause to reflect on what colleges and universities can do to increase the impact of the education they provide. We have the opportunity not to just return to business as usual or to develop a modestly redesigned approach to providing educational content, but instead to create a new beginning. We can start anew by explicitly considering the life outcomes that an institution intends to impart—the purposes to be fulfilled. For instance, is it to create contributing citizens? Then our research findings suggest that a priority should be placed on enhancing and resourcing experiences to develop larger perspectives and community involvement. Is it to have graduates live a fulfilled life, or be culturally involved, or continue to advanced study? Then focusing on enhancing and resourcing the full range of liberal arts practices inside and outside of class should take priority. If it is to facilitate individual success, then ensuring that students take a large proportion of courses outside their major and enhancing and resourcing community involvement should take priority.

At the same time, as students and their parents think about college life after the disorienting hiatus of a distanced pandemic experience, they should take the opportunity to think afresh about their goals for the higher education they seek. And politicians and policymakers, with some wisdom, should do likewise. And finally, given the many uncertainties facing humanity today, an outcomes-based way of thinking about higher education, as suggested in the section of this chapter titled "Implications for College or University Purpose and Priorities," will better prepare us to address whatever disruptive event next comes our way.

Implications for Faculty

The findings of this research provide real opportunities for faculty. The opportunities lie in the fact that the research demonstrates that many of the things that committed teachers and professors already do are important, including the use of challenging and effective approaches to teaching. In addition, the time they invest in students that has little or nothing to do directly with students' mastery of the subject matter of their coursework is very important, including talking with students about nonacademic matters outside of class time and providing mentoring. Kathryn Wentzel's description of how to be a good teacher, based on current research on student learning, nicely mirrors the experience-based opinions of scholars a millennium ago: "Effective teachers are typically described as those who develop relationships with students that are emotionally close, safe, and trusting, that provide access to instrumental help, and that foster a more general ethos of community and caring."[22]

At the same time, these findings present challenges. Professors are specialists, having typically spent between four and ten years in graduate school learning in depth about a particular subject. They have completed a dissertation that usually analyzes a very narrow topic within their subject area. The professional respect they receive from fellow academics, both inside and outside their school, is based on the degree to which they are recognized experts on a specific disciplinary topic. This does not mean that they can't also be committed teachers, nor that they aren't excited by seeing their students learn—many are, especially at teaching-oriented colleges—but there is a real tension between allocating their scarce time to interacting with students as opposed to doing internally and externally valued professional work.

The kinds of activities identified in this research that have impacts on the ways that students live their lives take up precious faculty time: talking with students outside of class time about both academic and nonacademic matters, knowing students' first names, having students write papers in most classes (which are time consuming to grade), and challenging students to examine the strengths and weaknesses of their own views (which can mean that a professor needs to understand each student's views and question each one individually). This type of mentoring role* involves not only spending more time on interacting with students outside of class and academic advising, but also lending them social support, life coaching, career counseling, and attentiveness to helping students identify and accomplish their life dreams.[23]

Professors also need to learn to use teaching methods that actively involve students, which take more time to prepare than lectures

---

*Many administrators and staff of a college or university also play an important role in the mentoring process—a description of mentoring should be part of their job requirements, and they should receive appropriate training, support, and constructive feedback on this responsibility.

and also require constant fine-tuning to implement effectively. An added insult is that students' developing specialized knowledge—learning the information in the professor's cherished, specialized area of knowledge—is not related to their long-term success. On the contrary, positive life outcomes are associated with learning about issues for which right answers do not necessarily exist, and with spending course time in all disciplines allocated to the larger philosophical and ethical issues associated with areas of study rather than focusing strictly on specialized knowledge. A professor also needs to convince students that they should spend less time studying one discipline (the one that the professor most loves) and take more than half their courses in other subjects. Content teaching is comparatively straightforward and easy for a professor to do, while achieving the full and active engagement of students in their learning is tremendously challenging and time consuming.

Yet the work required of professors for professional advancement typically involves research and writing, and this happens in the same out-of-class time as does involvement with students. Demands on professors' time far outstrip the number of hours available in a day. And it is commonly the case that, even at teaching institutions, advancement and salary for teachers are more closely tied to putting out published works (which are professionally valued and easily quantifiable) than to the number of hours spent outside of class talking with students about nonacademic matters (an activity that is far more difficult to measure and usually less valued).

From a faculty perspective, all of this can be frustrating at best and depressing on occasion at worst, especially when requirements to serve on college committees are added to the list of research and teaching expectations. There seems only one workable solution* to this dilemma: a professor should be clear about their professional

---

*See also the section titled "Implications for College or University Purpose and Priorities" earlier in this chapter.

goals, work at a college or university that values those same goals, and allocate time to activities that accomplish those goals. That is, if having an impact on the future lives of graduates is what motivates a professor, even if there is never an opportunity to observe the long-term impact of time with students or to receive thanks for it, then a liberal arts–based college is the place to work. If scholarly work in a discipline is what motivates a professor, then a position at a research-based university or professional school would be better suited. If both are valued—student life impact and scholarship— then a well-endowed, liberal arts–based college or university that has a modest teaching load is the place to be. And whichever choice a professor makes, vigilance about time allocation is essential so that their personal purpose can be fulfilled, whether that be more time spent in those content and context activities associated with life impact for graduates, more time allocated to the scholarly activities associated with professional contributions, or more time spent on committees as a way to improve the educational institution.

Of course, few get to make the choice of their perfect job or institution to work at, so this counsel to professors may well feel empty, except for the idea of being mindful of how one's time is allocated toward fulfilling valued personal goals—it is easy to become involved in the many competing demands on faculty time and do too little of what matters most to you. But there are things that an institution can be encouraged to do to help ensure that faculty have productive ways to fulfill their life goals, the purposes of a higher education, and the futures of their students. I review some of these in other sections of this chapter, and faculty can also be constructive advocates for them.

Implications for the Use of Part-Time Faculty

In relatively recent years, the use of contingent faculty—those often labeled as "adjunct" instructors or professors, who work part time and without long-term contracts with a college or university—has grown substantially.[24] Recent estimates are that 73% of instructional positions at American colleges and universities are not long-term (i.e., tenure-track) appointments.[25] While contingent faculty may be effective teachers and can provide the content of learning, part-time instructors without a continuing relationship with a school and who are paid minimally to teach only specific courses are not typically available for the extensive out-of-class time with students that is a central aspect of creating an authentic educational community.*

These observations are not meant to be a critique of contingent faculty members themselves, for most are committed instructors who add valuable knowledge and experience to their course offerings, and many would choose a more significant and/or permanent teaching position if it were available. Rather, it is a caution about the likely implications of institutions that increasingly choose to use part-time, noncontinuing professionals to impart instruction. Given the substantial relationship of an authentic educational community to the long-term impact of higher education, institutions may well be choosing to decrease the value of the education that they provide when they cut expenses by hiring contingent faculty and fail to compensate them adequately for time spent in outside-of-class involvement with students. Faculty have long been concerned about the greater use of contingent instructors, and it appears that there is justification for their worry in terms of educational impact. Likewise, prospective students who have choices about what college to attend should consider whether the life outcomes they are seeking are well served by less-available contingent faculty.

---

*The use of contingent faculty has implications for the discussions on faculty, college choice, institutional priorities, and marketing elsewhere in this chapter.

Implications for Study in the Humanities

It is clear from our research that college majors themselves bear little relationship to long-term life outcomes. The good news for the humanities is that, contrary to the common critique that the humanities are useless and lead to nothing of value—and indeed, to unemployment—study in the humanities is equally as valuable as other college areas of study. That is, graduates in the humanities fare no worse or better than those in other majors. While it may be disappointing to humanists that being a humanities major per se, or taking many courses in the humanities, is not systematically related to many distinctively positive outcomes in this research, it does include a number of key humanities-related findings that underline their importance to an impactful education.

When topics of central importance to the humanities are more frequently included in the broader educational experience for all students—that is, the span of study—then many positive life outcomes occur. In addition, two humanities-related college experiences, as described in chapter 4, frequently related to life impact are "discussed philosophical and ethical perspectives on the human condition in most classes" and "had frequent discussions with others of very different religious beliefs, political opinions, or personal values outside of class time." What these responses suggest is that while the humanities as a separate topic of study may not have a unique impact, when the types of issues of central importance to the humanities are an integral part of the overall educational experience, then much positive life impact accrues. Given that faculty in nonhumanities disciplines are often hesitant to include philosophical, ethical, or values-based issues in their coursework, real potential may lie in developing "humanities across the curriculum" initiatives involving courses in the sciences and social sciences, as well as in professional fields; increasing the degree to which humanities courses tangibly link their content to other disciplines; and/or developing strategies to encourage meaningful outside-of-class student engagement with diverse ideas and people, such as holding forums, debates, or other opportunities to engage with the area community.

Implications for Documenting Life Outcomes and the Marketing of Colleges

As the distinguished professor and foundation president Andrew Delbanco says, "Perhaps the most daunting challenge facing those of us who believe in the universal value of liberal education is the challenge of conveying its value to anyone—policymakers, public officials, and even many academics—who has not personally experienced it."[26] Because of the contemporary emphasis on having a highly paid job upon graduation, the marketing challenge is a complicated one. That is, while many educational practices associated with an education in the tradition of the liberal arts are very impactful in the short and long term, first job income is not. Longer-term success is associated with liberal arts education, as is leadership, fulfillment, and so forth. But persuading people that outcomes besides first job income matter is a real challenge, especially when government agencies, state and federal politicians, and news reports emphasize short-term job and income as the most important considerations.

On the other hand, generational research indicates that the newest generation of young people (Gen Z), while competitive, are more interested in service and want to effect lasting social change[27]—ideals that are very consistent with the purpose of education in the liberal arts tradition. As such, there may be a new opportunity to reframe marketing messages away from the prestige-oriented claims characteristic of much college marketing and toward the longer-term purposes served by a liberal arts education.

Imagine if *every* liberal arts–based college began documenting the ways in which the educational context and content are liberal arts in character, and the life outcomes that they seek to engender in their graduates? Then, with candor, they might communicate the choices that students must make when selecting a college—whether the priority is on short- or long-term outcomes, whether their priority is on serving their own private good or a public good—and tell students that the liberal arts is not a good choice for them if their individual goals do not align with liberal arts purposes. And finally, they might objectively and persuasively document the specific kinds of liberal arts educational experiences that students would be guaranteed to have at their institution: close out-of-class relationships with faculty (including little use of adjunct faculty), engaging classroom learning, many courses outside of the major, and the other benefits that have been discussed throughout this book. If every liberal arts institution did this, might we not begin to reframe the college search and choice process?

Implications for Government and Educational Policymakers

In 2011, the National Governor's Association issued a major report that made the argument that higher-education "students' academic success is linked to the needs of the marketplace"[28]—words directly mimicking the arguments of the Prussian bureaucrats in the early 1800s as they developed an anti–liberal arts approach designed to serve the immediate needs of the monarch and the state. In the years since that report came out, this assertion has been adopted and echoed by elected officials and government policymakers around the United States. As was clear during the development of higher education in the United States, that approach was rejected because its short-term benefit to the state did not match the longer-term interests of American society or its people, nor the development of the responsible and productive citizenry required for the success of our democracy.

Given the long-term impact of an education in the tradition of the liberal arts in serving the higher, common good by advancing the success and constructive development of both the individual and the nation, policymakers must place a renewed emphasis on educational practices that have a demonstrated positive impact. What is now frequently used as a key indicator of the quality of a college or university—first job income—must be supplemented or replaced by indicators of longer-term value to both the individual and society, as well as short-term personal or economic outcomes.

Implications for College Cost

While it might seem self-evident that a more highly personalized educational experience, with smaller classes and extensive out-of-class involvement as offered in the liberal arts tradition, would be more expensive than the more specialized education offered at a research university, this is not necessarily the case. In fact, many impactful practices of liberal arts education are budget neutral: they focus on having faculty and staff spend more time with students outside of class, limiting major requirements and broadening graduation requirements, increasing the use of student-involving approaches to teaching and learning, and developing strategies to increase meaningful student interaction with both faculty and each other. None of these require money to accomplish.

It is the case, however, that if an "and" strategy is used by a college—"we are going to continue doing everything we did before *and* add liberal arts practices"—then costs could increase. For example, if faculty are expected to (or want to) continue meeting current research and publication goals and committee assignment responsibilities and *also* spend more time on meaningful involvement with undergraduate students, then the only solution will be to increase costs by reducing the teaching courseload, thereby needing to add faculty to teach more class sections.*

In reality, the cost of education at student-focused colleges is actually lower than at other types of institutions. When you examine the expenditure for instruction and student services combined (indicating the total expenditures for student-educating and -involving activities), the average undergraduate-only college spends 47% less for these purposes than does the average research university,[29] where the educational context and content are less liberal arts in nature (see the section titled "Finding an Impactful Higher Education: The Liberal Arts Ideal," earlier in this chapter). The larger expenditure for the less liberal arts–oriented institutions is the result of a number of factors. First, faculty at research universities teach less because a major priority for the use of their time is for research instead of teaching, so more professors may be needed for the same number of courses. Second, because professors' reputations are based on their research productivity, the more they publish (and hence the less time they spend with undergraduate students), the more they are paid. Indeed, more research produced typically leads to both fewer courses taught and higher salaries for professors. Third, some specialized majors and professional programs—those involving expensive equipment, requiring especially highly paid faculty, or both—can be more expensive to offer than many nonvocational majors.

Finally, remember that a number of aspects of the educational context—including developing larger perspectives and significant

---

*There does exist a no-cost solution that is also often available: eliminate the more specialized course offerings within each department that are not really necessary at the undergraduate level. In practice, though, this is difficult, both because faculty are often reluctant to give up courses that are dear to their professional heart and because students usually feel that greater depth of study is more valuable than greater breadth of study, even though breadth has been shown to be so impactful over the longer term.

components of an authentic educational community—relate to how educational life is organized, not how much money is spent on salaries. This idea may be clearer by carrying out a thought experiment, in which you imagine designing a college based solely on creating the three categories of life outcome investigated in this research: lives of consequence, inquiry, and accomplishment. This would require designing a college education in which resources are allocated only to the following three attributes:

1. Maximizing interactions among faculty and students
2. Having a broad curriculum (without many specialized courses within majors) that features the sciences, social sciences, and humanities
3. Graduation requirements that include taking a majority of courses outside the major and outside-of-class involvement on campus and in the local community

Could you then, for example, accomplish this with a ratio of ten students per faculty member and with an additional staff member for every twenty students? If so, then the tuition required to cover this expense could be about half the current average. Now, of course, there are many other expenses that one could argue would have to be added to the college designed in this thought experiment, but the point being made is that those costs probably have little or nothing to do with the educational practices associated with long-term life impact, so they could be eliminated or minimized if one is committed to maximizing positive life outcomes.

Each type of institution allocates its resources not only to serve its missional priorities, but other priorities as well (ranging from the amenities that are thought necessary to attract and retain students to the pricey equipment, facilities, and faculty that are required to support many specialized programs). A student-centered, liberal arts–oriented institution can deliver an education of value to the individual and to society—an education of life impact—in a cost-efficient and effective manner.

Implications for the Value of Higher Education

There is a substantial current concern that higher education is a route to nowhere—it has no value because it is too often not directly connected to the needs of students for gainful employment upon graduation. If, indeed, the purpose of a higher education is to meet this short-term need, then this research tells us that much of education in the liberal arts tradition can be ignored. The sure path to the first postcollege job is paved with certifications and specialization. We know this because we found, as has other research, that first job income is higher for those with specialized and professional degrees. For example, engineering, business, and accounting majors most often do very well in their early careers; and training certifications of various sorts that are responsive to immediate market needs are also immediately lucrative (e.g., computer, web, or game programming at this moment).

For these immediate purposes, a higher education may be greatly streamlined through a narrow course of study designed to meet immediate job demands (requiring fewer faculty and few courses outside the major), little cocurricular activities (which are generally unrelated to the development of specialized competencies), and much greater use of competency or mastery-based instruction (e.g., computer-based teaching modules).* Some impactful practices, such

---

*To be sustainable, such specialized institutions will have to be flexible. For example, whereas today there is enormous demand for programmers and computer scientists, it was only a couple of decades ago that numerous colleges and universities eliminated their computer science major as interest declined and graduates could not find jobs. A similar story can be told about other specialized training, such as

as close relationships with faculty and other students, could still be involved, but they are generally less related to the development of specialized knowledge. As a result, not only might the cost of education be lower, but the knowledge necessary for admission could be clearly defined, with high school education tailored to those needs and remediation targeted to specific required competencies. The result of this Prussianized approach (as described in chapter 3) could be greater access for students at a lower cost, as well as a more sustainable financial model for the schools. Quality assurance by government agencies or college ratings organizations groups would be simple for these institutions: measure employment rate and average salary of students after graduation, and it is clear whether a program is a good one.

Education in the tradition of the liberal arts fulfills a different purpose, however: rather than focusing only on individual benefit and near-term employment and income, it is designed to benefit both the individual and society over the longer term. As this research has found, longer-term outcomes for not only individual success, but also leadership, contribution to society, cultural involvement, life fulfillment, and continued learning, are consistently related to liberal arts educational practices. These positive life outcomes are associated with learning in an educational community, developing larger perspectives, experiencing engaging pedagogy, developing intellectual skills, studying a broader span of knowledge, and having a nonvocational major. Indeed, while first job placement and income may be better for those with specialized training, this advantage disappears rather quickly.

---

nursing, teaching, various engineering specialties, and business, among many other majors. Predictions of future demand in these rapidly changing times are impossible; specialized schools will remain sustainable only if they are quick to replace programs and faculty where demand is dropping with programs of growing demand—which is not always easy to do.

There is an opportunity for higher education to bridge the apparent gap between the liberal arts and technical/professional education. Examples of this exist at a number of institutions, with the clearest example being "3/2" liberal arts–engineering programs. In these programs, students spend three years at a liberal arts college, followed by an automatic transfer into an engineering school with which there is an articulation agreement; the student receives a degree from both institutions. Of course, there is no reason why these dual educational programs can't exist within a single institution; the major challenge is typically that professional programs feel the need to have most of their courses of study be within the professional school, and the liberal arts courses are seen as separate service courses. It is instructive and significant that 3/2 programs effectively have 60% of their study occurring in the context of the liberal arts and 40% in that of the professional school; students thereby experience the span of study and development of broader perspectives associated with long-term fulfillment and success.

For liberal arts education, becoming higher educated is not based on the accumulation of facts in a person's head that may lead to their first job; rather, it is preparation for life success, as opportunities and challenges inevitably change. This liberal arts outcome is accomplished through a comprehensive educational ecology involving a full set of in-class and out-of-class learning experiences. Quality assurance by government agencies or private ratings groups is more challenging in this case: rather than measuring first job salary, quality indicators must examine current educational practices (e.g., degree of faculty and student involvement, span of student learning, engagement with new perspectives) and the longer-term success, contributions, and life satisfaction of graduates.

So, what is the value of a liberal arts education? It depends on one's goal. For the student whose priority is that first job, and for a society that is most concerned with employability upon graduation, the liberal arts may have only limited value. However, for the student whose goal is a life of consequence, inquiry, and accomplishment over the longer term, and for a society that is concerned with growing and supporting an economically and socially successful democracy, the liberal arts has great value.

For two centuries, American-style colleges and universities have been distinguished by their commitment to the common good—to the well-being and advancement of both the individual and the society. It is clear that a refocus on the impactful long-term practices of the liberal arts, rather than the Prussianized specialization that is currently in vogue, is essential for the health and longevity of the ideals upon which this nation was founded.

12

Becoming Higher Educated and the Liberal Arts

Be not simply good. Be good for something.
—Henry David Thoreau, "The Higher Life: From Thoreau's Private Letters," 35

What is education in the tradition of the liberal arts? We can now draw some clear conclusions about how its *purpose, content,* and educational *context* combine to create an unusually impactful approach to higher education—in many ways the most practical form of education for the individual and for society.

*   *   *

In the late 1800s—fifty or so years after the American-style liberal arts college movement began—the Englishman Rudyard Kipling, himself a visitor to the United States and too poor in his youth to have attended college, wrote a novel about a young American. This man, Harvey (known as "Harve") ran off to become a deep sea fisherman, a choice of apparent courage, as he was defying his father's dictates. The culmination of his story of adventure occurs when the young man's father—himself financially successful, but not college educated—tells his son that the truly courageous choice that he must make is to leave the sea to attend college, so he can live a more valued and fruitful life. The father describes himself as a "mucker"—a coarse and uneducated man—who will never have the opportunity to be meaningfully involved in society. He says to his son, "Now you've got your chance. You've got to soak up all the learning that's around, and you will live with a crowd that are doing the same thing . . . above all, you'll have to stow away the plain, common, sit-down-with-your-chin-on-your-elbows book learning. Nothing pays like that, Harve, and it's bound to pay more and more each year in our country in business and in politics."[1] This description, in colloquial terms, is a compelling statement about the impact of a liberal arts education— the dominant and respected approach to higher learning that characterized American-style education at that time.

Yet this path to education is not universally acclaimed, and this book opened with a puzzle: in the United States, education in the tradition of the liberal arts is now often disparaged and seen as useless, while it is often admired and seen as enormously valuable by leading voices in other countries. In the United States, many influential people advocate for replacing the liberal arts with specialized, vocation-based education, even as other nations are increasingly recognizing the shortcomings of the specialization approach to undergraduate education that they adopted a century or two ago in the era of European colonialism. Influential people outside the United States are advocating for replacing specialization with a liberal arts approach. Interestingly, American business executives and educational innovators, like non-US leaders, agree in their advocacy for liberal arts education.

Why is this? To an important degree, it is because the meaning of the terms "liberal arts" and "liberal arts education" is confusing. Not only do some see them as political labels, but they lack clear and commonly agreed-upon definitions. With literally hundreds of descriptions available, is it any wonder that there is controversy about the value of this approach to higher learning?

This book, therefore, has explored two fraught, yet very simple questions: what is liberal arts education, and what difference, if any, does it make? Rather than adding one more description to the hundreds that already exist, I sought to use what I hoped would be a more persuasive and productive approach, comprising four steps. First, describe the purposes, content of study, and educational context of the liberal arts as it has existed and evolved from the time of its inception. Second, use the mission statements and educational practices of current colleges to describe the purpose, content, and context of liberal arts–based higher education today. Third, assess whether there is a statistical relationship between liberal arts content of study and educational context and the long-term life outcomes of graduates, utilizing a large sample of people from a diverse range of types of institutions. Finally, based on these research outcomes, draw conclusions about the relationships between aspects of study in the tradition of the liberal arts and particular life outcomes.

What conclusions have we reached about education in the tradition of the liberal arts? Four key conclusions have emerged through the historical and empirical analyses reported in this book.

1. Purpose: Liberal arts education is designed for life impact; it serves a higher, common good

The axiom "Lift as you climb" nicely summarizes the idea behind the first conclusion of this book. In relatively recent years, a view has strongly emerged that higher education serves the selfish goal of helping individuals maximize personal success—money, power, fame, and other accoutrements—without much care for how that success affects the lives of others or society more generally. These outcomes are called a private good, in that the primary benefit of education accrues to the individual. On the other hand, higher education can be understood to have a more unselfish goal: helping individuals not only to do well for themselves, but, very importantly, to develop a corresponding and deeper commitment to the well-being of others and the progress of society more broadly. These outcomes are called a public good because benefits accrue to humanity.

We would never think to make this distinction between private and public good when it comes to primary or secondary education—it is good for the individual and society. Thomas Jefferson's advocacy for education, as well as his assertion that public education is essential, were based on his belief that "no other sure foundation can be devised for the preservation of freedom and happiness."[2] Throughout American history, furthering this higher good has resulted in the commitment of every community to support public education for their children.

Until the last few decades, higher education was thought of in this same way—it served the public good. However, as people increasingly recognized the income disparity between those with and without a college education, government policymakers concluded that income at first job is the most important indicator of the value of a college education. The thinking shifted, with the result that today, higher education is often considered a private good, not a public good—it is believed to bolster the success of individuals rather than the strength of society more broadly.

A liberal arts education, unlike other approaches to higher education, demonstrably serves a higher purpose—the common good—by benefiting both the individual and society.

2. Content: Liberal arts education requires study of the full span of human knowledge and insight into the complex interrelations among the various domains of knowledge

Education in the liberal arts tradition views the content of study (i.e., what is studied) differently than is the norm. Rather than seeing learning as defined by specialized knowledge—ideas and facts believed to be necessary for a particular job or profession—the liberal arts has a different focus. It deliberately sees higher learning as acquiring awareness of the full span of human knowledge, including the humanities, social sciences, and sciences. Eliminate study of the humanities, and a liberal arts education can no longer occur. Just as important, though, drop the social sciences or sciences and a liberal arts education can no longer occur either. Further, and very importantly, the liberal arts requires people to develop insight into ways that various areas of knowledge relate to one another, which necessitates the development of intellectual habits and skills of reasoning and critical thinking. For example, philosophical and ethical implications are involved in aspects of psychology and biology, just as there are scientific and sociological issues involved in an understanding of history or art.

3. Context: Liberal arts education requires a learning environment that is socially and affectively powerful

While people typically focus strictly on the subjects studied in college (its content), from the historical review and the research reported in this book, we see that education in the tradition of the liberal arts places equal (if not greater) emphasis on the context within which leaning occurs (the educational environment). Indeed, it is an error to consider higher education simply as the mastery of more information. Approaches to teaching that directly engage students and their emotions in the learning process are essential.

But a liberal arts education does not occur only in the classroom; a deeply engaging, out-of-class experience is essential through extensive relationships with faculty and staff, meaningful engagement with other students who contribute different values and life experiences, and involvement in campus activities. Impactful learning occurs from experiences that are intellectually, personally, and emotionally engaging.

4. Educational ecology: The higher, common good purposes of a liberal arts education—to educate people for lives of consequence, inquiry, and accomplishment—are fulfilled only when study involves liberal arts content in a liberal arts educational context

The methods and content of a liberal arts education are related to valued life outcomes. A liberal arts education requires a combination of purpose, content, *and* context. Any one or two of these do not constitute a liberal arts education; *all three are required.* Indeed, in our research, those who did not experience all aspects of an education in the tradition of the liberal arts were less likely to be leaders, altruists, continuing learners, culturally involved, fulfilled, and successful as adults. Education in the tradition of the liberal arts provides true value—*long-term* value—for the individual and for society.

*   *   *

We can now return to the question that began this book: what is a liberal arts education? While it is common to think of the liberal arts simply as describing what a person studies while in college, it turns out to be more complicated than that. The liberal arts indeed includes the content of study, but unless that content is learned in a particular educational context and with a larger purpose, it is not a liberal arts education. In our journey through the past and present of the liberal arts we have learned the following lesson:

> *A bona fide liberal arts education is impactful—fulfilling the common good and serving the future of both the individual and society—by educating people for lives of consequence, inquiry, and accomplishment. This impact is brought about through a learning environment that is*

socially and affectively engaging and involves the study of the full span of human knowledge, intellectual challenge, and the exploration of different perspectives on issues of significance to humanity.

This may not be the kind of inspiring definition you would find in a glossy college brochure or on a slick website—but it does give a practical description intended to capture the essential character of a liberal arts education. While the liberal arts is not for all people or all institutions—individual purposes can and should differ—individual colleges and universities that are committed to advancing both the individual and humanity at large have the ability to write inspiring statements of their mission and character in ways that clearly describe their higher purpose, as well as the content and context of the liberal arts educational experience they offer. And then, critically, they must establish priorities and take actions that provide the educational content and context that fulfill this purpose.

The Lessons of History is a slender volume written many years ago by two historians, Will and Ariel Durant, who attempted to summarize all human history in just a few pages. In their conclusion, they express their belief that each generation has the responsibility to ensure that its best knowledge and wisdom are passed to the next generation—that this must happen for humanity to progress constructively:[3]

> Civilization is not inherited; it has to be learned and earned by each generation anew; if the transmission should be interrupted for one century, civilization would die, and we should be savages again . . . Consider education not as the painful accumulation of facts and dates and reigns, nor merely the necessary accumulation of facts and dates and reigns, nor merely the necessary preparation of the individual to earn his keep in the world, but as the transmission of our mental, moral, technical, and aesthetic heritage as fully as possible, to as many as possible, for the enlargement of man's understanding, control, embellishment, and enjoyment of life.

Consider the liberal arts not as an accumulation of facts, nor merely as the preparation of people for particular jobs or professions; think of education in the tradition of the liberal arts as the necessary preparation for a life well lived, for both individuals and the society in which they live.

Most fundamentally, this book is a call for courage. Those colleges and universities that seek to serve the common good must be courageous by ensuring that they are truly fulfilling the purpose, content, and context of a liberal arts education. The legacy to be protected is not the continuation of business as usual, but the legacy of education in the tradition of the liberal arts and the common good outcomes it seeks to create. Colleges and universities must be diligent in not making priority choices designed simply to maintain their current structure, operations, and programs, nor to chase the easiest available revenue. Rather, they must convincingly assert the importance and long-term value of education in the liberal arts tradition for both the individual and society, develop and support policies and programs that clearly and specifically fulfill this larger purpose, and allocate resources accordingly.

Students must courageously choose colleges that will help them fulfill their life aspirations and ignore those that seek to influence their choice based on criteria unrelated to those goals. Those who place a priority on living lives of consequence, inquiry, and accomplishment over the longer term need to make college choices based on the educational attributes associated with those outcomes: learning in an authentic educational community characterized by personal, out-of-class relationships with both faculty and other students, the development of larger perspectives, engaging and involving approaches to teaching and learning, experiences that develop intellectual skills, study of the broad span of human knowledge, and support for a nonvocational college major.

And those who seek to shape the direction of higher education must courageously reject changes to higher education based on simple, short-term understandings of what college is for. Rather than deferring to the demand that colleges work simply on preparing students to take today's jobs, focus instead on the ways that both the individual and our society are advanced over the longer term through study in the tradition of the liberal arts and its deliberate educational ecology of purpose, content, and context—an education that is the best preparation for a life well lived in this complex and demanding era, characterized by relentless change.

We can—we must—strengthen and extend a higher education of life impact—an education for a higher, common good.

Appendix 1: The Question of Cause and Effect

It is reasonable to question whether this research tells us anything about whether specific college experiences cause particular life outcomes. Throughout this book, I have been careful to describe the relationship between college experiences and life outcomes; on the other hand, I have not stated that the college experiences caused the adult outcomes. Does this mean that liberal arts education is not impactful? Is it possible that those who seek out liberal arts–type experiences in college already possess the individual attributes that lead to adult lives of leadership, inquiry, and achievement? If this is the case, then college isn't what makes the difference—it is the nature of people who are more involved and successful as adults to have chosen liberal arts college experiences. While this is a reasonable argument to make, it doesn't eliminate the value of the liberal arts—should we not provide meaningful college experiences for those people with the traits or interests that lead to a successful and meaningful adult life?

However, I believe that there is a strong case to be made for a cause-and-effect relationship between college experiences and life outcomes. After all, it seems odd to argue that the kinds of experiences that one has during four years of living and learning made no difference in one's life. At minimum, people will get the opportunity to master a number of important life skills, including the ability to learn new and different material, live and work constructively with people who have different backgrounds and values, and be mentored by more experienced adults. A causal impact of merely graduating from college on income is well established; why wouldn't there be a causal impact for specific types of college experience?

But it is possible to make a reasonably strong case for a cause-and-effect relationship between liberal arts college experiences and adult life. Doing this is analogous to asking whether smoking causes lung cancer in humans. The only way to prove a causal link is to randomly assign a representative sample of people to two groups: for one group, the researcher requires participants to smoke for a number of years, and for the other group, the members would be required not to smoke. The obvious ethical issues involved here make this strategy impossible. Thus, to test smoking's effects, scientists used a number of other strategies, including analog studies using rats (which did develop lung cancer when forced to smoke), epidemiological research (comparisons between humans who chose to smoke and those who did not, including looking for other related variables, such as diet or living location), and biological studies of the impact of smoking components on cell development.

We face the same challenge in trying to understand the long-term relationship between experiencing the attributes of a liberal arts education and how an adult lives. The only sure way to prove cause-and-effect for college experiences would be the random assignment of a representative sample of seventeen- and eighteen-year-olds to two types of college: some required to attend schools that are highly liberal arts in character and others required to attend schools that are not. And then, wait forty years and see what happens. In addition to the complete impracticality of getting a representative sample of young people to agree to participate in such a process, this author won't live long enough to find out the results.

So, the results reported here, like all epidemiological research on the causes of diseases, are based on a cross-sectional research design: comparisons are made between those who have had one kind of experience with those who have had another type of experience. How can we support the idea that there is a cause-and-effect relationship between liberal arts experiences and adult life? Following the smoking and lung cancer example, we can look for both theories and related empirical research consistent with causal explanations. The neuroscientific work reported in chapter 9 gives both a strong theoretical and a research-based foundation for the results that were found: human learning occurs best in a socially meaningful, affectively active environment. This is directly parallel to the most consistently strong relationship found between the liberal arts learning environment and adult outcomes.

We can then buttress these findings with related research: there are a very large number of other studies, often nonexperimental (like this study), and less often experimental (with random assignment). These studies most often document the shorter-term effects of various educational practices. Examples of experimental studies range from a study of physics students in which a lecture by an inexperienced instructor who applied principles of cognitive psychology was more successful than an experienced and highly rated instructor in increasing student attendance and learning,[1] to educational challenge interventions that result in increased retention and grades, fewer doctor visits, and improved reports of well-being.[2]

Undoubtedly the most systematic work involves the National Survey of Student Engagement (NSSE),[3] which relates aspects of educational engagement to various dimensions of learning or perceptions of the college experience. An exhaustive analysis of these and other "high-impact educational practices" is summarized by George Kuh.[4] Additional extensive work on college impact has also been done by the Wabash National Study of Liberal Arts Education,[5] which consistently reports that a college education yields changes in measures of intercultural effectiveness, lifelong learning, well-being, and leadership.

Richard Light's decades of interviews of thousands of college students provide deep insight into the impact of the choices that students make during college.[6] Richard Arum and Josipa Roksa's book *Academically Adrift*, which reviews extensive research and provides new analyses of college impact, also reports effects that are highly consistent with the results reported in this book, including the very important impact of faculty interaction, peer interaction, and involvement with college life. Finally, Arum and Roksa's subsequent book, which follows up on students two years after graduation, concludes the following:

> While those committed to traditional models of liberal arts education have long argued that the development of generic competencies is useful for citizenship and for graduates' capacity to live full and meaningful individual lives, we have shown that these skills also have labor market payoffs over and above the specific fields of study chosen.[7]

Among the indicators of this effect is "avoidance of unemployment, underemployment, and job loss."[8]

The research cited here, like most educational impact research, is characterized by a focus on outcomes while in college or shortly after graduation. But do these effects last? There are relatively fewer efforts to assess long-term impact. For example, Ken Bain[9] combines a review of research on learning with stories based on interviews of people who have, in their adult lives, been unusually successful. Ernest Pascarella and colleagues[10] compare samples of graduates of twenty-six institutions five, fifteen, and twenty-five years after graduation, including both liberal arts colleges and other institution types. While their analyses focused on institution type rather than specific educational practices per se, they did document a substantial long-term impact, with findings consistent with the results reported in this study.

It is also useful to note that Gallup–Purdue University research involving 30,000 college graduates finds that *"what* students are doing in college and *how* they are experiencing it . . . more than any other [factor] has a profound relationship to life and career." Further, "if graduates had a professor who cared about them as a person, made them excited about learning, and encouraged them to pursue their dreams, their odds of being engaged at work more than doubled, as did their odds of thriving in their well-being."[11]

Finally, as Gardner has summarized, there is a remarkable compendium of three decades of research on how college affects students, which reports that "critical thinking, analytic competences, and general intellectual development thrive in college environments that emphasize close relationships and frequent interaction between faculty and students as well as faculty concern about student growth and development."[12] Again, this finding is highly consistent with the liberal arts relationships reported in this book.

And, of course, there is a plethora of research that demonstrates the positive effects of attending and graduating from college—on income, health, and other aspects of life. What this research does is to extend all the findings summarized here by examining which particular types of college experiences seem to be important for causing a number of different effects over one's lifetime.

In sum, then, there is good reason to feel confident that the results reported in this book indicate that an education in the tradition of the liberal arts is causally related to aspects of adult life: the long-term results reported in this research are highly consistent with the short-term effects reported in wide varieties of other research; where research on long-term effects exists, their results are also consistent with the liberal arts–specific results reported here; the results are consistent across a number of differences in student background and experience; and cognitive neuroscience research provides an empirically supported theoretical basis for why effects occur. Of course, no single research project is proof of any phenomena—my hope is that this work will stimulate others to design and carry out many more research projects that will focus on the relationship between specific higher education practices and long-term life outcomes.

Appendix 2: Attributes of Participants and Colleges Attended

There were three goals in developing the sample of people to be interviewed in this study: (1) college graduates ranging in age from twenty-five to sixty-five years old, who (2) attended a range of institution types and (3) experienced different amounts of six categories of liberal arts educational experience. A total of 600 interviewees were randomly drawn from a nationally representative panel sample, with the requirement that they be college graduates in the right age range categories. While this approach satisfied the first two goals, because of the small number of graduates who would have experienced the full range of liberal arts experiences (between 5% and 10% of college graduates nationally, as described in chapter 5) 400 additional interviewees were randomly selected from the total of 84,000 living alumni of twelve liberal arts institutions. It is important to emphasize that the purpose of this added sample was *not* to oversample liberal arts colleges per se, but rather to increase the number and range of liberal arts practices that could be analyzed through this research. (The analyses were not designed to compare institution type, but rather to compare differences in educational practice.)

The demographic characteristics of the respondents are shown in figure A2.1—age, gender, race/ethnicity, standardized test scores, and family socioeconomic status (SES) at the time that they were in high school. For SES, a description of various socioeconomic groups was read to participants that included the information reported in the chart, and respondents indicated which one best fit their family.

Attributes of the colleges and universities attended by respondents are shown in figure A2.2, including type of college or university attended, institution size and ranking, and undergraduate major of the respondents.

Age	
25 to 35	34.0%
36 to 45	32.5%
55 to 65	33.5%
Gender	
Female	58.2%
Male	41.8%
Race/ethnicity	
Nonwhite	11.3%
White	88.7%
SAT scores (ACT converted to SAT equivalent)	
1100 and lower	27.2%
1110 to 1200	26.4%
1210 to 1300	35.6%
1310 to 1400	23.4%
1410 to 1500	7.1%
1510 to 1600	7.5%
(Note: 73.2% of interviewees reported a score)	
High school family SES	
Less than $25,000 family income, or unemployed, public assistance, work part time	2.6%
About $25,000 to $60,000 family income, or manual, retail, service workers	21.5%
About $60,000 to $75,000 family income, or retail sales, administrative work	17.8%
About $75,000 to $150,000 family income, or lower-level professionals or managers, craftsmen, nonretail sales	39.1%
About $150,000 to $350,000 family income, or upper-level professionals, managers, own medium-size businesses	17.8%
Over $350,000 family income, or presidents/owners of large companies, or inherited wealth	1.7%

Figure A2.1
Student background

College type (Carnegie classification)	
Bachelors (Liberal arts)	46.1%
Masters	16.4%
Doctoral/research	32.9%
Other	4.6%
Control	
Public	35.0%
Private	65.0%
Enrollment of institution attended	
1,500 or fewer	13.4%
1,501 to 2,500	31.1%
2,501 to 5,000	13.5%
5,001 to 10,000	14.2%
10,001 to 20,000	13.7%
20,001 and more	13.9%
Ranking of institution attended (U.S. News and World Report)	
Top (best 50 within each institution type)	26.8%
Middle (rank of 51 to 120)	58.1%
Lower (rank of 121 and higher)	15.1%
Respondent major	
Math/science	19.6%
Humanities or arts	22.8%
Social sciences	27.7%
Professional	22.5%
Other	7.4%

Figure A2.2
College/university attributes

Appendix 3: Liberal Arts Practices, Not Institutions

The purpose of this book is to identify particular liberal arts practices and educational experiences to gain insight into whether these practices are related to adult life outcomes. As such, it is important to note that the project's unit of analysis is not liberal arts institutions per se, but rather six liberal arts educational practices that could occur at *any* institution.

However, it is reasonable to ask whether the results reported in this book are, in fact, related to the six educational experiences that were examined, or if the findings are possibly an artifact of including (and indeed oversampling, as described in chapter 5 and appendix 2) liberal arts colleges in this study.

As shown in figure A3.1, and as expected, liberal arts practices are on average twice as common at liberal arts colleges as at other types of institutions, with the use of engaging pedagogy especially prevalent and the development of larger perspectives only somewhat more prevalent (note that a 100% increase means a doubling of the frequency of the practice).

So, does the inclusion of the liberal arts colleges in this study bias the reported results? This concern arises for a number of reasons. First, some might argue that the characteristics of students who attend liberal arts colleges are fundamentally different from those who attend other types of institutions. For example, perhaps they are people who have attributes, experiences, or family support that predestines them to roles of leadership, altruism, cultural involvement, and so forth. Second, some liberal arts colleges are wealthy and selective, and some argue that they provide educational opportunities and relationships with peers that are richer than the

	Chi square	df	Significance	Incident risk ratio	Percent relative effect
Nonvocational college major	54.51	1,1000	<.001	1.98	98%
Span of study	98.25	1,998	<.001	2.11	111%
Intellectual skills development	95.71	1,1000	<.001	2.37	137%
Engaging pedagogy	217.36	1,1000	<.001	3.05	205%
Larger perspectives experiences	14.29	1,1000	<.001	1.30	30%
Authentic learning community	134.62	1,1000	<.001	2.24	124%

Note: Items preceded by a star are substantial, as described in chapter 5 and appendix 5 with $p < .05$ and relative effect $\geq 20\%$. Items that do not fulfill these criteria are treated as statistically significant.

Figure A3.1
Frequency of liberal arts practices at liberal arts versus non–liberal arts institutions

kinds of experiences available elsewhere. That is, the education at these institutions might be fundamentally different in ways unrelated to liberal arts practices themselves. Third, respondents from liberal arts colleges were oversampled in this research (see chapter 5 for a description of the participants in this study). Nearly half of the participants come from liberal arts colleges and a majority of those come from a set of twelve specific colleges. It is possible, therefore, that the book's findings are the result of the data being dominated by people from these colleges—that is, an artifact of the nature of these particular colleges rather than the liberal arts practices and experiences being studied.

Fortunately, the project's sampling provides a way to rule out these concerns. To evaluate whether the book's findings are a possible artifact of the inclusion of a large number of respondents from liberal arts colleges, we conducted a separate set of analyses eliminating the 461 participants in the study who attended a liberal arts college (i.e., not only the 400 respondents from the liberal arts sample, but also the 61 graduates of small undergraduate colleges included in the representative panel sample). The primary analyses reported in the book were then repeated using only graduates of the broader range of institutions.

Figure A3.2 presents a summary of the findings based on the full analyses of the 1,000 participants' responses as reported in the book, side by side with the same analyses based on the 539 respondents from the non–liberal arts college subgroup. In the full analysis, there are twenty statistically significant findings demonstrating the benefits of six types of educational

		Total Sample			No Liberal Arts Colleges		
		Chi square df = 1,994 to 1,1000	Sig	Percent relative effect	Chi square df = 1,537 to 1,539	Sig	Percent relative effect
Life of consequence	**On being leaders**						
	Nonvocational college major	0.03	.87	1%	1.32	.25	–6%
	Span of study	16.10	<.001	17%	5.32	.02	13%
	Intellectual skills development	11.13	.001	15%	2.60	.11	9%
	Engaging pedagogy	8.25	.004	11%	2.63	.11	10%
	* *Larger perspectives experiences*	42.31	<.001	28%	* 23.55	<.001	29%
	* *Authentic learning community*	36.40	<.001	25%	* 10.57	.001	20%
	On being altruists						
	Nonvocational college major	0.06	.81	2%	0.09	.77	–3%
	Span of study	3.66	.06	14%	0.31	.58	6%
	Intellectual skills development	0.28	.60	4%	0.84	.36	–9%
	Engaging pedagogy	0.02	.88	7%	0.17	.68	–4%
	Larger perspectives experiences	4.85	.03	16%	2.41	.12	17%
	* *Authentic learning community*	12.16	.001	26%	* 4.93	.03	26%
Life of inquiry	**Continued learning**						
	* *Nonvocational college major*	13.97	<.001	29%	x 1.34	.25	11%
	* *Span of study*	19.71	<.001	29%	* 10.03	.002	31%
	* *Intellectual skills development*	24.23	<.001	37%	* 10.02	.002	32%
	* *Engaging pedagogy*	20.10	<.001	29%	* 3.93	.047	28%
	* *Developing larger perspectives*	38.63	<.001	42%	* 21.81	<.001	50%
	* *Authentic learning community*	23.00	<.001	31%	* 9.96	.002	33%
	Cultural engagement						
	* *Nonvocational college major*	16.96	<.001	36%	* 9.77	.002	34%
	* *Span of study*	29.99	<.001	42%	* 10.03	.002	31%
	* *Intellectual skills development*	23.45	<.001	40%	* 13.57	<.001	39%
	* *Engaging pedagogy*	12.93	<.001	25%	x 3.22	.072	18%
	* *Developing larger perspectives*	10.66	.001	22%	* 4.43	.035	21%
	* *Authentic learning community*	30.60	<.001	40%	* 22.03	<.001	52%
Life of accomplishment	**Fulfillment**						
	* *Nonvocational college major*	20.61	<.001	44%	* 11.38	.001	45%
	* *Span of study*	46.04	<.001	59%	* 13.74	<.001	44%
	* *Intellectual skills development*	43.89	<.001	66%	* 21.97	<.001	63%
	* *Engaging pedagogy*	19.12	<.001	33%	x 2.82	.105	19%
	Larger perspectives	7.19	.007	19%	0.04	.847	2%
	* *Authentic learning community*	34.06	<.001	46%	* 10.90	.001	41%
	Personal success						
	Nonvocational college major	0.00	.95	0%	2.15	.14	–12%
	Span of study	1.48	.22	8%	0.00	.96	0%
	Intellectual skills development	0.43	.52	4%	0.05	.83	–2%
	Engaging pedagogy	0.01	.94	0%	0.29	.59	–5%
	Larger perspectives experiences	1.03	.31	6%	0.16	.69	4%
	Authentic learning community	0.13	.72	2%	2.90	.09	–16%

Note: An asterisk means that the result was substantial, as described in chapter 5 and appendix 5, with $p < .05$ and relative effect $\geq 20\%$. Items that do not fulfill these criteria are treated as statistically insignificant. An *x* means that the result was significant and substantial for total but not for non–liberal arts only.

Figure A3.2

Comparative results: Total study and non–liberal arts institutional respondents experience that are derived from the liberal arts tradition. Identical analyses of the 539 non–liberal arts college participants replicated seventeen of the same twenty statistically significant findings. The three effects that did not reach a conventional level of statistical significance nevertheless showed very clear trends in the same direction as the results reported in this book, and no results contradicted the reported results. Those that follow current replication efforts in the social sciences would see this level of internal replication of this book's overall findings as extremely strong.

Taken as a whole, this replication of the book's overall results among the 539 non–liberal arts college participants provides strong evidence that the book's overall findings are not an artifact of the inclusion of liberal arts colleges in the research, nor of the unique characteristics of students who choose to attend liberal arts colleges. Rather, the findings pertain to six types of educational experiences that are derived from the liberal arts tradition, but practiced to a greater or lesser degree by all American institutions, ranging from small undergraduate institutions to major research universities. Although students who seek these educational experiences might be more likely to attend a liberal arts college, what matters for the research findings presented in this book is the liberal arts practices that a student may experience in any college. Indeed, these have been the defining characteristics of most of American higher education for nearly two centuries.

Appendix 4: Data Considerations, Demographics, and Statistical Approach

Data Considerations

The questions that we asked interviewees, as described in chapters 4 through 7, were specifically developed as indicators of six aspects of a liberal arts education (nonvocational study, span of study, developing intellectual skills, engaging pedagogy, larger perspectives, and authentic community), and six categories of adult life outcome (leadership, altruism, continued learning, cultural involvement, fulfillment, and success). These questions (a total of fifty-five) were designed to assess *behaviors* rather than attitudes—that is, specific experiences that people have while in college and activities they participate in as adults.

Coding of responses and scale of measurement differed depending on the question (e.g., "Did you have a mentor in college?" was recorded as "Yes/No," frequency of voting recorded as an ordinal "Never/Occasionally/Sometimes/Always," and "How many hours do you spend volunteering each month?" was recorded as a number of hours). This resulted in a more naturalistic interview, but it influenced how the subsets of items could be combined to serve as composite measures of the six aspects of a liberal arts education and six categories of adult life outcomes. Simply adding or averaging item responses was not possible, given the variety of scale types and range of response options, and data normalization transformations were expected, and confirmed, to be ineffective in many cases. As such, an a priori decision was made to carry out median splits on each individual item, resulting in a code of "Lower" (below the median score) or "Higher" (above the median score). Whenever a response option coincided with the median, it was coded as :Lower" or "Higher," depending on which coding resulted in a more equal division of respondents.

The study's indicators of the six aspects of a liberal arts education and the six categories of adult life outcomes were computed by adding each individual item's score of 0 ("Lower") or 1 ("Higher"), resulting in unit-weighted composite scores ranging from 0 (all individual items coded as "Lower" for a respondent) to N (all individual items coded as "Higher" for a respondent, where N is the number of items included in the measure, which varied by the attribute being assessed). The composite indicators of the six educational experiences and six life outcomes were again coded as "Lower" (that is, experienced less often than average) or "Higher" (experienced more often than average).

This last step was taken for a number of reasons. First, many of the composite scores were not normally distributed, and transformations did not rectify this issue. Second, this is a conservative approach because the loss of score variability reduces the likelihood of finding significant effects. Third, the question behind this study is to learn whether there is any relationship between specific types of liberal arts educational experiences and various life outcomes—not to establish some required level of experience or outcome. Finally and importantly, the author's experience presenting the analyses to its intended audience—a broad range of educators and other informed stakeholders—made it clear that relationships described in this manner far more understandably answered the essential questions regarding findings than other statistical approaches.

Analyses

Before proceeding with the primary statistical analyses of the study (i.e., relating educational experiences to life outcomes), it was essential to determine whether and to what extent various demographic variables might account for the life outcomes being tested. To the extent that four such variables—gender, race/ethnicity, socioeconomic status (SES) while in college, and SAT/ACT test score—predict life outcomes, they might provide alternative explanations for this project's findings. However, as shown in figure A4.1, these variables are generally *not* predictive of the specific adult outcomes reported in the book. Of the twenty-four statistically substantial findings reported in the book, only four revealed a possible role for these demographic variables. Three of these four analyses were for the study's measure of success (individual's position and income) in which the six liberal arts attributes were *not* predictive. (Note: Attributes with an asterisk are meaningful in the context of this research because they satisfy the criteria used in all other analyses reported: they are statistically significant at the $p < .05$ level and the magnitude of the difference between groups is 20% or greater. See appendix 5 for more information.)

The few significant effects for these demographic variables may seem surprising, given the fact that these individual differences are commonly associated with life outcomes. Indeed, they are predictive for the measure of success (income and position). But the other outcome measures as defined here, assessed over decades of life, are not commonly investigated and may indeed be nonpredictive: leadership (in nonwork settings); altruistic involvement in society (indicated by donations, volunteering, and voting); continued learning (time spent reading and discussing the news, graduate study); cultural involvement (going to museums and concerts, reading and discussing culture); and fulfillment (time spent reflecting on life and its meaning).

Given the dichotomous data (for the reasons described here) and the low prevalence of demographic variables as confounding variables (obviating the need for analyses including covariates in most analyses), we decided to present the analyses in the most straightforward way by testing the statistical significance of relationships between educational experiences and life outcomes using tabular chi-square tests and reporting the magnitude of significant effects using incident risk ratios. Risk ratios are commonly used in cross-sectional and epidemiological research to report the effects of exposure to specific experiences on later outcomes. For disease, an example would be the percentage of people who develop lung cancer who smoked divided by the percentage of people who develop lung cancer who did not smoke. In the table given in figure A4.1, the number of graduates who came from lower–socioeconomic (SES) families who were more successful as adults (196) divided by the total number of lower-SES people (429) is .46. That is, 46% of those from a lower-SES family were more successful as adults. The number of graduates who came from a higher-SES family who were more successful (328) divided by the total number of higher-SES people (571) is .57. Therefore, 57% of those from a higher-SES family were more successful as adults.

The ratio of these two percentages (57% / 46%) is 1.26 (and is called the incident risk ratio) which means that those from higher-SES families were 26% more likely to be more successful as adults than those from lower-SES

Gender

Outcome: Liberal arts experience	Number of Cases in Each Condition				Chi square	df	Signficance	Incident risk ratio	Percent relative effect
	Lower female	Higher female	Lower male	Higher male					
Leadership	157	420	99	318	1.52	1,994	.22	1.05	5%
Altruism	312	270	219	199	0.14	1,1000	.70	1.03	3%
Continued learning	273	309	171	247	3.55	1,1000	.06	1.11	11%
Cultural engagement	273	309	209	209	0.93	1,1000	.33	0.94	−6%
Fulfillment	283	299	229	189	3.69	1,1000	.06	0.88	−12%
*Personal success	305	277	171	247	12.89	1,1000	<.001	1.24	24%

Race/ethnicity

Outcome: Individual attribute	Number of Cases in Each Condition				Chi square	df	Signficance	Incident risk ratio	Percent relative effect
	Lower nonwhite	Higher nonwhite	Lower white	Higher white					
Leadership	29	84	227	654	0.01	1,994	.98	1.00	0%
*Altruism	70	43	461	426	4.00	1,1000	.05	1.26	26%
Continued learning	51	62	393	494	0.03	1,1000	.87	1.02	2%
Cultural engagement	56	57	426	461	0.09	1,1000	.76	1.03	3%
Fulfillment	58	55	454	433	0.01	1,1000	.98	1.00	0%
*Personal success	70	43	406	481	10.51	1,1000	.001	1.43	43%

Figure A4.1a
Demographics and life outcomes

SES

Outcome: Individual attribute	Number of Cases in Each Condition				Chi square	df	Significance	Incident risk ratio	Percent relative effect
	Lower Lower	Higher Lower	Lower Higher	Higher Higher					
Leadership	124	303	132	435	4.23	1,994	.04	1.08	8%
Altruism	229	200	302	269	0.02	1,1000	.88	1.01	1%
Continued learning	193	236	251	320	0.11	1,1000	.75	1.02	2%
Cultural engagement	224	205	258	313	4.85	1,1000	.03	1.15	15%
Fulfillment	239	190	273	298	6.12	1,1000	.013	1.18	18%
Personal success	233	196	243	328	13.57	1,1000	<.001	1.26	26%

SAT/ACT score

Outcome: Individual attribute	Number of Cases in Each Condition				Chi square	df	Significance	Incident risk ratio	Percent relative effect
	Lower SAT Lower SAT	Higher SAT Lower SAT	Lower SAT Higher SAT	Higher SAT Higher SAT					
Leadership	78	246	82	225	0.58	1,631	.45	0.97	-3%
Altruism	182	142	187	121	1.34	1,632	.25	0.90	-10%
Continued learning	141	183	129	179	0.17	1,632	.68	1.03	3%
Cultural engagement	153	171	126	182	2.55	1,632	.11	1.12	12%
Fulfillment	162	162	152	156	0.03	1,632	.87	1.01	1%
Personal success	160	164	153	155	0.05	1,632	.82	0.99	-1%

Note: Attributes marked with an asterisk (*) are meaningful, as they satisfy the criteria used in all reported analyses: they are statistically significant at the $p < .05$ level and the magnitude of the difference between groups is 20% or greater. (See appendix 5 for more information.)

Figure A4.1b (continued)

families; this final percentage is called the percent relative effect. The percent relative effect is more useful and meaningful to the intended audience of this book because the goal is to describe changes in probability of a particular adult behavior as associated with college experiences rather than to indicate (or imply) that a specific percentage of individuals with a liberal arts experience or a particular family background will exhibit this adult behavior.

In the handful of instances where the demographic variables are related to the study's outcome measures, appropriate additional analyses using the demographic variables are reported in appendix 5 to account for and better understand the results that are reported. As an example, while those from lower-SES families were less likely to be more successful as adults, as reported in chapter 8 taking a higher percentage of courses outside the major was particularly impactful for this group; lower-SES graduates who took more than half of their courses outside their major were 72% more likely to be successful than adults than those lower-SES graduates who took most of their courses within their major.

In summary, as a consequence of the measurement and analytic approach used in this research, readers' attention is focused where it should be for the purpose of this book—not on predicting any specific level of desirable adult behavior based on different levels of educational experience, but on identifying the kinds of liberal arts educational experiences that are more often associated with desired liberal arts outcomes. It is our hope that the book's reported pattern of findings will stimulate further investigations into the aspects of education in the tradition of the liberal arts that make a difference in people's lives.

Appendix 5: Statistical Results

The statistical analyses for all the effects reported in chapters 6, 7, and 8 are listed in figures A5.1 through A5.6, in the same order as they are presented in the chapters. All results reported are substantial, meaning that (1) the difference between groups are statistically significant at the $p < .05$ level based on a two-tailed chi-square test, and (2) the magnitude of the difference (the percent relative effect) between groups is 20% or greater. While requiring both statistical significance and a relatively larger effect magnitude meant that some statistically significant results are not reported, by considering only larger effects, our attention is focused on those attributes that make a bigger difference and thus might be considered more meaningful.

The magnitude statistic is calculated by incident risk ratios. This statistic is commonly used in cross-sectional and epidemiological research to report on the effects of exposure to specific experiences on later outcomes. The ratio is the probability of the adult behavior among the group that had a high level of a particular liberal arts experience divided by the probability of the adult behavior for those who had a low level of that experience. For example, in the first line of figure A5.1, the incidence of leadership is reported for those who experienced lesser or greater perspective development in college. The difference in leadership is significant at the $p < .001$ level (chi-square $= 42.31$, df $= 1,994$). The incidence of adult leadership among those with a higher perspective development experience in college was 86% (328 of the 383 people who had the liberal arts experience of more perspective development in college were leaders as adults); contrarily the incidence of high leadership among those with less perspective development while in college was 67%

(410 of the 611 people who experienced less perspective development in college were leaders as adults). Therefore, the incident risk ratio is 1.28 (86/67). This ratio is then expressed in percentage terms—percent relative effect—as 28% ([1.28–1]/100), or a 28% increase in the probability that a person who experienced more perspective development in college is a leader as an adult.

This ratio is more meaningful in this research than the mere difference between two percentages because the goal is to describe changes in probability of adult behavior as related to a college experience, not to indicate (or imply) that a specific percentage of individuals with a liberal arts experience will exhibit the adult behavior.

Adult outcome: leadership Liberal arts experience	Number of Cases in Each Condition				Chi square	df	Significance	Incident risk ratio	Percent relative effect
	Low Low	High Low	Low High	High High					
Overall									
Nonvocational college major	69	195	187	543	0.03	1,994	.87	1.01	1%
Span of study	140	297	115	441	16.10	1,994	<.001	1.17	17%
Intellectual skills development	105	219	151	519	11.13	1,994	.001	1.15	15%
Engaging pedagogy	146	344	110	394	8.25	1,994	.004	1.11	11%
Larger perspectives experiences	201	410	55	328	42.31	1,994	<.001	1.28	28%
*Discussed issues such as peace/justice with students outside of class	107	176	149	560	29.79	1,992	<.001	1.27	27%
*Frequent conversations with others of different religious/political/personal values	186	378	70	380	35.58	1,994	<.001	1.26	26%
Authentic learning community	183	367	73	371	36.40	1,994	<.001	1.25	25%
*Frequently talked with faculty about academic subjects outside of class	180	378	76	360	28.14	1,994	<.001	1.22	22%
*Frequently talked with faculty about nonacademic subjects outside of class	214	500	42	238	23.58	1,994	<.001	1.21	21%
*Had a college mentor with lasting impact	142	253	114	485	35.63	1,994	<.001	1.26	26%

Liberal arts attributes

Note: Items preceded by an asterisk (*) are substantial, as described in the introduction to this appendix ($p < .05$ and relative effect $\geq 20\%$). Items that do not fulfill these criteria are treated as statistically insignificant.

Figure A5.1
Leadership

ALTRUISM

Adult outcome: level of altruism / Liberal arts experience	Number of Cases in Each Condition				Chi square	df	Significance	Incident risk ratio	Percent relative effect
	Low Low	High Low	Low High	High High					
Overall									
Nonvocational college major	144	124	387	345	0.06	1,1000	.81	1.02	2%
Span of study	248	190	283	277	3.66	1,1000	.06	1.14	14%
Intellectual skills development	177	149	354	320	0.28	1,1000	.60	1.04	4%
Engaging pedagogy	264	231	237	238	0.02	1,1000	.88	1.07	7%
Larger perspectives experiences	344	272	187	197	4.85	1,1000	.03	1.16	16%
Authentic learning community	321	232	210	237	12.16	1,1000	.001	1.26	26%
*Frequently talked with faculty about nonacademic subjects outside of class	402	317	129	152	8.12	1,1000	.005	1.23	23%
*Lived in college housing	210	138	321	326	10.47	1,995	.001	1.27	27%
*Had a college mentor with lasting impact	231	167	300	302	6.48	1,1000	.012	1.20	20%
*Actively participated in college or university organizations	287	197	244	272	14.47	1,1000	<.001	1.30	30%
*Led a college or university organization	403	319	128	149	7.42	1,1000	.007	1.22	22%
Donate a larger percentage of income									
Authentic learning community	392	86	262	102	11.99	1,842	.001	1.56	56%
*Actively participated in college or university organizations	350	72	304	116	13.53	1,842	<.001	1.62	62%
*Lived in campus housing for at least three years	256	52	394	136	8.62	1,838	.003	1.52	52%
*Most professors know the student's first name	123	23	528	165	4.50	1,839	.003	1.51	51%
*Led a college or university organization	493	121	161	67	8.98	1,842	.003	1.49	49%
*Had a college mentor with lasting impact	278	62	376	126	5.51	1,842	.023	1.38	38%
*Nonvocational major	488	125	166	63	4.87	1,842	.032	1.35	35%
Time volunteering									
Authentic Learning Community	305	178	239	263	24.03	1,985	<.001	1.42	42%
*Frequently talked with faculty about non-academic subjects outside of class	381	326	102	176	23.62	1,985	<.001	1.37	37%
*Actively participated in college or university organizations	272	206	211	296	23.01	1,985	<.001	1.35	35%
*Led a college or university organization	379	333	104	168	17.71	1,984	<.001	1.32	32%
*Had a college mentor with lasting impact	220	170	263	332	14.05	1,985	<.001	1.28	28%
*Most professors know the student's first name	92	69	390	431	5.01	1,982	.031	1.22	22%
*Frequently talked with faculty about academic subjects outside of class	295	253	188	246	10.15	1,985	.002	1.23	23%
*Lived in campus housing for at least three years	190	156	291	344	7.40	1,981	.007	1.20	20%

Liberal arts attributes

Figure A5.2a
Altruism

Ethnicity and Altruism

	Number of Cases in Each Condition				Chi square	df	Significance	Incident risk ratio	Percent relative effect
Outcome: Liberal arts experience	Lower Low	Higher Low	Lower High	Higher High					
Nonvocational college major	144	124	387	345	0.06	1,1000	.81	1.02	2%
White	128	117	333	309	0.01	1,887	.92	1.01	1%
Nonwhite	16	7	54	36	0.71	1,113	.40	1.31	31%
Span of study	248	190	283	277	3.66	1,998	.06	1.14	14%
White	212	171	249	253	2.88	1,885	.09	1.13	13%
Nonwhite	36	19	34	34	0.56	1,113	.06	1.45	45%
Intellectual skills development	177	149	354	320	0.28	1,1000	.60	1.04	4%
White	144	139	317	287	0.20	1,887	.66	0.97	-3%
*Nonwhite	33	10	37	33	6.45	1,113	.011	2.03	103%
Engaging pedagogy	264	231	267	238	0.02	1,1000	.88	1.01	1%
White	224	209	237	217	0.02	1,887	.89	0.99	-1%
Nonwhite	40	22	30	21	0.39	1,381	.54	1.16	16%
Larger perspectives experiences	344	272	187	197	4.85	1,1000	.028	1.16	16%
White	311	257	150	169	4.89	1,887	.03	1.17	17%
Nonwhite	33	15	37	28	1.64	1,113	.20	1.38	38%
Authentic learning community	321	232	210	237	12.16	1,1000	<.001	1.26	26%
*White	281	212	180	214	11.23	1,820	.001	1.26	26%
Nonwhite	40	20	30	23	1.21	1,113	.27	1.30	30%

Liberal arts attributes

Note: Items preceded by an asterisk (*) are substantial, as described in the introduction to this appendix ($p < .05$ and relative effect $\geq 20\%$). Items that do not fulfill these criteria are treated as statistically insignificant.

Figure A5.2b (continued)

Ethnicity and Altruism: Authentic Learning Community

Adult outcome: altruism Liberal arts experience	Number of Cases in Each Condition				Chi square	df	Significance	Incident risk ratio	Percent relative effect
	Lower Low	Higher Low	Lower High	Higher High					
*Authentic learning community	321	232	210	237	12.16	1,000	<.001	1.26	26%
*White	281	212	180	214	11.23	1,887	.001	1.26	26%
Nonwhite	40	20	30	23	1.21	1,113	.27	1.30	30%
*Frequently talked with faculty about nonacademic subjects	402	317	129	152	8.12	1,000	.004	1.23	23%
*White	352	288	109	138	8.44	1,887	.004	1.24	24%
Nonwhite	50	29	20	14	0.20	1,113	.65	1.12	12%
*Lived three or more years on campus	210	138	321	326	10.47	1,995	.001	1.27	27%
*White	177	124	284	297	7.83	1,882	.005	1.24	24%
Nonwhite	33	14	37	29	2.33	1,113	.13	1.48	48%
*Had a mentor with lasting impact	231	167	300	302	6.48	1,000	.011	1.20	20%
*White	202	150	259	276	6.85	1,887	.009	1.21	21%
Nonwhite	29	17	41	26	0.04	1,113	.84	1.05	5%
*Actively participated in college or university organizations	287	197	244	272	14.47	1,000	<.001	1.30	30%
*White	254	182	207	244	13.57	1,887	<.001	1.30	30%
Nonwhite	33	15	37	28	1.64	1,113	.20	1.38	38%
*Led a college or university organization	403	319	128	149	7.42	1,999	.006	1.22	22%
*White	355	292	106	133	7.74	1,886	.005	1.23	23%
Nonwhite	48	27	22	16	0.40	1,113	.53	1.17	17%

Liberal arts attributes

Note: Items preceded by an asterisk (*) are substantial, as described in the introduction to this appendix (p < .05 and relative effect ≥ 20%). Items that do not fulfill these criteria are treated as statistically insignificant.

Figure A5.2c (continued)

CONTINUED LEARNING

Liberal arts attributes

Adult outcome: degree of continued learning — Liberal arts experience	Number of Cases in Each Condition				Chi square	df	Significance	Incident risk ratio	Percent relative effect
	Low Low	High Low	Low High	High High					
Overall									
*Nonvocational college major	145	123	299	433	13.97	1, 1000	<.001	1.29	29%
*Not business nor accounting majors	66	48	378	508	9.49	1, 1000	0.003	1.36	36%
*Span of study	229	209	214	346	19.71	1, 998	<.001	1.29	29%
*Discussed philosophical/ethical perspectives in most classes	184	161	256	390	17.11	1, 991	<.001	1.29	29%
*More than half of courses outside major area of study	316	341	125	205	9.28	1, 987	.003	1.20	20%
*Intellectual skills development	181	145	263	411	24.23	1, 1000	<.001	1.37	37%
*Professors encouraged students to examine strengths/weaknesses of their views	81	59	363	494	11.71	1, 997	<.001	1.37	37%
*Required to write papers in most classes	76	59	366	495	8.99	1, 996	.003	1.32	32%
*Coursework frequently involved questions with no right answer	119	104	324	450	9.28	1, 997	.003	1.25	25%
*Engaging pedagogy	255	240	189	316	20.10	1, 1000	<.001	1.29	29%
*Classes with twenty to thirty students or fewer during the first year at college	192	182	252	373	11.50	1, 999	.001	1.23	23%
*In first two years, took seminar classes with discussion	119	104	324	450	9.28	1, 997	.003	1.25	25%
*Developing larger perspectives	321	295	123	261	38.63	1, 1000	<.001	1.42	42%
*Discussed issues such as peace/justice/human rights with students outside of class	172	113	272	440	40.42	1, 997	<.001	1.56	56%
*Frequent conversations with others of different religious/political/personal values	297	272	146	284	33.03	1, 999	<.001	1.38	38%
*Learning about people from other cultures was a very important part of college	119	98	324	456	12.16	1, 997	.001	1.29	29%
*Authentic learning community	283	270	161	286	23.00	1, 1000	<.001	1.31	31%
*College experiences involving activism	225	199	217	355	22.58	1, 996	<.001	1.32	32%
*Frequently talked with faculty about nonacademic subjects outside of class	351	368	93	188	20.23	1, 1000	<.001	1.31	31%
*Most professors know the student's first name	91	72	352	482	10.25	1, 997	.001	1.31	31%
*Frequently talked with faculty about academic subjects outside of class	284	277	160	279	20.05	1, 1000	<.001	1.29	29%
*Had a college mentor with lasting impact	204	194	240	362	12.59	1, 1000	<.001	1.23	23%
Earn advanced degrees									
*Coursework frequently involved questions with no right answer	120	102	342	430	6.59	1, 994	.012	1.21	21%
*In first two years, took seminar classes with discussion	120	102	342	430	6.59	1, 994	.012	1.21	21%
*Discussed issues such as peace/justice with students outside of class	170	114	293	417	28.18	1, 994	<.001	1.46	46%
*Had a college mentor with lasting impact	211	185	252	349	12.37	1, 997	<.001	1.24	24%
*Most professors know the student's first name	89	74	373	458	5.17	1, 994	.026	1.21	21%

Note: Items preceded by an asterisk (*) are substantial, as described in the introduction to this appendix ($p < .05$ and relative effect $\geq 20\%$). Items that do not fulfill these criteria are treated as statistically insignificant.

Figure A5.3
Continued learning

CULTURAL ENGAGEMENT

Adult outcome: degree of cultural engagement / Liberal arts experience	Number of Cases in Each Condition				Chi square	df	Significance	Incident risk ratio	Percent relative effect
Overall	Low Low	High Low	Low High	High High					
*Nonvocational college major	158	110	324	408	16.96	1,1000	<.001	1.36	36%
*Attend concerts, theaters, and/or museums	269	52	463	216	27.10	1,1000	<.001	1.96	96%
*Reading about, watching, or discussing the arts	180	39	552	229	11.56	1,1000	.001	1.65	65%
*Span of study	254	184	227	333	29.99	1,998	<.001	1.42	42%
*Many courses in the humanities	256	176	224	336	36.22	1,992	<.001	1.47	47%
*Discussed philosophical/ethical perspectives in most classes	195	150	281	365	15.28	1,991	<.001	1.30	30%
*Intellectual skills development	193	133	289	385	23.45	1,1000	<.001	1.40	40%
*Required to write papers in most classes	86	49	394	467	15.05	1,996	<.001	1.49	49%
*Coursework frequently involved questions with no right answer	133	90	347	427	15.21	1,997	<.001	1.37	37%
*Engaging pedagogy	267	228	215	290	12.93	1,1000	<.001	1.25	25%
*Students played a large role in discussion in most classes	61	35	421	483	10.01	1,1000	.002	1.47	47%
*In first two years, took seminar classes with discussion	133	90	347	427	15.21	1,997	<.001	1.37	37%
*Developing larger perspectives	322	294	160	224	10.66	1,1000	.001	1.22	22%
*Learning about people from other cultures was a very important part of college	131	86	350	430	16.33	1,997	<.001	1.39	39%
*Discussed issues such as peace/justice/human rights with students outside of class	166	119	316	396	15.67	1,997	<.001	1.33	33%
*Frequent conversations with others of different religious/political/personal values	304	265	177	253	14.76	1,999	<.001	1.26	26%
*Authentic learning community	310	243	172	275	30.60	1,1000	<.001	1.40	40%
*Activism important part of college life	230	194	249	323	11.20	1,996	.001	1.23	23%
*Frequently talked with faculty about nonacademic subjects outside of class	383	336	99	182	26.33	1,1000	<.001	1.39	39%
*Had a college mentor with lasting impact	224	174	258	344	17.29	1,1000	<.001	1.31	31%
*Frequently talked with faculty about academic subjects outside of class	302	259	180	259	16.24	1,1000	<.001	1.28	28%
*Lived in campus housing for at least three years	192	156	286	361	10.91	1,995	.001	1.24	24%

Liberal arts attributes

Note: Items preceded by an asterisk (*) are substantial, as described in the introduction to this appendix (p < .05 and relative effect ≥ 20%). Items that do not fulfill these criteria are treated as statistically insignificant.

Figure A5.4
Cultural engagement

FULFILLMENT

Adult outcome: degree of fulfillment / Liberal arts experience	Number of Cases in Each Condition				Chi square	df	Significance	Incident risk ratio	Percent relative effect
	Low Low	High Low	Low High	High High					
Overall									
Nonvocational college major	169	99	343	389	20.61	1,1000	<.001	1.44	44%
Span of study	277	161	233	327	46.04	1,998	<.001	1.59	59%
*Discussed philosophical/ethical perspectives in most classes	223	122	282	364	39.63	1,991	<.001	1.59	59%
*Many courses in the humanities	260	172	245	315	26.36	1,992	<.001	1.41	41%
Intellectual skills development	216	110	296	378	43.89	1,1000	<.001	1.66	66%
*Professors encouraged students to examine strengths/weaknesses of their views	110	30	400	457	49.00	1,997	<.001	2.49	149%
*Coursework frequently involved questions with no right answer	149	74	360	414	28.56	1,997	<.001	1.61	61%
*Write papers in most classes	89	46	419	442	13.92	1,996	<.001	1.51	51%
Engaging pedagogy	288	207	224	281	19.12	1,1000	<.001	1.33	33%
*Large student role in discussions in most classes	64	32	448	456	10.17	1,1000	.002	1.51	51%
*In first two years, seminar classes where discussion was a critical part of learning	149	74	360	414	28.56	1,997	<.001	1.61	61%
*Classes with twenty to thirty students or fewer during the first year at college	212	162	300	325	7.06	1,999	.009	1.20	20%
Larger perspectives	336	280	176	208	7.19	1,1000	.007	1.19	19%
Authentic learning community	329	224	183	264	34.06	1,1000	<.001	1.46	46%
*Most professors know the student's first name	112	51	398	436	24.01	1,997	<.001	1.67	67%
*College experiences involving activism	255	169	254	318	24.13	1,996	<.001	1.39	39%
*Had a college mentor with lasting impact	237	161	275	327	18.44	1,1000	<.001	1.34	34%
*Frequently talked with faculty about academic subjects outside of class	321	240	191	248	18.53	1,1000	<.001	1.32	32%
*Frequently talked with faculty about non-academic subjects outside of class	391	328	121	160	10.36	1,1000	.002	1.25	25%
*Led a college or university organization	388	334	123	154	6.98	1,999	<.001	1.20	20%

(Left margin labels: Liberal arts attributes)

Note: Items preceded by an asterisk (*) are substantial, as described in the introduction to this appendix ($p < .05$ and relative effect $\geq 20\%$). Items that do not fulfill these criteria are treated as statistically insignificant.

Figure A5.5
Fulfillment

SUCCESS

Adult outcome: degree of fulfillment	Number of Cases in Each Condition				Chi square	df	Significance	Incident risk ratio	Percent relative effect
	Low	High	Low	High					
Gender	Female 305	Female 277	Male 171	Male 247	12.89	1,1000	<.001	1.24	24%
Ethnicity	Nonwhite 70	Nonwhite 43	White 406	White 481	10.51	1,1000	.001	1.43	43%
SES	Lower 233	Lower 196	Higher 243	Higher 328	13.57	1,1000	<.001	1.26	26%
SAT/ACT score	Lower 160	Lower 164	Higher 153	Higher 155	0.05	1,632	.82	0.99	–1%

INCOME

Outcome:	Income				Chi square	df	Significance	Incident risk ratio	Percent relative effect
	Lower	Higher	Lower	Higher					
Gender	Female 350	Female 232	Male 219	Male 199	5.95	1,1000	.015	1.19	19%
Ethnicity	Nonwhite 84	Nonwhite 29	White 485	White 402	15.79	1,1000	<.001	1.77	77%
SES	Lower 272	Lower 157	High 297	High 274	12.96	1,1000	<.001	1.31	31%
SAT/ACT score	Lower 190	Lower 134	Higher 185	Higher 123	0.13	1,632	.72	0.97	–3%

POSITION

Outcome:	Position				Chi square	df	Significance	Incident risk ratio	Percent relative effect
	Lower	Higher	Lower	Higher					
Gender	Female 308	Female 122	Male 200	Male 130	10.23	1,760	.001	1.39	39%
Ethnicity	Nonwhite 61	Nonwhite 25	White 447	White 227	0.73	1,760	.39	1.16	16%
SES	Lower 217	Lower 94	Higher 291	Higher 158	2.04	1,760	.15	1.16	16%
SAT/ACT score	Lower 170	Lower 84	Higher 177	Higher 79	0.29	1,510	.59	0.93	–7%

Figure A5.6a
Personal success

MORE THAN HALF OF COURSES OUTSIDE MAJOR: INCOME

Outcome: More than half of courses outside major	Number of Cases in Each Condition				Chi square	df	Significance	Incident risk ratio	Percent relative effect
	Lower No	Higher No	Lower Yes	Higher Yes					
Overall	396	261	168	162	7.87	1,987	.005	1.24	24%
SAT/ACT Score									
*Lower	262	158	113	97	4.27	1,630	.039	1.23	23%
*Higher	140	83	50	50	4.66	1,323	.031	1.34	34%
Higher	122	75	63	47	0.64	1,301	.42	1.12	12%
Ethnicity	396	281	168	162	7.87	1,987	.005	1.18	18%
Nonwhite	57	23	27	6	1.37	1,113	.24	0.63	−37%
*White	339	238	141	156	10.07	1,874	.002	1.27	27%
Gender	396	261	168	162	7.87	1,987	.005	1.24	24%
Female	250	147	95	77	3.01	1,569	.083	1.21	21%
*Male	146	114	73	85	3.90	1,418	.048	1.23	23%
SES	396	261	168	162	7.87	1,987	.005	1.24	24%
*Lower	198	97	72	56	4.57	1,423	.033	1.33	33%
Higher	198	164	96	106	2.67	1,564	.10	1.16	16%

OLDER PARTICIPANTS AND DEMOGRAPHIC CHARACTERISTICS: SUCCESS

Outcome:	Number of Cases in Each Condition				Chi square	df	Significance	Incident risk ratio	Percent relative effect
	Lower	Higher	Lower	Higher					
SAT/ACT score	Lower 27	Lower 62	Higher 13	Higher 45	1.11	1,147	.29	1.11	11%
Ethnicity	Nonwhite 8	Nonwhite 10	White 97	White 220	1.52	1,335	.22	1.25	25%
Gender	Female 57	Female 108	Male 48	Male 122	1.55	1,335	.21	1.10	10%
SES	Lower 56	Lower 90	Higher 49	Higher 140	5.91	1,335	.015	1.20	20%

Note: Items preceded by an asterisk (*) are substantial, as described in the introduction to this appendix ($p < .05$ and relative effect $\geq 20\%$). Items that do not fulfill these criteria are treated as statistically insignificant.

Figure A5.6b (continued)

Adult outcome: level of personal success Liberal arts experience	Number of Cases in Each Condition				Chi square	df	Significance	Incident risk ratio	Percent relative effect
	Low Low	High Low	Low High	High High					
Overall									
Nonvocational college major	42	68	63	162	3.56	1,335	.059	1.16	16%
Span of study	56	107	49	122	1.26	1,334	.262	1.09	9%
Intellectual skills development	54	89	51	141	4.78	1,335	.029	1.18	18%
Engaging pedagogy	78	148	27	82	3.24	1,335	.072	1.15	15%
Larger perspectives experiences	70	131	35	99	2.83	1,335	.092	1.13	13%
*Authentic learning community	85	139	20	91	13.70	1,335	<.001	1.32	32%

Adult outcome: level of personal success Liberal arts experience	Number of Cases in Each Condition				Chi square	df	Significance	Incident risk ratio	Percent relative effect
	Low Low	High Low	Low High	High High					
*Authentic learning community	85	139	20	91	13.70	1,335	<.001	1.32	32%
*Lower family SES in high school	42	53	9	97	10.03	1,145	.002	1.64	64%
*Higher family SES in high school	38	86	11	54	4.18	1,189	.011	1.20	20%
Frequently talk with faculty—academic subjects outside of class	84	125	21	105	20.22	1,335	<.001	1.39	39%
*Lower family SES in high school	43	46	13	44	9.56	1,146	.002	1.49	49%
*Higher family SES in high school	41	79	8	61	11.62	1,189	.001	1.34	34%
Frequently talk with faculty—nonacademic outside of class	90	166	15	64	7.33	1,335	.007	1.25	25%
*Lower family SES in high school	47	62	9	28	4.13	1,145	.042	1.33	33%
*Higher family SES in high school	43	104	6	36	3.81	1,189	.05	1.21	21%
*Had a college mentor with lasting impact	56	94	39	136	13.97	1,335	<.001	1.24	24%
*Lower family SES in high school	34	34	22	56	7.30	1,146	.007	1.44	44%
*Higher family SES in high school	32	60	17	80	7.32	1,189	.007	1.26	26%

Figure A5.6c (continued)

OLDER PARTICIPANTS AND COURSES UNRELATED TO THE MAJOR: SUCCESS AND INCOME

Outcome: More than half courses	Number of Cases in Each Condition				Chi square	df	Significance	Incident risk ratio	Percent relative effect
	Lower No	Lower Yes	Higher No	Higher Yes					
*Success	77	27	134	88	5.80	1,326	.016	1.53	53%
*Lower SES	42	13	51	35	4.35	1,141	.037	1.72	72%
Higher SES	35	14	83	53	1.69	1,185	.19	1.36	36%
*Current income	105	35	106	80	11.35	1,326	.001	1.72	72%
*Lower SES	52	17	41	31	5.32	1,141	.021	1.75	75%
*Higher SES	53	18	65	49	5.89	1,185	.015	1.70	70%

Note: Items preceded by an asterisk (*) are substantial, as described in the introduction to this appendix ($p < .05$ and relative effect $\geq 20\%$). Items that do not fulfill these criteria are treated as statistically insignificant.

Figure A5.6d (continued)

Notes

Chapter 1

1. International Trade Administration, *Department of Commerce Report 2016 Top Markets Report*.

2. Wildavsky, "The Rise of Liberal Arts in Hong Kong."

3. Aggarwal, "The New Wave of Liberal Arts."

4. Sharma, "Liberal Arts Universities on Par with IITs, IIMs Are Next on Modi Govt's Education Plan."

5. Purinton and Skaggs, *American Universities Abroad*.

6. Nishimura and Sasao, *Doing Liberal Arts Education*.

7. See Global Liberal Arts Alliance at www.LiberalArtsAlliance.org.

8. Kam, "Finding Myself Through My College Major."

9. Association of American Colleges and Universities, "It Takes More than a Major: Employer Priorities for College Learning and Student Success."

10. Cuban, "Because of AI, the Value of a Computer Science Degree Will Diminish over Time."

11. Zakaria, *In Defense of the Liberal Arts*, 151.

12. Brooks, "The Humanist Vocation."

13. Brooks, *The Road to Character*.

14. Lydgate, "Visionary Technologist, Prodigal Son."

15. Microsoft, *The Future Computed*.

16. Detweiler, "Lessons from Middle East 'de Tocquevilles.'"

17. Kimball, *Orators & Philosophers*.

18. Doerr, *Measure What Matters*.

19. Gardner, *The Mind's New Science*, 388.

20. Neem, *What's the Point of College?*, 9.

21. US Department of Education National Center for Education Statistics, "Digest of Education Statistics 2016," 643.

22. US Department of Education National Center for Education Statistics, "National Postsecondary Student Aid Study Features," 14.

23. US Department of Education, "National Center for Education Statistics, Baccalaureate and Beyond."

24. US Department of Education Office of Federal Student Aid Programs, "Official Cohort Default Rates for Schools."

Chapter 2

Some of the insights contained in this chapter were previously summarized in Detweiler, "International Perspectives on Liberal Education: International Insights on the Essence of the Liberal Arts"; Harward, "Is the Civic a Culturally Dependent Concept?"; and Purinton and Skaggs, *American Universities Abroad*.

1. Detweiler et al., "Creating Liberal Learners."

2. Kimball, *Orators & Philosophers*, 21.

3. For an in-depth exploration of the content and character of classical Greek education at all levels—primary, secondary, and higher—see Marrou, *A History of Education in Antiquity*.

4. Marrou, *A History of Education in Antiquity*, 186–187.

5. Marrou, *A History of Education in Antiquity*, 187.

6. Kimball, *Orators & Philosophers*, 17.

7. Marrou, *A History of Education in Antiquity*, 217, 219, 225.

8. Marrou, *A History of Education in Antiquity*, 67, 165–166, and 221, respectively.

9. Marrou, *A History of Education in Antiquity*, 67.

10. Thomas *Literacy and Orality in Ancient Greece*.

11. Marrou, *A History of Education in Antiquity*, 239.

12. Marrou, *A History of Education in Antiquity*, 246.

13. Marrou, *A History of Education in Antiquity*, 284.

14. Kimball, *Orators & Philosophers*, 13.

15. For an English translation, see Stahl and Johnson, *Martianus Capella and the Seven Liberal Arts*.

16. Stahl and Johnson, *Martianus Capella and the Seven Liberal Arts*, 65.

17. Stahl and Johnson, *Martianus Capella and the Seven Liberal Arts*, 67.

18. Nakosteen, *History of Islamic Origins of Western Education*, 17.

19. Nakosteen, *History of Islamic Origins of Western Education*, 21.

20. Lyons, *The House of Wisdom*, 66.

21. Freely, *Aladdin's Lamp*, 72–75.

22. For a full description, see Lyons, *The House of Wisdom*, ch. 3.

23. Morgan, *Lost History*, 10–11.

24. Morgan, *Lost History*, 59–60.

25. Lyons, *The House of Wisdom*, 65.

26. Freely, *Aladdin's Lamp*, 107.

27. Nakosteen, *History of Islamic Origins of Western Education*, 56.

28. Nakosteen, *History of Islamic Origins of Western Education*, 50–51.

29. Berkey, *The Transmission of Knowledge*, 21.

30. Nakosteen, *History of Islamic Origins of Western Education*, 57.

31. Nakosteen, *History of Islamic Origins of Western Education*, 57 and 46, respectively.

32. Nakosteen, *History of Islamic Origins of Western Education*, 38.

33. Nakosteen, *History of Islamic Origins of Western Education*, 179 and 53, respectively.

34. Brown, *The Abacus and the Cross*, 14.

35. Brown, *The Abacus and the Cross*, 36.

36. Lyons, *The House of Wisdom*, 36.

37. Brown, *The Abacus and the Cross*, 50.

38. Brown, *The Abacus and the Cross*, 53.

39. Personal communication, March 5, 2018.

40. Brown, *The Abacus and the Cross*, 159.

41. Freely, *Aladdin's Lamp*, 83.

42. Kimball, *Orators & Philosophers*, 39.

43. Bisaha, *Creating East and West*, 107.

44. Lyons, *The House of Wisdom*, 161.

45. H. O. Taylor, *The Mediaeval Mind*, 379.

46. Pederson, *The First Universities*, 295.

47. Lucas, *American Higher Education*, 42.

48. Lucas, *American Higher Education*, 47.

49. Kimball, *Orators & Philosophers*, 41.

50. Taylor, *The Mediaeval Mind*, 377–378.

51. Pederson, *The First Universities*, 127.

52. Pederson, *The First Universities*, 143.

53. Lucas, *American Higher Education*, 44.

54. Pederson, *The First Universities*, 248–249.

55. Haskins, *The Rise of Universities*, 54–55.

56. Pederson, *The First Universities*, 250–251.

57. Rudolph, *The American College & University*, 4 and 7.

58. Lucas, *American Higher Education*, 104.

59. Lucas, *American Higher Education*, 109–110.

60. Schmidt, *The Liberal Arts College*, 7.

61. Schmidt, *The Liberal Arts College*, 78.

62. Rudolph, *The American College & University*, 87.

63. Schmidt, *The Liberal Arts College*, 79–80.

64. Morison, *The Founding of Harvard College*, 250.

65. Lucas, *American Higher Education*, 105.

66. Lucas, *American Higher Education,* 112.

67. Reich, *The Common Good,* 18.

Chapter 3

1. Delbanco, *College,* 177.

2. Ruegg, *A History of the University in Europe,* 3.

3. Kohli, *State-Directed Development,* 1.

4. Menard, Reitter, and Wellmon, *The Rise of the Research University,* 106.

5. Hohendorf, "Wilhelm von Humboldt, 1767–1835," 665; M. C. Taylor, *Crisis on Campus,* 18.

6. Hohendorf, "Wilhelm von Humboldt, 1767–1835," 665–666.

7. Wilhelm von Humboldt, as quoted by Hohendorf, "Wilhelm von Humboldt, 1767–1835," 673.

8. UNESCO, *Prospects,* 6.

9. Hohendorf, "Wilhelm von Humboldt, 1767–1835," 673.

10. Hohendorf, "Wilhelm von Humboldt, 1767–1835," 674.

11. Ash, "Bachelor of What, Master of Whom?," 246.

12. Ash, "Bachelor of What, Master of Whom?," 246.

13. Jarausch, "Graduation and Careers," 381.

14. Ruegg, *A History of the University in Europe,* 6.

15. Cocks and Jarausch, *German Professions, 1800–1950,* 4.

16. Jarausch, "Graduation and Careers," 373.

17. Menard et al., *The Rise of the Research University,* 138.

18. Taylor, *Crisis on Campus,* 18.

19. Menard et al., *The Rise of the Research University,* 139.

20. The actual name of the report was the *Reports on the Course of Instruction in Yale College,* by the Committee of the Corporation and the Academical Faculty.

21. Committee of the Corporation and the Academical Faculty, *Reports on the Course of Instruction in Yale College,* 29.

22. Committee of the Corporation and the Academical Faculty, *Reports on the Course of Instruction in Yale College,* 15.

23. Committee of the Corporation and the Academical Faculty, *Reports on the Course of Instruction in Yale College*, 7–8.

24. Committee of the Corporation and the Academical Faculty, *Reports on the Course of Instruction in Yale College*, 9.

25. Committee of the Corporation and the Academical Faculty, *Reports on the Course of Instruction in Yale College*, 10.

26. Lucas, *American Higher Education*, 117.

27. Lucas, *American Higher Education*, 117.

28. Geiger, *A History of American Higher Education*, 194.

29. Schmidt, *The Liberal Arts College*, 11.

30. As quoted by Geiger, *A History of American Higher Education*, 194.

31. Heins, *Throughout All the Years*.

32. A. Taylor, *William Cooper's Town*.

33. Heins, *Throughout All the Years*, 150.

34. As quoted by Lucas, *American Higher Education*, 119.

35. Geiger, *A History of American Higher Education*, 398.

36. Rudolph, *The American College & University*, 53–58.

37. Westmayer, *A History of American Higher Education*, 121.

38. Geiger, *A History of American Higher Education*, 193.

39. Chen and Kisker, *The Shaping of American Higher Education*, 24.

40. Rudolph, *The American College &University*, 62.

41. As quoted by Lucas, *American Higher Education*, 65.

42. Rudolph, *The American College & University*, 58–59.

43. Geiger, *A History of American Higher Education*, 205–206.

44. OurDocuments.gov, "An Act Donating Public Lands to the Several States and Territories Which May Provide Colleges for the Benefit of Agriculture and Mechanic Arts," section 4.

45. Founding university president Daniel Coit Gilman, as quoted in Hawkins, *Pioneer*, 37.

46. Hawkins, *Pioneer*, 217.

Chapter 4

1. Committee of the Corporation and the Academical Faculty, *Reports on the Course of Instruction in Yale College*, 15, 27.

2. Percentages add up to 101% due to rounding.

3. Committee of the Corporation and the Academical Faculty, *Reports on the Course of Instruction in Yale College*, 15.

4. Schmidt, *The Liberal Arts College*, 44.

5. Committee of the Corporation and the Academical Faculty, *Reports on the Course of Instruction in Yale College*, 8.

6. Committee of the Corporation and the Academical Faculty, *Reports on the Course of Instruction in Yale College*, 33–34.

7. Kimball, *Orators & Philosophers*, 270.

8. Dodge, *Muslim Education in Medieval Times*, 17.

9. Dodge, *Muslim Education in Medieval Times*, 79.

10. Committee of the Corporation and the Academical Faculty, *Reports on the Course of Instruction in Yale College*, 7, 30, respectively.

11. Committee of the Corporation and the Academical Faculty, *Reports on the Course of Instruction in Yale College*, 11, 13, respectively.

12. Marrou, *A History of Education in Antiquity*, 219.

13. Committee of the Corporation and the Academical Faculty, *Reports on the Course of Instruction in Yale College*, 15, 20, respectively.

14. Committee of the Corporation and the Academical Faculty, *Reports on the Course of Instruction in Yale College*, 9.

Chapter 5

1. See, for example, the research reported by the College Board Advocacy & Policy Center, *Five Ways Ed Pays*.

2. *U.S. News and World Report*, "Economic Diversity National Liberal Arts Colleges."

3. College Board, "Trends in Student Aid 2019," 27.

4. Olsen et al., *An Introduction to Epidemiology for Health Professionals*.

Chapter 6

1. Committee of the Corporation and the Academical Faculty, *Reports on the Course of Instruction in Yale College*, 29.

2. Committee of the Corporation and the Academical Faculty, *Reports on the Course of Instruction in Yale College*, 15.

Chapter 7

1. For an in-depth exploration of the content and character of classical Greek education at all levels—primary, secondary, and higher—see Marrou, *A History of Education in Antiquity*.

2. Committee of the Corporation and the Academical Faculty, *Reports on the Course of Instruction in Yale College*, 15.

Chapter 8

1. Isaacson, *Benjamin Franklin*.

2. Franklin, *The Autobiography of Benjamin Franklin*, 160.

3. Committee of the Corporation and the Academical Faculty, *Reports on the Course of Instruction in Yale College*, 14–15.

4. Committee of the Corporation and the Academical Faculty, *Reports on the Course of Instruction in Yale College*, 28.

5. Lucas, *American Higher Education*, 119.

6. This item was reverse coded—that is, those who are living a fulfilled life will report thinking more about their life and its direction.

7. Buffett, *Berkshire Hathaway Shareholders Report 2008*.

8. US Department of Labor, Bureau of Labor Statistics, "Number of Jobs, Labor Market Experience, and Earnings Growth Results from a National Longitudinal Survey."

Chapter 9

1. Grazer, *Face to Face*, 189.

2. Kaplan, *The Case against Education*.

3. Gardner, *The Mind's New Science*, 386.

4. Gardner, *The Mind's New Science*, 388.

5. Pascarella and Terenzini, *How College Affects Students*, 600.

6. "Cognition," *Oxford English Dictionary*, https://en.oxforddictionaries.com/definition/cognition.

7. Wentzel, "Students' Relationships with Teachers as Motivational Contexts," 301.

8. Bawa, "Retention in Online Courses."

9. Immordino-Yang, *Emotions, Learning, and the Brain*, 18 and 17, respectively.

10. Pekrun, "Emotions at School," 587.

11. Immordino-Yang, *Emotions, Learning, and the Brain*, 19.

12. Marrou, *A History of Education in Antiquity*, 67, 165–166, and 221, respectively.

13. Walton and Cohen, "A Brief Social-Belonging Intervention Improves Academic and Health Outcomes in Minority Students," 1447–1451.

14. Strayhorn, *College Students' Sense of Belonging*.

15. Morison, *The Founding of Harvard College*, 252.

Chapter 10

1. Mahew et al., *How College Affects Students*, 554.

Chapter 11

1. Arum and Roksa, *Aspiring Adults Adrift*, 34.

2. Chambliss and Takacs, *How College Works*, 157.

3. Gallup/Purdue University, "Great Jobs, Great Lives."

4. Crabtree, "Students at Smaller Colleges More Likely to Say Faculty Care."

5. Statista, "The Top Ten Most Important Factors Considered in Deciding upon a College in the United States 2015."

6. Art & Science Group, "College-Bound Students Use a Wide Variety of College Rankings Sources."

7. Michigan State University Collegiate Employment Research Institute, "Recruiting Trends 2016–2017."

8. Long, "The New Normal."

9. The Balance. "How Often Do People Change Jobs?"

10. Arum and Roksa, *Academically Adrift*, 104–109.

11. Anders, *You Can Do Anything*.

12. Stross, *A Practical Education*.

13. Harley, *The Fuzzy and the Techie*.

14. World Economic Forum. "Jobs of Tomorrow."

15. World Economic Forum. "Jobs of Tomorrow," 12.

16. Kumar S. and George, "Why Skills—Not Degrees—Will Shape the Future of Work."

17. Clydesdale, *The Purposeful Graduate*, xviii.

18. Walton and Cohen, "A Brief Social-Belonging Intervention Improves Academic and Health Outcomes in Minority Students," 1447–1451.

19. Strayhorn, *College Students' Sense of Belonging*.

20. Microsoft, *The Future Computed*, 19.

21. Casap, as quoted in Lederman, "A Silicone Valley 'Evangelist' Who Doesn't Bash Higher Ed."

22. Wentzel, "Students' Relationships with Teachers as Motivational Contexts," 301.

23. Johnson, *On Being a Mentor*.

24. Hurlburt and McGrath, "The Shifting Academic Workforce."

25. American Association of University Professors, "Data Snapshot."

26. Delbanco, *College*, 171.

27. See Miller and Meghan, *Generation Z Goes to College*.

28. National Governors Association, *Degrees for What Job?*

29. Association for Institutional Research, "Trends in College Spending," figure A3.

Chapter 12

1. Kipling, *Captains Courageous*.

2. Jefferson, "Letter to George Wythe," 243.

3. Durant and Durant, *The Lessons of History*, 101–102.

Appendix 1

1. Deslauriers, Schelew, and Wieman, "Improved Learning in a Large Enrollment Physics Class," 862–864.

2. Walton and Cohen, "A Brief Social-Belonging Intervention Improves Academic and Health Outcomes of Minority Students," 1447–1451.

3. For a listing of many of these reports, see NSSE, "Our Research: Projects, Publications, and More," https://nsse.indiana.edu/research/publications-presentations /index.html.

4. Kuh, *High-Impact Educational Practices*, esp. footnote 10.

5. See, for example, Seifert et al., "The Effects of Liberal Arts Experiences on Liberal Arts Outcomes," 107–125; and Pascarella and Blaich, "Lessons from the Wabash National Study of Liberal Arts Education."

6. See, for example, Light, *Making the Most of College*.

7. Arum and Roksa, *Aspiring Adults Adrift*, 134.

8. Arum and Roksa, *Aspiring Adults Adrift*, 80.

9. Bain, *What the Best College Students Do*.

10. Pascarella et al., *Liberal Arts Colleges and Liberal Arts Education*.

11. Gallup/Purdue University, "Great Jobs, Great Lives," 4 and 5 (emphasis added).

12. Pascarella and Terenzini, *How College Affects Students*, 600.

Bibliography

Aggarwal, Megha. "The New Wave of Liberal Arts." *The Hindu*, March 24, 2016. https://www.thehindu.com/features/education/college-and-university/the-new-wave-of-liberal-arts/article7980357.ece.

American Association of University Professors. "Data Snapshot: Contingent Faculty in US Higher Ed." 2018. https://www.aaup.org/sites/default/files/10112018%20Data%20Snapshot%20Tenure.pdf.

Anders, George. *You Can Do Anything: The Surprising Power of a "Useless" Liberal Arts Education*. New York: Little Brown, 2017.

Art & Science Group. "College-Bound Students Use a Wide Variety of College Rankings Sources." *studentPoll* 12, no. 3 (December 2016). https://www.artsci.com/insights/studentpoll/volume-12-issue-3.

Arum, Richard, and Josipa Roksa. *Academically Adrift: Limited Learning on College Campuses*. Chicago: University of Chicago Press, 2011.

Arum, Richard, and Josipa Roksa. *Aspiring Adults Adrift: Tentative Transitions of College Graduates*. Chicago: University of Chicago Press, 2014.

Ash, Mitchell G. "Bachelor of What, Master of Whom? The Humboldt Myth and Historical Transformations of Higher Education in German-Speaking Europe and the US." *European Journal of Education* 41, no. 2 (2006).

Association for Institutional Research. "Trends in College Spending: 2003–2013." Washington, DC, 2016. https://www.air.org/system/files/downloads/report/Delta-Cost-Trends-in-College%20Spending-January-2016.pdf.

Association of American Colleges and Universities. "It Takes More Than a Major: Employer Priorities for College Learning and Student Success." April 10, 2013. https://www.aacu.org/publications-research/periodicals/it-takes-more-major-employer-priorities-college-learning-and.

Bain, Ken. *What the Best College Students Do*. Cambridge, MA: Harvard University Press, 2012.

Balance, The. "How Often Do People Change Jobs?" https://www.thebalance.com/how-often-do-people-change-jobs-2060467.

Bawa, Papia. "Retention in Online Courses: Exploring Issues and Solutions—A Literature Review." SAGE Open, January 5, 2016. https://doi.org/10.1177/2158244015621777.

Berkey, Jonathan. *The Transmission of Knowledge in Medieval Cairo: A Social History of Islamic Education*. Princeton, NJ: Princeton University Press, 1992.

Bisaha, Nancy. *Creating East and West: Renaissance Humanists and the Ottoman Turks*. Philadelphia: University of Pennsylvania Press, 2004.

Brooks, David. "The Humanist Vocation." *New York Times*, June 20, 2013.

Brooks, David. *The Road to Character*. New York: Random House, 2016.

Brown, Nancy Marie. *The Abacus and the Cross: The Story of the Pope Who Brought the Light of Science to the Dark Ages*. New York: Basic Books, 2010.

Buffett, Warren. *Berkshire Hathaway Shareholders Report 2008*. http://www.berkshirehathaway.com/letters/2008ltr.pdf.

Carroll, Lewis. *Alice's Adventures in Wonderland*. New York: D. Appleton and Co., 1866.

Chambliss, Daniel F., and Christopher G. Takacs. *How College Works*. Cambridge, MA: Harvard University Press, 2014.

Chen, Arthur, and Carrie Kisker. *The Shaping of American Higher Education*. San Francisco: Jossey-Bass, 2010.

Cheng, Leonard K., and Xiangdong Wei. "Boya Education in China: Lessons from Liberal Arts Education in the U.S. and Hong Kong." In Ka Ho Mok and Simon Marginson, "Expansion of Higher Education in China for Two Decades: Critical Reflections from Comparative Perspectives," special issue, *International Journal of Education Development* 84 (July 2021).

Clydesdale, Tim. *The Purposeful Graduate: Why Colleges Must Talk to Students about Vocation*. Chicago: University of Chicago Press, 2015.

Cocks, Geoffrey, and Konrad H. Jarausch. *German Professions, 1800–1950*. New York and Oxford: Oxford University Press, 1990.

College Board. "Trends in Student Aid 2019." https://research.collegeboard.org/pdf/trends-student-aid-2019-full-report.pdf.

College Board Advocacy & Policy Center. "Five Ways Ed Pays: Five Powerful Ways a College Degree Can Transform Your Life." New York: College Board, 2011. http://youcango.collegeboard.org/sites/default/files/11b_4427_5waysedpays_eng_web_111107.pdf.

Committee of the Corporation and the Academical Faculty. *Reports on the Course of Instruction in Yale College*. New Haven, CT: Hezekian Howe, 1828.

Crabtree, Steve. "Students at Smaller Colleges More Likely to Say Faculty Care." Gallup Education Insights, January 30, 2019. https://news.gallup.com/poll/246083/students -smaller-colleges-likely-say-faculty-care.aspx.

Cuban, Mark. "Because of AI, the Value of a Computer Science Degree Will Diminish over Time." Interview by Eric Johnson, Vox.com, May 29, 2019. https://www.vox.com /recode/2019/5/29/18644652/mark-cuban-ai-computer-science-coding-liberal-arts-kara -swisher-steve-case-decode-podcast-interview.

Delbanco, Andrew. *College: What It Was, Is, and Should Be*. Princeton, NJ: Princeton University Press, 2012.

Deslauriers, L., E. Schelew, and C. Wieman. "Improved Learning in a Large Enrollment Physics Class." *Science* 332, no. 6031 (May 13, 2011): 862–864. https://science .sciencemag.org/content/332/6031/862.

Detweiler, Richard A. "International Perspectives on Liberal Education: International Insights on the Essence of the Liberal Arts." In Harward, *Transforming Undergraduate Education*, 225–238.

Detweiler, Richard A. "Lessons from Middle East 'de Tocquevilles.'" *Inside Higher Ed*, October 30, 2006. https://www.insidehighered.com/views/2006/10/30/lessons -middle-east-de-tocquevilles.

Detweiler, Richard A., Lori Collins-Hall, William Vining, Jerusha Detweiler-Bedell, and Brian Detweiler-Bedell. "Creating Liberal Learners." Meeting of the Association of American Colleges and Universities. Long Beach, CA, Spring 2004.

Dodge, Bayard. *Muslim Education in Medieval Times*. Washington, DC: Middle East Institute, 1962.

Doerr, John. *Measure What Matters: How Google, Bono, and the Gates Foundation Rock the World with OKRs*. New York: Portfolio/Penguin, 2018.

Durant, Will, and Ariel Durant. *The Lessons of History*. New York: Simon & Schuster, 1986.

Emerson, Ralph Waldo. *Select Writings of Ralph Waldo Emerson*. London: Walter Scott, 1888.

Franklin, Benjamin. *The Autobiography of Benjamin Franklin*. Edited by Frank Woodworth Pine. New York: Garden City Publishing, 1916.

Freely, John. *Aladdin's Lamp*. New York: Vintage Books, 2009.

Gallup/Purdue University. "Great Jobs, Great Lives: The 2014 Gallup-Purdue Index Report." Washington, DC: Gallup, 2014. http://www.gallup.com/services/176768 /2014-gallup-purdue-index-report.aspx.

Gardner, Howard. *The Mind's New Science*. New York: Basic Books, 1986.

Gates, Bill. "The Future of College." National Association of College and University Business Officers Annual Meeting, 2014. https://www.gatesnotes.com/Education/The -Future-of-College-NACUBO-Remarks.

Geiger, Roger L. *A History of American Higher Education*. Princeton, NJ: Princeton University Press, 2015.

Grazer, Brian. *Face to Face: The Art of Human Connection*. New York: Simon and Schuster, 2019.

Harley, Scott. *The Fuzzy and the Techie: Why the Liberal Arts Will Rule the Digital World*. New York: Houghton Mifflin Harcourt, 2017.

Harward, Donald. "Is the Civic a Culturally Dependent Concept? Are Democratic Practices?" In *Civic Provocations*, edited by Donald Harward, 57–62. Washington, DC: Bringing Theory to Practice, 2012.

Harward, Donald, ed. *Transforming Undergraduate Education: Theory That Compels and Practices That Succeed*. New York: Rowan and Littlefield, 2011.

Haskins, Charles Homer. *The Rise of Universities*. New Brunswick, NJ: Transaction Publishers, 2002. Originally published in 1923.

Hawkins, Hugh. *Pioneer: A History of the Johns Hopkins University, 1874–1889*. Ithaca, NY: Cornell University Press, 1960.

Heins, Henry Hardy. *Throughout All the Years*. Oneonta, NY: Hartwick College, 1946.

Hohendorf, Gerd. "Wilhelm von Humboldt, 1767–1835." *Prospects: The Quarterly Review of Comparative Education* 23, no. 3/4 (1993): 665–676.

Hurlburt, Steven, and Michael McGrath. "The Shifting Academic Workforce: Where Are the Contingent Faculty?" TIAA-CREF and the Delta Cost Project, 2016. https://www.air.org/sites/default/files/downloads/report/Shifting-Academic-Workforce-November-2016.pdf.

Immordino-Yang, Mary Helen. *Emotions, Learning, and the Brain*. New York: W. W. Norton, 2016.

International Trade Administration. *Department of Commerce Report 2016 Top Markets Report*. Accessed February 21, 2021. https://legacy.trade.gov/topmarkets/pdf/Education_Top_Markets_Report.pdf.

Isaacson, Walter. *Benjamin Franklin: An American Life*. New York: Simon and Schuster, 2003.

Jarausch, Konrad H. "Graduation and Careers." In Ruegg, *A History of the University in Europe*, 363–389.

Jefferson, Thomas. "Letter to George Wythe," August 13, 1786. In *The Papers of Thomas Jefferson*, vol. 10, edited by Julian P. Boyd, Charles T. Cullen, John Catanzariti, Barbara B. Oberg, et al., 243–245. Princeton, NJ: Princeton University Press, 1954.

Johnson, W. Brad. *On Being a Mentor: A Guide for Higher Education Faculty*. New York: Lawrence Erlbaum Associates, 2007.

Kam, Joshua. "Finding Myself through My College Major." *New York Times*, January 16, 2017, Opinion.

Kaplan, Bryan. *The Case against Education*. Princeton, NJ: Princeton University Press, 2018.

Kimball, Bruce A. *Orators & Philosophers*. New York: College Entrance Examination Board, 1995.

Kipling, Rudyard. *Captains Courageous: A Story of the Grand Banks*. New York: The Century Co., 1897.

Kohli, Atul. *State-Directed Development: Political Power and Industrialization in the Global Periphery*. Cambridge: Cambridge University Press, 2004.

Kuh, George D. *High-Impact Educational Practices: What They Are, Who Has Access to Them, and Why They Matter*. Washington, DC: Association of American Colleges and Universities, 2008.

Kumar S., Ravi, and Steve George. "Why Skills—Not Degrees—Will Shape the Future of Work." World Economic Forum COVID Action Platform, September 21, 2020. https://www.weforum.org/agenda/2020/09/reckoning-for-skills/.

Lederman, Doug. "A Silicone Valley 'Evangelist' Who Doesn't Bash Higher Ed." *Inside Digital Learning*, April 25, 2018. https://www.insidehighered.com/digital -learning/article/2018/04/25/technology-evangelist-believes-colleges-can-teach -their-digital.

Light, Richard J. *Making the Most of College: Students Speak Their Minds*. Cambridge, MA: Harvard University Press, 2001.

Long, Heather. "The New Normal: 4 Job Changes by the Time You're 32." CNN Money, 2016. http://money.cnn.com/2016/04/12/news/economy/millennials-change -jobs-frequently/index.html.

Lucas, Christopher J. *American Higher Education: A History*. 2nd ed. New York: Palgrave Macmillan, 2006.

Lydgate, Chris. "Visionary Technologist, Prodigal Son." *Reed Magazine*, December 2011. https://www.reed.edu/reed-magazine/in-memoriam/obituaries/december2011 /steve-jobs-1976.html.

Lyons, Jonathan. *The House of Wisdom*. New York: Bloomsbury, 2009.

Mahew, M., A. Rockenbach, N. Bowman, T. Seifert, G. Wolniak, E. Pascarella, and P. Terenzini. *How College Affects Students*. Vol. 3. San Francisco: Jossey-Bass, 2016.

Marrou, H. I. *A History of Education in Antiquity*. Madison: University of Wisconsin Press, 1948.

Menard, L., P. Reitter, and C. Wellmon. *The Rise of the Research University*. Chicago: University of Chicago Press, 2017.

Michigan State University Collegiate Employment Research Institute. "Recruiting Trends 2016–2017: Brief 3; Starting Salaries." https://files.eric.ed.gov/fulltext /ED586487.pdf.

Microsoft. *The Future Computed: Artificial Intelligence and Its Role in Society*. Redmond, WA: Microsoft, 2018.

Miller, Corey, and Grace Meghan. *Generation Z Goes to College*. New York: John Wiley & Sons, 2016.

Morgan, Michael Hamilton. *Lost History. The Enduring Legacy of Muslim Scientists, Thinkers, and Artists*. Washington, DC: National Geographic, 2007.

Morison, Samuel Eliot. *The Founding of Harvard College*. Cambridge, MA: Harvard University Press, 1935.

Nakosteen, Mehdi. *History of Islamic Origins of Western Education*. Boulder: University of Colorado Press, 1964.

National Governors Association. *Degrees for What Job?* Washington, DC: NGA Center for Best Practices, 2011.

Neem, Johann N. *What's the Point of College?* Baltimore: Johns Hopkins University Press, 2019.

Nishimura, Mikiko, and Toshiaki Sasao. *Doing Liberal Arts Education*. Singapore: Springer, 2019.

Olsen, J., K. Christensen, J. Murray, and A. Ekbom. *An Introduction to Epidemiology for Health Professionals*. New York: Springer, 2010.

OurDocuments.gov. "An Act Donating Public Lands to the Several States and Territories Which May Provide Colleges for the Benefit of Agriculture and Mechanic Arts." Transcript of Morrill Act. Accessed January 23, 2021. http://www.ourdocuments.gov/print_friendly.php?page=transcript&doc=33&title=Transcript+of+Morrill+Act+(1862.

Pascarella, Ernest, and Charles Blaich. "Lessons from the Wabash National Study of Liberal Arts Education." *Change: The Magazine of Higher Learning* 45, no. 2 (2013): 6–15.

Pascarella, Ernest, C. Gregory, Tricia A. Wolniak, Ty M. Seifert, M. Cruce, and Charles F. Blaich. *Liberal Arts Colleges and Liberal Arts Education: New Evidence on Impacts*. San Francisco: Wiley, 2005.

Pascarella, Ernest, and Patrick Terenzini. *How College Affects Students*. Vol. 2. San Francisco: Jossey-Bass, 2005.

Pederson, Olaf. *The First Universities*. Translated by Richard North. Cambridge: Cambridge University Press, 1997.

Pekrun, R. "Emotions at School." In *Handbook of Motivation at School*, edited by Kathryn R. Wentzel and Allan Wigfield, 575–604. New York: Routledge, 2009.

Peters, Gerhard, and John T. Woolley. "The American Presidency Project: Proclamation 3422." *American Education Week*, July 25, 1961. http://www.presidency.ucsb.edu/ws/?pid=24146.

Purinton, Ted, and Jennifer Skaggs. *American Universities Abroad: The Leadership of Independent Transnational Higher Education Institutions*. Cairo: American University in Cairo Press, 2017.

Reich, Robert. *The Common Good*. New York: Alfred A. Knopf, 2018.

Roth, Michael S. *Beyond the University: Why Liberal Education Matters*. New Haven, CT: Yale University Press, 2014.

Rudolph, Frederick. *The American College & University: A History*. New York: Alfred Knopf, 1962.

Ruegg, Walter. *A History of the University in Europe.* Vol. 3. Cambridge: Cambridge University Press, 2004.

Schmidt, George P. *The Liberal Arts College: A Chapter in American Cultural History.* New Brunswick, NJ: Rutgers University Press, 1957.

Seifert, Tricia A., Kathleen M. Goodman, Nathan Lindsay, James D. Jorgensen, Gregory Wolniak, Ernest T. Pascarella, and Charles Blaich. "The Effects of Liberal Arts Experiences on Liberal Arts Outcomes." *Research in Higher Education* 49 (2008): 107–125.

Seldes, George. *The Great Thoughts.* New York: Ballantine Books, 1985.

Seuss, Dr. *I Can Read with My Eyes Shut!* New York: Random House, 1978.

Sharma, Kritika. "Liberal Arts Universities on Par with IITs, IIMs Are Next on Modi Govt's Education Plan." *The Print,* October 28, 2019. https://theprint.in/india/education/liberal-arts-universities-par-iits-iims-next-modi-govts-plan/312263/.

Stahl, W. H., and R. Johnson. *Martianus Capella and the Seven Liberal Arts.* Vol. 2, *The Marriage of Philology and Mercury.* New York: Columbia University Press, 1977.

Statista, the Statistics Portal. "The Top Ten Most Important Factors Considered in Deciding upon a College in the United States 2015." https://www.statista.com/statistics/706268/top-10-factors-in-deciding-on-a-specific-college-us/.

Strayhorn, Terrell L. *College Students' Sense of Belonging: A Key to Educational Success for All Students.* New York, Routledge, 2012.

Stross, Randall. *A Practical Education: Why Liberal Arts Majors Make Great Employees.* Stanford, CA: Redwood Press, 2017.

Taylor, Alan. *William Cooper's Town: Power and Persuasion on the Frontier of the Early American Republic.* New York: Knopf, 1995.

Taylor, Henry Osborn. *The Mediaeval Mind.* Vol. 2. New York: Macmillan Co., 1911.

Taylor, Mark C. *Crisis on Campus.* New York: Alfred A. Knopf, 2010.

Thomas, Rosalind. *Literacy and Orality in Ancient Greece.* Cambridge: Cambridge University Press, 1992.

Thoreau, Henry David. "The Higher Life: From Thoreau's Private Letters." In *Life without Principle,* 31–38. London: Arthur C. Fifield, 1905.

UNESCO. *Prospects: The Quarterly Review of Comparative Education* 23, no. 3 (1993): 613–623.

US Department of Education National Center for Education Statistics. "Baccalaureate and Beyond: A First Look at the Employment and Educational Experiences of College Graduates, 1 Year Later." 2019. https://nces.ed.gov/pubsearch/pubsinfo.asp?pubid=2019241.

US Department of Education National Center for Education Statistics. "Digest of Education Statistics 2016." https://nces.ed.gov/pubsearch/pubsinfo.asp?pubid=2017094.

US Department of Education National Center for Education Statistics. "National Postsecondary Student Aid Study Features." January 2018. https://nces.ed.gov/surveys/npsas/.

US Department of Education Office of Federal Student Aid Programs. "Official Cohort Default Rates for Schools." October 8, 2020. https://www2.ed.gov/offices/OSFAP/defaultmanagement/cdr.html.

US Department of Labor, Bureau of Labor Statistics. "Number of Jobs, Labor Market Experience, and Earnings Growth Results from a National Longitudinal Survey." August 22, 2019; revised October 7, 2020. https://www.bls.gov/news.release/pdf/nlsoy.pdf.

U.S. News and World Report. "Economic Diversity: National Liberal Arts Colleges." 2020. https://www.usnews.com/best-colleges/rankings/national-liberal-arts-colleges/economic-diversity.

Walton, Gregory M., and Gregory L. Cohen. "A Brief Social-Belonging Intervention Improves Academic and Health Outcomes in Minority Students." *Science* 331, no. 6023 (March 18, 2011): 1447–1451.

Wentzel, Kathryn R. "Students' Relationships with Teachers as Motivational Contexts." In *Handbook of Motivation at School,* edited by Kathryn R. Wentzel and Allan Wigfield, 301–322. New York: Routledge, 2009.

Westmayer, Paul. *A History of American Higher Education.* Springfield, IL: Charles C. Thomas, 1985.

Wildavsky, Ben. "The Rise of Liberal Arts in Hong Kong." *Atlantic,* March 20, 2015. https://www.theatlantic.com/education/archive/2016/03/the-rise-of-liberal-arts-in-china/474291/.

World Economic Forum. "Jobs of Tomorrow: Mapping Opportunity in the New Economy." Cologny/Geneva Switzerland, 2020. http://www3.weforum.org/docs/WEF_Jobs_of_Tomorrow_2020.pdf.

Zakaria, Fareed. *In Defense of a Liberal Education.* New York: W. W. Norton, 2015.

Index